THE PEOPLE OF EDINBURGH
1725-1775

The People of
EDINBURGH
1725-1775

By
David Dobson

CLEARFIELD

Copyright © 2012
by David Dobson
All Rights Reserved

Printed for Clearfield Company by
Genealogical Publishing Company
Baltimore, Maryland
2012

ISBN 978-0-8063-5573-3

Made in the United States of America

INTRODUCTION

The period 1725 to 1775 was one of continuity and change for Edinburgh. For much of the period the majority of the population lived in the Old Town, its medieval site, but by 1770 the elite of the burgh were beginning to move to the New Town of Edinburgh which lay to the north. Edinburgh had once been the capital of Scotland but lost that role after the political union of Scotland and England in 1707. It remained the centre of the Scottish legal system, the Church of Scotland, brewing, printing, university education, medicine, and a wide range of specialised crafts. Immediately to the east of the old burgh of Edinburgh lay the burgh of Canongate which was a center for skilled craftsmen. To the north lay Leith, a distinct burgh, which acted as the port of Edinburgh. Leith contained a significant number of merchants, seafarers, and shipbuilders. Leith and Canongate, among other localities, are now integrated within the City of Edinburgh. This book identifies many of the inhabitants of Edinburgh, Canongate and Leith living at home and abroad during the mid eighteenth century and is based on research in both manuscript and published sources.

During the medieval and early modern period a minority of the inhabitants of the Scottish burghs were burgesses. They were the urban elite, only burgesses could operate businesses, vote, or train apprentices. To become a burgess a man had either to serve an apprenticeship under an existing burgess, inherit the right from his father, marry the daughter of a burgess, sometime purchase the right or be awarded burgess –ship in recognition of some service to the community. Burgesses were either craftsmen or merchants and were members of the relevant craft or merchant guild which supervised the training of apprentices, standards of work, and the interests of members. It was therefore essential that records be maintained and these were major sources of data for this work. The book also is based on records of the Commissariat Court, the High Court of the Admiralty, the Court of Session, the burgh sasines [property], the register of deeds, monumental inscription lists, and miscellaneous published sources.

David Dobson

Dundee, Scotland, 2011.

The People of Edinburgh, 1725-1775

ABBREVIATIONS

Appr. = Apprentice
C.E. = Commissariat of Edinburgh
Dau. = Daughter
M.I. = Monumental Inscription
Test. = Testament

GLOSSARY

Baxter = baker
Cordiner = shoemaker
Flesher = butcher
Indweller = resident
Litster = dyer
Sklaiter = slater
Tack = lease
Writer = lawyer

The People of Edinburgh, 1725-1775

SOURCES

ActsPCCol	=	Acts of the Privy Council, Colonial
AJ	=	Aberdeen Journal
ANY	=	St Andrews Society of New York
AP	=	St Andrews Society of Philadelphia
BI	=	Burgess Roll of Inveraray
CBR	=	Canongate Burgess Roll
CCMC	=	Colonial Clergy of the Middle Colonies
CLRO	=	City of London Record Office
DUAS	=	Dundee University Archival Service
EBR	=	Edinburgh Burgess Roll/Edinburgh Burgh Records
ECL	=	Register of the Episcopal Congregation in Leith
EEC	=	Edinburgh Evening Courant
EMA	=	List of Emigrant Ministers to America
ERA	-	Edinburgh Register of Apprentices
F	=	Fastii Ecclesiae Scoticanae
FPA	=	Fulham Papers, American
ESG	=	Early Settlers of Georgia
GaGaz	=	Georgia Gazette
HBRS	=	Hudson Bay Record Society
ImmNE	=	Immigrants to New England
LER	=	Leith Episcopal Records
MAGU	=	Matriculation Albums of Glasgow University
MSA	=	Maryland State Archives
NLS	=	National Library of Scotland
NRS	=	National Records of Scotland
NYGaz	=	New York Gazette
P	=	Prisoners of the '45
PCC	=	Prerogative Court of Canterbury
PCCol	=	Calendar of the Privy Council, Colonial
SCS	=	Scots Charitable Society of Boston
SL	=	Calendar of Irregular Marriages in South Leith
SM	=	Scots Magazine
StABR	=	St Andrews Burgess Roll
TNA	=	The National Archives of UK
VMHB	=	Virginia Magazine of History and Biography
WED	=	Williamson's Edinburgh Directory of 1773
WMQ	=	William and Mary Quarterly

COCK OF THE GREEN.

WHA'L O CALLER OYSTERS

The People of Edinburgh, 1725-1775

ABELL, GEORGE, son of James Abell, a tailor in Canongate, test., 1726, C.E. [NRS]
ABERCROMBY, JAMES, a vintner in Edinburgh, test., 1748, C.E. [NRS]
ABERCROMBIE, MARY, wife of Andrew Darling a coachmaker in Leith, heir to her uncle Robert Abercrombie a saddler there, 1774. [NRS.S/H]
ABERCROMBIE, ROBERT, born in Edinburgh during 1712, a minister in Pelham, New England, from 1744 to 1755, died there on 3 March 1780. [ImmNE#1]
ABERCROMBY, ROBERT, a portioner in Leith, testamtnt, 1778, C.E. [NRS]
ABERDOUR, ALEXANDER, a founder in Edinburgh, test., 1765, C.E. [NRS]
ABERDOUR, JAMES, son of Alexander Aberdour, appr. to William Smith a founder burgess, 1747, [ERA]; a founder, a burgess of Edinburgh, 1763, by right of his wife Isobel, dau. of George Aitken a smith burgess. [EBR]
ABERDOUR, WILLIAM, a founder, a burgess of Edinburgh, 1761, by right of his wife Helen, dau. of John Burns a merchant burgess. [EBR]
ADAM, ANDREW, a sailor in Leith, husband of Eupham Douglas, 1761. [ECL#14]
ADAM, ELIZABETH, relict of Charles Haigs a baxter burgess of Canongate, test., 1731, C.E. [NRS]
ADAM, JAMES, appr. to David Robertson a locksmith in Edinburgh 1768-1773. [ERA]
ADAM, JANET, relict of Colin McIntyre a merchant in Edinburgh, test., 1740, C.E. [NRS]
ADAM, JOHN, an architect in Edinburgh, a sasine, 1751; son of William Adam, a burgess and guildsbrother of Edinburgh, 1755; heir to Thomas Thornton who died in January 1769; a deed, 1772. [NRS.RS27.138.242; S/H; RD4.216/415]
ADAM, JOHN, a merchant, a burgess and guilds-brother of Edinburgh, 1762, husband of Katherine, dau. of Charles Stalker a burgess and guilds-brother. [EBR]
ADAM, JOHN, in Edinburgh, a deed, 1773. [NRS.RD3.232/274]
ADAM, WILLIAM, an architect in Edinburgh, a burgess and guildsbrother in 1728, [EBR]; 1735; sasine, 1742; test., 1748, C.E. [NRS.AC10.215; RS27.127.414]
ADAMS, WILLIAM, a printer in Edinburgh, test., 1736, C.E. [NRS]
ADAMSON, CHRISTIAN, sometime relict of Ninian Miln, and thereafter relict of David Anderson a cooper in Leith, test., 1743, C.E. [NRS]
ADAMSON, GEORGE, a surgeon apothecary in Edinburgh, test., 1749, C.E. [NRS]
ADAMSON, GEORGE, a barber & wigmaker burgess of Edinburgh, 1778. [EBR]
ADAMSON, JOHN, a baker in Canongate, a sasine, 1753. [NRS.RS27.142.321]
ADAMSON, LAURENCE, a wright in Leith, son and heir of Thomas Adamson usher at New College, S t Andrews, 1763. [NRS.S/H]

The People of Edinburgh, 1725-1775

ADAMSON, MARY, spouse of John Young a tailor in Edinburgh, a sasine, 1742. [NRS.RS27.127.325]

ADDISON, JAMES, a sailor in Leith, husband of Rachel Robertson, 1759; a deed, shipmaster in Queen Street, Leith, 1773. [SL#86][NRS.RD4.215/772]

ADDISON, JOHN, a music teacher in Jamaica, later in Leith, 1776. [NRS.CS16.1.170]

ADDISON, ROBERT, son of Peter Addison in Liberton, appr. of James Caddel an upholster in Edinburgh, 1762-1768. [ERA]

ADIE, MARY, relict of Alexander Campbell of Aenachan a writer in Edinburgh, test., 1739, C.E. [NRS]

ADIE, WILLIAM, son of William Adie in Portsburgh, appr. to James Seton a merchant in Edinburgh 1768-1773. [ERA]

AGNEW, Sir JAMES, of Lochnaw, a resident of Canongate, test., 1736. C.E. [NRS]

AIKEN, WILLIAM, a wright burgess of Edinburgh, 1767, husband of Catherine, dau. of Patrick Cunningham a wright burgess. [EBR]

AIKENHEAD, ALEXANDER, a writer in Edinburgh, test., 1751, C.E. [NRS]

AIKENHEAD, DAVID, a surgeon in Edinburgh, test., 1774, C.E. [NRS]

AIKENHEAD, HELEN, relict of James Rigg a merchant in Edinburgh, test., 1745, C.E. [NRS]

AIKENHEAD, JAMES, a shoemaker in Ninian's Row, Edinburgh, 1743. [NRS.AC10.301]

AIKENHEAD, JAMES, a merchant in Edinburgh, a sasine, 1749; later resident in Leith, test., 1770, C.E. [NRS.RS27.135.186]

AIKENHEAD, JAMES, a merchant and guildsbrother of Edinburgh, 1766, son of James Aikenhead a merchant burgess. [EBR]

AIKMAN, DAVID, a sail/ropemaker in North Leith, test., 1725, C.E. [NRS]

AIKMAN, WILLIAM, a shoemaker in St Mary Wynd, Edinburgh, test., 1745, C.E. [NRS]

AINSLIE, ALEXANDER, a merchant in Leith, 1731, 1732; test., 1743, C.E. [NRS.AC10.189; AC11.58]

AINSLIE, JOHN, a merchant in Rotterdam, a burgess of Edinburgh, 1777.[EBR]

AINSLIE, PHILIP, in Edinburgh, a deed of factory, 1773. [NRS.RD2.214.428]

AINSLIE, WALTER, a merchant in Edinburgh, a decreet, 1767. [NRS.CS16.1.130]

AIRD, GEORGE, in Edinburgh, test., 1738, C.E. [NRS]

AIRD, THOMAS, a flesher in Edinburgh, test., 1738, C.E. [NRS]

AIRTH, ALEXANDER, a cowfeeder in Canongate, and his spouse Jean Livingston, test., 1752, C.E. [NRS]

The People of Edinburgh, 1725-1775

AITCHISON, ALEXANDER, a goldsmith and Jeweller in Edinburgh, son and heir of Alexander Aitchison a goldsmith and jeweller in Edinburgh, 1777. [NRS.S/H]; a burgess and guildsbrother of Edinburgh, 1778. [EBR]

AITCHISON, JAMES, a horse-hirer in Edinburgh, test., 1769, C.E. [NRS]

AITCHISON, JOHN, a merchant burgess and guilds-brother of Edinburgh, 1775. [EBR]

AITCHISON, ROBERT, a clock and watchmaker burgess of Edinburgh, 1770, son of James Aitchison a merchant burgess. [EBR]

AITKEN, DOROTHY, dau. of Andrew Aitken a merchant in Edinburgh, a bond, 1750. [NRS.RD2.168.320]

AITKEN, GEORGE, a writer in Edinburgh, sasines, 1751; test., 1778, C.E. [NRS.RS27.139.105/107]

AITKEN, GEORGE, a smith in Edinburgh, a sasine, 1758. [NRS.RS27.152.441]

AITKEN, HUGH, a merchant burgess and guilds-brother of Edinburgh, 1763.[EBR]

AITKEN, JAMES, a stabler burgess of Edinburgh, 1763. [EBR]

AITKEN, JAMES, clerk in the Annexed Estates office in Edinburgh, test., 1767, C.E. [NRS]

AITKEN, JOHN, a wright in Canongate, 1742. [NRS.AC11.154A]

AITKEN, JOHN, son of John Aitken a wright in Canongate, appr. to John Stiell a watch and clock-maker in Edinburgh, 1750. [ERA]

AITKEN, JOHN, a book-seller in Edinburgh, a sasine, 1752. [NRS.RS27.139.254]

AITKEN, JOHN, a merchant burgess of Edinburgh, 1765. [EBR]

AITKEN, JOHN, a surgeon burgess of Edinburgh, 1770. [EBR]

AITKEN, MARGARET, relict of George Galloway a maltman in Portsburgh, Edinburgh, test., 1739, C.E. [NRS]

AITKEN, ROBERT, a distiller in Canongate, test., 1756, C.E. [NRS]

AITKIN, ROBERT, son of James Aitkin a wright in Canongate, appr. to Robert Boog a cutler in Edinburgh, 1763-1769. [ERA]

AITKEN, THOMAS, a flesher burgess of Edinburgh, test., C.E. [NRS]

AITKEN, WILLIAM, a wright in Edinburgh, test., 1768, C.E. [NRS]

AKERS, ARRELAS, of Paradise, St Kitts, a burgess and guilds-brother of Edinburgh, 1765. [EBR]

ALCORN, HENRY, Essay master of the Royal Mint in Scotland, test., 1766, C.E. [NRS]

ALCORN, JAMES, son of R. Alcorn a watchmaker in Edinburgh, heir to his grandmother Margaret Henderson, wife of H. Alcorn the Mint Master, 1765. [NRS.S/H]

ALCORN, RICHARD, a watchmaker in Edinburgh, test., 1769, C.E. [NRS]

ALEXANDER, AGNES, in Edinburgh, test., 1754, C.E. [NRS]

The People of Edinburgh, 1725-1775

ALEXANDER, ALEXANDER, a sailor in Leith, 1768; a shipmaster in Bernard Street, Leith, 1773. [SL#106][WED#2]

ALEXANDER, ALEXANDER, a skipper from Leith, husband of Elizabeth Murray, a Loyalist in Charleston, South Carolina, 1776, killed in Delaware, 1777. [TNA.AO13.96.6]

ALEXANDER, CHARLES, a vintner in Edinburgh, test., 1753, C.E. [NRS]

ALEXANDER, CHRISTOPHER, a merchant and vintner in Edinburgh, a bond, 1728. [NRS.RD4.176/2.212]

ALEXANDER, ELIZABETH, spouse of Andrew Spalding a brewer in Leith, a sasine, 1749. [NRS.RS27.136.212]

ALEXANDER, HELEN, spouse of Alexander Hay a weaver in Leith, a sasine, 1749. [NRS.RS27.135.304]

ALEXANDER, JAMES, a coach-builder in Canongate, a sasine, 1755; a burgess of Edinburgh, 1773, son of Christopher Alexander a vintner burgess, [EBR]; test., 1786, C.E. [NRS.RS27.146.51]

ALEXANDER, JOHN, a brewer and maltman in Leith, test., 1758, C.E. [NRS]

ALEXANDER, JOHN, a sailor in Leith, husband of Johan McGrigor, 1758. [SL#84]

ALEXANDER, JOHN, a merchant in Edinburgh, a decreet, 1777. [NRS.CS16.1.171]

ALEXANDER, MARGARET, at the Water of Leith, test., 1738, C.E. [NRS]

ALEXANDER, ROBERT, a merchant in Edinburgh, heir to his cousin Jane Alexander of Blackhouse who died in May 1750.[NRS.S/H]

ALEXANDER, ROBERT, in Leith, a bond, 1775. [NRS.RD3.233/141]

ALEXANDER, ROBERT, a shipmaster in Bernard Street, Leith, 1773; master of the American Planter, test., 1775, Comm. Edinburgh. [WED#3]

ALEXANDER, THEODORE, in Edinburgh, a bond, 1773. [NRS.RD2.214.2/644]

ALEXANDER, WILLIAM, a merchant in Edinburgh, a burgess and guilds-brother in 1733, [EBR]; a sasine, 1744. [NRS.RS27.130.196]; trading between Ayr and Virginia, 1749, [NRS.E504.4.1]; 1777. [NRS.CS16.1.171]

ALEXANDER, WILLIAM, of the Edinburgh Ropery Company, 1754. [NRS.AC8.822]

ALISON, ANDREW, a mariner in Leith, husband of Janet Wright, 1764. [SL#99]

ALISON, COLIN, son of George Alison a merchant, a wright in Edinburgh, a burgess and guilds-brother in 1725, [EBR]; a sasine, 1749. [NRS.RS27.135.394]

ALISON, DAVID, a journeyman tailor in Edinburgh, test., 1764, C.E. [NRS]

ALISON, HENRY, a merchant in Edinburgh, a sasine, 1742. [NRS.RS27.127.56]

ALISON, JOHN, a ship-builder in Leith, a sasine, 1753. [NRS.RS27.142.231]

ALISON, ROBERT, a writer in Edinburgh, test.s, 1757/1759, C.E. [NRS]

ALISON, ROBERT, son of James Alison in Leith, appr. to James Wallace a barber in Edinburgh, 1773-1779. [ERA]

The People of Edinburgh, 1725-1775

ALISON, THOMAS, son of George Alison a merchant, a glazier in Edinburgh, a burgess in 1721, [EBR]; a sasine, 1754. [NRS.RS27.144.147]

ALISON, WILLIAM, son of Robert Alison a writer, appr. to Henry Hardie a baxter burgess of Edinburgh, 1741. [ERA]

ALISON, WILLIAM, a physician from Edinburgh, settled in Virginia, a decreet, 1748. [NRS.CS16.1.80]

ALLAN, ALEXANDER, a glover in Edinburgh, heir to his father William Allan a slater in Elgin, 1767. [NRS.S/H]

ALLAN, ALEXANDER, a merchant burgess and guilds-brother of Edinburgh, 1772/1775, [EBR]; a decreet, 1783. [NRS.CS17.1.2]

ALLAN, ANDREW, son of John Allan, a baker in Edinburgh, a sasine, 1742. [NRS.RS27.127.49]

ALLAN, ANN, relict of William Miln a skipper in Leith, test., 1732, C.E. [NRS]

ALLAN, BENJAMIN, a writer in Edinburgh, test., 1728, C.E. [NRS]

ALLAN, CHARLES, born 1728, a cooper's servant from Leith, transported to Jamaica on 31 March 1747, landed there. [P.2.8][TNA.CO137.58]

ALLAN, CHARLES, son of Robert Allan a merchant, a surgeon in Edinburgh, a burgess and guilds-brother in 1722, [EBR]; a sasine, 1741. [NRS.RS27.126.113]

ALLAN, DAVID, a sailor in Leith, 1739. [SL#44]

ALLAN, ELIZABETH, spouse of John Sinclair a writer in Edinburgh, a sasine, 1745; heir to her father Charles Allan a surgeon in Edinburgh, 1761. [NRS.RS27.131.320; S/H]

ALLAN, EUPHAN, widow of John MacEwan in Edinburgh, test., 1763, C.E. [NRS]

ALLAN, GEORGE, born 2 December 1676, messenger in Edinburgh, died 16 February 1749, husband of Elizabeth Belfrag, born 1670, died 27 March 1729. [St Cuthbert's MI]; tests., 1749/1762, C.E. [NRS]

ALLAN, GEORGE, in Edinburgh, test., 1746, C.E.

ALLAN, HENRY, a writer in Edinburgh, burgess of Canongate, 1731. [CBR]; test., 1774, C.E. [NRS]

ALLAN, HENRY, a baker burgess of Edinburgh, 1768, [EBR]; son and heir of John Allan a baker burgess there, 1774. [NRS.S/H]

ALLAN, JAMES, a wright in Edinburgh, test., 1731, C.E. [NRS]

ALLAN, JANET, spouse to Thomas Bowie a baxter in Edinburgh, test., 1755, C.E. [NRS]

ALLAN, JOHN, sr., a baxter in Edinburgh, test., 1749, C.E. [NRS]

ALLAN, JOHN, a baker burgess of Edinburgh, test., 1753, C.E. [NRS]

ALLAN, JOHN, a burgess of Edinburgh, 1761, son of William Allan a merchant. [EBR]

ALLAN, JOHN, workman at the Glass Works, test., 1775, C.E. [NRS]

The People of Edinburgh, 1725-1775

ALLAN, MARGARET, dau. of William Allan a writer in Edinburgh, a bond. 1735. [NRS.RD2.168.321]
ALLAN, RICHARD, a merchant bailie of Glasgow, a burgess and guilds-brother of Edinburgh, 1743. [EBR]
ALLAN, RICHARD, a weaver in Leith, a sasine, 1753. [NRS.RS27.142.261]
ALLAN, RICHARD, a former student of physics in Edinburgh, settled in North America, a decreet, 1778. [NRS.CS16.1.174]
ALLAN, ROBERT, a merchant burgess of Edinburgh, test., 1725, C.E. [NRS]
ALLAN, ROBERT, a deed, 1769. [NRS.RD3.753/263]
ALLAN, ROBERT, a merchant burgess and guilds-brother of Edinburgh, 1771. [EBR]
ALLAN, THOMAS, son of Thomas Allan, a merchant and baillie of Edinburgh, a burgess and guilds-brother in 1724, [EBR]; a deed, 1742. [NRS.RD4.330]
ALLAN, THOMAS, late merchant in Edinburgh and shore-master in Leith, test., 1763, C.E. [NRS]
ALLAN, WILLIAM, son of Hugh Allan a cooper in Leith, appr. to James Smith a skinner burgess of Edinburgh, 1741. [ERA]
ALLARDICE, MARY, in Edinburgh, test., 1760, C.E. [NRS]
ALLARDICE, WILLIAM, son of James Allardice a merchant in Edinburgh, heir to his sister Euphemia Allardice, 1760. [NRS.S/H]
ALSTON, Dr CHARLES, Professor of Botany at Edinburgh University, a burgess and guilds-brother in 1749, [EBR]; a deed, 1750. [NRS.RD2.167.231]
ALSTON, DAVID, son of James Alston a merchant, appr. to James Crawford a glazier burgess, 1739. [ERA]
ALVES, ALEXANDER, a surgeon apothecary in Edinburgh, test., 1738, C.E. [NRS]
ALVES, ANDREW, a Writer to the Signet in Edinburgh, a deed, 1750. [NRS.RD2.168.392]
ALVES, BASIL, son of Andrew Alves WS, and Fort Major of Edinburgh Castle, a burgess and guilds-brother of Edinburgh, 1766. [EBR]
ALVES, DAVID, a burgess and guilds-brother of Edinburgh, 1761, son of William Alves WS and husband of Jean dau. of Thomas Mercer a burgess and guilds-brother. [EBR]
ALVES, MARGARET, in Edinburgh, a deed, 1773. [NRS.RD4.214/298]
ALVES, RICHARD, son of David Alves in Edinburgh, appr. to Hugh Hamilton a merchant and guilds-brother of Edinburgh, 1755. [ERA]
ALVES, THOMAS, a writer in Edinburgh, a sasine, 1759. [NRS.RS27.153.209]
AMBROSE, CHARLES, a burgess of Edinburgh, 1762. [EBR]
ANCRUM, MICHAEL, a merchant in Edinburgh, decreets, 1757, 1763; a burgess and guilds-brother, 1759, test., 1762, C.E. [NRS.CS16.1.100/117; AC7.53] [EBR]

The People of Edinburgh, 1725-1775

ANDERSON, ADAM, a pewterer in Edinburgh, husband of Margaret Raitt, a burgess, 1734, a deed, 1750. [NRS.RD3.210.431][EBR]

ANDERSON, ADAM, a sailor in Leith, 1751. [SL#66]

ANDERSON, AGNES, relict of Robert Mutter a merchant in Leith, test., 1758, C.E. [NRS]

ANDERSON, ALEXANDER, a sailor in Leith, husband of Christian Chalmers, 1768. [SL#104]

ANDERSON, ALEXANDER, a merchant burgess and guilds-brother of Edinburgh, 1772, son of James Anderson of Newbigging an advocate burgess and guilds-brother. [EBR]

ANDERSON, ANDREW, a writer in Edinburgh, test., 1733, C.E. [NRS]

ANDERSON, ANDREW, appr. to Henry Antonius a wright, a wright in Edinburgh, a burgess in 1742, a deed, 1749. [EBR] [NRS.RD2.167.17]

ANDERSON, ANDREW, a merchant from Edinburgh, settled in Jappahannock, Virginia, before 1755, died 1760 in Virginia. [NRS.RD4.198.558]

ANDERSON, ANDREW, a shoemaker in Leith, test., 1766, C.E. [NRS]

ANDERSON, ANDREW, of Rashiegrain, a wright burgess of Edinburgh, test., 1769, C.E. [NRS]

ANDERSON, ANDREW, a sailor in Leith, 1767; a shipmaster at Sheriffbrae, Leith, 1773; in Leith, 1779-1785. [ECL#43][WED#2] [NRS.GD226.18.247-248]

ANDERSON, DANIEL, a shoemaker burgess of Edinburgh, 1764, [EBR]; test., 1771, C.E. [NRS]

ANDERSON, DAVID, a writer in Edinburgh, a burgess and guilds-brother in 1726, a sasine, 1743; a deed, 1750. [EBR][NRS.RS27.128.122; RD3.210.51]

ANDERSON, DAVID, a slater in Leith, a burgess of Edinburgh in 1759, a sasine, 1760. [NRS.RS27.155.273][EBR]

ANDERSON, DAVID, a tiler in Leith, son and heir of David Anderson a cooper there, 1760. [NRS.S/H]

ANDERSON, DAVID, son of William Anderson, a hatmaker in Edinburgh, a burgess and guilds-brother in 1739, a sasine, 1760. [EBR][NRS.RS27.157.1]

ANDERSON, DAVID, a sailor from Leith, a housebreaker, transported to the colonies in April 1774. [AJ#1374]

ANDERSON, GABRIEL, a sailor in Leith, wife Christian Findlay, 1763. [SL#95]

ANDERSON, GEORGE, born 1727, from Canongate, emigrated in August 1745. [NRS.B59.29.82]

ANDERSON, GEORGE, a merchant in Leith, a deed, 1750. [NRS.RD4.176/2.412]; trading with South Carolina, 1745, 1755. [NRS.E504.22]

ANDERSON, GEORGE, a barber in Crosscauseway, Edinburgh, heir to his father James Anderson, a maltster in Cupar, Fife, 1760. [NRS.S/H]

The People of Edinburgh, 1725-1775

ANDERSON, GEORGE, a candlemaker burgess of Edinburgh, 1762, former apprentice to James Tod a candlemaker burgess. [EBR]

ANDERSON, GEORGE, son of George Anderson a pressman, appr. to Duncan McQueen a white-ironsmith, 1768-1775. [ERA]

ANDERSON, GEORGE, a barber and wigmaker burgess of Edinburgh, 1771. [EBR]

ANDERSON, HELEN, widow of James Gordon in Edinburgh, test., 1755, C.E. [NRS]

ANDERSON, HENRY, appr. to Robert Herron a cordiner, a shoemaker in Edinburgh, a burgess in 1741, a sasine, 1746. [EBR][NRS.RS27.128.122]

ANDERSON, ISABELLA, wife of John Haddoway a merchant in Leith, heir to her brother John Anderson, son of Patrick Anderson a merchant in Leith, 1762. [NRS.S/H]

ANDERSON, JAMES, son of Alexander Anderson a comb-maker, appr. to Alexander and John Learmont tanners in Edinburgh, 1748. [ERA]

ANDERSON, JAMES, of Newbigging, an advocate burgess and guilds-brother of Edinburgh, 1763, husband of Janet dau. of Patrick Lindsay late Lord Provost. [EBR]

ANDERSON, JAMES, a merchant from Leith, settled at Brokesbank, Rappahannock, Essex County, Virginia, before 1772, died 1788, test., deeds, C.E. [NRS.RD3.231; RD4.21.288; CC8.8.127]

ANDERSON, JAMES, a tailor in Colonton, a burgess of Edinburgh, 1767. [EBR]

ANDERSON, JAMES, a shipmaster in James Street, Leith, 1773. [WED#3]

ANDERSON, Mrs JANET, milliner in Edinburgh, test., 1761, C.E. [NRS]

ANDERSON, JOHN, son of John Anderson a tailor, appr. to Alexander Orem a cordiner, 1728. [ERA]

ANDERSON, JOHN, a writer in Edinburgh, a decreet, 1749. [NRS.CS16.1.81]

ANDERSON, JOHN, a merchant in Edinburgh, test., 1752, C.E. [NRS]

ANDERSON, JOHN, son of Adam Anderson a pewterer, appr. to Edward Lothian a goldsmith burgess of Edinburgh, 1753. [ERA]; a burgess, 1763.[EBR]

ANDERSON, JOHN, a merchant in Edinburgh, test., 1759, C.E. [NRS]

ANDERSON, JOHN, son of Daniel Anderson in Edinburgh, appr. to James Thomson a merchant in Edinburgh, 1765-1770. [ERA]

ANDERSON, JOHN, a shoemaker in Canongate, test., 1770, C.E. [NRS]

ANDERSON, JOHN, a writer in Edinburgh, test., 1772, C.E. [NAS]

ANDERSON, JOHN, a gunsmith in Edinburgh, test., 1775, C.E. [NRS]

ANDERSON, LILIAS, wife of Alexander Thomson a merchant in Edinburgh, heir to her sister Janet, dau. of Alexander Anderson a merchant there, 1779. [NRS.S/H]

The People of Edinburgh, 1725-1775

ANDERSON, MICHAEL, a merchant in Pleasance, burgess of Canongate, 1729. [CBR]
ANDERSON, MICHAEL, in Edinburgh, a bond, 1773. [NRS.RD3.232/629]
ANDERSON, PATRICK, a merchant in Leith, test., 1744, C.E. [NRS]
ANDERSON, PATRICK, a merchant in Leith, a sasine, 1759. [NRS.RS27.154.178]
ANDERSON, REBECCA, relict of John Anderson a baker in Edinburgh, a sasine, 1750. [NRS.RS27.137.265]
ANDERSON, ROBERT, a maltman and brewer in Leith, test., 1727, C.E. [NRS]
ANDERSON, ROBERT, a brewer in Leith, a sasine, 1759. [NRS.RS27.154.111]
ANDERSON, ROBERT, a merchant in Edinburgh, test., 1765, C.E. [NRS]
ANDERSON, ROBERT, born 1758, a clerk from Edinburgh, from London to Antigua in November 1774. [TNA.T47.9.11]
ANDERSON, THOMAS, son of Baillie Alexander Anderson, a merchant in Edinburgh, test., 1741, C.E. [NRS]
ANDERSON, THOMAS, late Keeper of the Advocates Library in Edinburgh, a sasine, 1756. [NRS.RS27.147.60]
ANDERSON, THOMAS, a merchant in South Leith, test., 1758, C.E. [NRS]
ANDERSON, THOMAS, a shoemaker in Leith Wynd, test., 1764, C.E. [NRS]
ANDERSON, WALTER, book-keeper to John Hope and Company, merchants in Edinburgh, test., 1750, C.E. [NRS]
ANDERSON, WILLIAM, son of George Anderson, appr. to Thomas Forrest a glazier burgess of Edinburgh, 1739. [ERA]
ANDERSON, WILLIAM, son of John Anderson a baker in Edinburgh, a sasine, 1742. [NRS.RS27.127.49]
ANDERSON, WILLIAM, in Edinburgh, test., 1744, C.E. [NRS]
ANDERSON, WILLIAM, son of William Anderson in Edinburgh, appr. to Adam Anderson a barber and wigmaker burgess of Edinburgh, 1748. [ERA]
ANDERSON, WILLIAM, in Leith, previously in Bristol, heir to John Livingston, a candlemaker in Leith, 1768. [NRS.S/H]
ANDERSON, WILLIAM, son of John Anderson a journeyman shoemaker, appr. to William Murray and James Clerk shoemakers in Edinburgh, 1771-1778. [ERA]
ANDREW, ALEXANDER, a skipper in Leith, test., 1762, Comm. Edinburgh.
ANDREW, DAVID, a sailor in Leith, heir to his uncle Laurence Andrew a wright in Edinburgh, 1771. [NRS:S/H]
ANDREWS, GEORGE, teller in the Royal Bank, second son of George Andrews a minister in Edinburgh, test., 1742, C.E. [NRS]
ANGUS, ANDREW, a flesher in Canongate, test., 1741, C.E. [NRS]
ANGUS, ARCHIBALD, appr. to Patrick Murray, a merchant in Edinburgh, a burgess and guilds-brother in 1732, a deed, 1750; test., 1758, C.E. [EBR][NRS.RD2.168.218]

The People of Edinburgh, 1725-1775

ANGUS, ELIZABETH, dau. of Andrew Angus a flesher in Canongate, test., 1759, C.E. [NRS]

ANGUS, ELIZABETH, relict of John Lyle a merchant in Edinburgh, test., 1762, C.E. [NAS]

ANGUS, JAMES, a wright in Edinburgh, test., 1753, C.E. [NRS]

ANGUS, MARGARET, relict of George Skinner a merchant in Edinburgh, test., 1740, C.E. [NRS]

ANGUS, ROBERT, a flesher burgess of Canongate, test.s, 1745 and 1754, C.E. [NRS]

ANGUS, WILLIAM, a merchant in Edinburgh, 1730. [NRS.AC10.155]; test., 1756, C.E. [NRS]

ANGUS, WILLIAM, a sailor on the Elizabeth of Leith, test., 1766, C.E. [NRS]

ANIGUS, EDWARD, a merchant in Edinburgh, test., 1737, C.E. [NRS]

ANSWORTH, JOHN, a merchant, burgess of Canongate, 1726. [CBR]

ANTONIUS, HENRY, a wright in Edinburgh, test., 1750, C.E. [NAS]

ARBUTHNOTT, ALEXANDER, a tailor in Edinburgh, test., 1725, C.E. [NRS]

ARBUTHNOTT, ALEXANDER, a bailie of Edinburgh, 1731. [NRS.AC10.185]; a merchant in Edinburgh, test., 1764, C.E. [ERA]

ARBUTHNOTT, ARCHIBALD, son of bailie Alexander Arbuthnott a merchant, a merchant in Edinburgh, a burgess and guilds-brother in 1750, a deed, 1750; test., 1775, C.E. [NRS.RD3.210.577][EBR]

ARBUTHNOTT, ELIZABETH, dau. of Thomas Arbuthnott a merchant in Edinburgh, test., 1758, C.E. [NRS]

ARBUTHNOTT, GEORGE, a merchant in Edinburgh, a burgess and guilds-brother of Edinburgh in 1737, a sasine, 1753.[EBR][NRS.RS27.142.62]

ARBUTHNOTT, JAMES, a merchant in Edinburgh, test., 1729, C.E. [NRS]

ARCHIBALD, JAMES, son of William Archibald a tanner, a tanner in Portsburgh, Edinburgh, a burgess in 1747, a sasine, 1751. [NRS.RS27.138.183][EBR]

ARCHIBALD, WILLIAM, son of John Archibald a lint-dresser, appr. to James Waugh a merchant in Edinburgh, 1766-1771. [ERA]

ARMSTRONG, HENRY, a merchant in Leith, 1725. [NRS.CS228/A.1/10]

ARMSTRONG, JOHN, a sailor in Leith, husband of Christian Mitchell, 1748. [ECL#32]

ARMSTRONG, JOHN, heir to his mother Mary Lautie, wife of James Armstrong a wigmaker in Leith, 1777. [NRS.S/H]

ARMSTRONG, JOHN, a writer from Edinburgh, in Jamaica, a decreet, 1778. [NRS.AC7.56; CS.GMB.56]

ARMSTRONG, WILLIAM, a coppersmith burgess and guilds-brother of Edinburgh, 1768, son of William Armstrong a coppersmith burgess. [EBR]

ARNOT, GEORGE, a sailor in Leith, husband of Eliza Birnie, 1731. [SL#30]

The People of Edinburgh, 1725-1775

ARNOT, GEORGE, a brewer in Leith, a letter, 1749. [NRS.CH2.716.265]
ARNOT, HUGO, an advocate burgess and guilds-brother of Edinburgh, 1779. [EBR]
ARTHUR, ALEXANDER, boxmaster of the Tailors of Edinburgh, a deed, 1750. [NRS.R4.176/1.389]
ARTHUR, GEORGE, coachman to the Duchess of Gordon, burgess of Canongate, 1725. [CBR]
ARTHUR, HELEN, born 1753, a servant from Edinburgh, from Leith to Philadelphia, Pennsylvania, in May 1775. [TNA.T47.12]
ARTHUR, ISABEL, born 1748, a servant from Edinburgh, from Leith to Philadelphia, Pennsylvania, in May 1775. [TNA.T47.12]
ARTHUR, JAMES, master's mate aboard HMS Prince Frederick, son and heir of Alexander Arthur a burgess of Edinburgh, 1762. [NRS.S/H]
ASHER, JOHN, born 1745, a gardener from Edinburgh, to Virginia in December 1773. [TNA.T47.9.11]
ATCHISON, WILLIAM, a sailor in Leith, dead by 1756. [ECL#14]
AUCHENLECK, CHARLES, son of Robert Auchenleck a white-ironsmith, appr. to Duncan McQueen a white-ironsmith in Edinburgh, 1766-1772. [ERA]
AUCHENLECK, GILBERT, son of James Auchenleck, a cutler in Edinburgh, a burgess 1750, a sasine, 1759. [NRS.RS27.154.447][EBR]
AUCHENLECK, ROBERT, appr. to Messrs Martin and Wetherspoon printers in Edinburgh, 1770-1774. [ERA]; a burgess of Edinburgh, 1770. [EBR]
AUCHTERLONY, JAMES, a smith burgess of Edinburgh, 1763, former apprentice to William Balfour a smith burgess. [EBR]
AULD, WILLIAM, born 1770, a surgeon in Edinburgh, at Hudson Bay from 1790 to 1815, died in Edinburgh after 1830. [HBRS.2.204]
AUSTIN, Dr ADAM, in Edinburgh, deeds, 1755, 1773. [NRS.RD4.214/878/890, 895]
AYTON, GEORGE, son of George Ayton a skinner, appr. to John Dalgleish a skinner burgess of Edinburgh, 1736. [ERA]
AYTON, WILLIAM, a goldsmith in Edinburgh, a burgess and guilds-brother in 1718, an indenture, 1746; test., 1755, C.E. [NRS.RD3.210.203][EBR]
BACHOPE, JOHN, a skipper in Leith, test., 1730, C.E. [NRS]
BACHOPE, WILLIAM, a skipper in Leith, a burgess of Inveraray, 1742. [BI#44]
BADEN, JOHN, an ale-seller burgess of Canongate, 1727. [CBR]
BAILLIE, ALEXANDER, a shoemaker burgess of Edinburgh, 1765, son of Angus Baillie a burgess. [EBR]
BAILLIE, ALEXANDER, a merchant burgess and guilds-brother of Edinburgh, 1766. [EBR]

The People of Edinburgh, 1725-1775

BAILLIE, BLINSHALL, son of Robert Baillie a mason in Canongate, appr. to Baillie Blinshall a saddler in Edinburgh, 1769-1775. [ERA]

BAILLIE, GEORGE, a merchant from Edinburgh, settled in Georgia 1733, [TNA.CO5.670.106]; a merchant in Savannah, 1763, [GaGaz#15]; a Loyalist in 1776, returned to Edinburgh. [TNA.AO12.74.101][NRS.RD3.279.116]

BAILLIE, JAMES, son of Alexander Baillie a writer, appr. to George Murray a surgeon apothecary burgess of Edinburgh, 1733. [ERA]

BAILLIE, JAMES, son of Robert Baillie a merchant in Edinburgh, a merchant in Jamaica, 1740. [NRS.GD1.1155.64]

BAILLIE, JAMES, a merchant in Edinburgh, a deed, 1750. [NRS.RD4.176/2.258]

BAILLIE, JOHN, son of Michael Baillie a writer, a merchant from Edinburgh, a burgess and guilds-brother in 1724, to Georgia in 1733. [TNA.CO5.70.106][EBR]

BAILLIE, JOHN, an upholsterer burgess of Edinburgh, 1776, son of Thomas Baillie millwright burgess at the Water of Leith. [EBR]

BAILLIE, PATRICK, a writer in Edinburgh, a deed, 1750. [NRS.RD4.176/1.67]

BAILLIE, ROBERT, a merchant in Edinburgh, 1728; a deed, 1750, 1757, a sasine, 1751; from Leith aboard the <u>Elizabeth and Peggy of Leith</u>, master Walter Scott, bound for Charleston, South Carolina, 1757. [NRS.AC10.141; RD2.168.256; AC7.49.1293; RS27.138.84; AC9.1591/7]

BAILLIE, ROBERT, a merchant burgess and guilds-brother of Edinburgh, 1770, former apprentice to William Hogg merchant burgess and guilds-brother.[EBR]

BAILLIE, THOMAS, a millwright burgess of Edinburgh, 1771, husband of Helen dau. of William Gordon a baxter burgess. [EBR]

BAILLIE, WILLIAM, son of William Baillie a coach-master in Canongate, appr. to Robert Thomson a coach and harness maker in Canongate, 1738. [ERA]

BAILLIE, WILLIAM, a merchant in Jamaica, a burgess and guilds-brother of Edinburgh, 1757. [EBR]

BAIN, GEORGE, a vintner burgess of Edinburgh, 1774. [EBR]

BAIN, THOMAS, son of David Bain in Canongate, appr. to John Mylne a founder in Edinburgh, 1773-1781. [ERA]

BAIRD, CESSFORD, appr. to his uncle John Kennedy a surgeon in Edinburgh, 1747. [ERA]

BAIRD, DAVID, son of William Baird a merchant, a merchant in Edinburgh, a burgess and guilds-brother in 1730, a deed, 1740; trading with Maryland, a decreet, 1748. [NRS.RD2.167.435; CS16.1.80][EBR]

BAIRD, GEORGE, son of Alexander Baird in Edinburgh, appr. to William Gray a cordiner burgess of Edinburgh, 1733. [ERA]

BAIRD, JAMES, son of Alexander Baird a shoemaker, appr. to James McCoull a candlemaker in Edinburgh, 1771-1777. [ERA]

The People of Edinburgh, 1725-1775

BAIRD, JAMES, a painter burgess of Edinburgh, 1775, son of James Baird a baxter burgess. [EBR]
BAIRD, JAMES, a writer in Edinburgh, a decreet, 1779. [NRS.CS16.1.174]
BAIRD, THOMAS, a wright in Edinburgh, heir to his uncle John Kennedy of Dangart, a surgeon-apothecary in Edinburgh, 1761. [NRS.S/H]
BAIRDNER, ARCHIBALD, son of William Bairdner of Coltmill, appr. to Thomas Mitchell a goldsmith in Edinburgh, 1761-1768. [ERA]
BAIRNSFATHER, ALEXANDER, a baxter in Leith, a burgess of Edinburgh, 1767, husband of Eupham dau. of George Herriot a baxter burgess. [EBR]
BAIRNSFATHER, GEORGE, son of Hugh Bairnsfather, appr. to John Scott a plumber burgess of Edinburgh, 1724. [ERA]
BALDERSON, WILLIAM, a staymaker burgess of Edinburgh, 1762, son of George Balderston a feltmaker. [EBR]
BALDON, JOHN, a stabler in Leith, 1748. [NRS.CH2.716.264]
BALFOUR, ANDREW, a merchant in Edinburgh, land-owner in St Andrew's parish, South Carolina, 1741. [South Carolina Deeds, book W#469]
BALFOUR, ANDREW, born in Edinburgh during 1737, son of Andrew Balfour and his wife Margaret Robertson, a salt manufacturer in Charleston, South Carolina, died 1782, test., 1783, C.E. [NRS]
BALFOUR, ARCHIBALD, a merchant in Edinburgh, trading with Boston, 1738. [NRS.AC7.43.493; AC13.1; AC10.10.246]
BALFOUR, DAVID, a sailor from Leith, a house-breaker, transported in April 1774. [AJ#1374]
BALFOUR, GEORGE, son of George Balfour a Writer to the Signet, appr. to John Hope & Company merchants in Edinburgh, 1763-1768. [ERA]
BALFOUR, JANET, born 1757, a servant from Edinburgh, from Leith to Philadelphia, Pennsylvania, in May 1775. [TNA.T47.12]
BALFOUR, JOHN, a burgess and guilds-brother of Edinburgh, 1761, son of James Balfour of Pilrig an advocate burgess and guilds-brother. [EBR]
BALFOUR, JOHN, born 1748 in Edinburgh, son of Andrew Balfour of Braidwood and his wife Margaret Robertson, a merchant-planter in South Carolina, a Loyalist, died in South Carolina, 1781, test., 1783, C.E. [NA.AO12.48.238][NRS.CC8.8.126]
BALFOUR, ROBERT, a merchant in Leith, a deed, 1750. [NRS.RD3.210.183]
BALFOUR, ROBERT, in Edinburgh, a deed, 1769. [NRS.RD4.213/1251]
BALLANTYNE, JOHN, a wool merchant burgess of Edinburgh, 1776. [EBR]
BALLINGALL, DAVID, Lieutenant of Edinburgh City Guard, a burgess and guilds-brother. [EBR]
BALLINGAL, JOHN, a writer in Edinburgh, 1739. [NRS.AC11.114]

The People of Edinburgh, 1725-1775

BALLINGALL, THOMAS, son of Thomas Ballingall a journeyman baxter, appr. to George Gellis a barber and wig-maker burgess of Edinburgh, 1743. [ERA]

BALMAINE, ALEXANDER, born 1740 in Edinburgh, a minister educated at St Andrews and Edinburgh Universities 1757-1760, settled in Copley, Virginia, by 1772, died 1820 in Fredericksburg, Va. [EMA#12][FRA#310]

BANKHEAD, WILLIAM, a burgess and guilds-brother of Edinburgh, 1763.[EBR]

BANKS, CHARLES, a merchant in Leith, 1736. [NRS.AC10.241]

BANKS, DAVID, a skipper in Leith, and his wife Isobel Christie, test., 1739, C.E. [NRS]

BANKS, JAMES, a sailor in Leith, 1762. [SL#95]

BANNATYNE, ANDREW, son of Andrew Bannatyne a merchant, appr. to James Buchanan a wright burgess of Edinburgh, 1734. [ERA]; a burgess and guilds-brother of Edinburgh, 1769. [EBR]

BANNATYNE, JAMES, a writer from Edinburgh, later in Jamaica, 1783. [NRS.CS17.1.2]

BANNATYNE, WILLIAM, a shipmaster at Coalhill, Leith, 1773. [WED#8]

BANNERMAN, JOHN, son of William Bannerman a ticket porter, appr. to James Wemyss a goldsmith in Edinburgh, 1763-1770. [ERA]

BAPTIE, DAVID, a skipper in Leith, test., 1729, C.E. [NRS]

BAPTIE, PETER, a sailor, married Elizabeth Carthrae in Leith, 1725. [SL#21]

BARCLAY, ALEXANDER, former appr. to the late Alexander Smitoun a hatter in Canongate, later appr. to Robert Oliphant a hatter in Edinburgh, 1747. [ERA]

BARCLAY, GEORGE, son of George Barclay a founder in Canongate, appr. to Robert Boog a cutler in Edinburgh, 1759-176. [ERA]

BARCLAY, HARRY ROBERTSON, son of James Robertson a Writer to the Signet, appr. to Mansfield, Hunter & Company, merchants in Edinburgh, 1767-1772. [ERA]

BARCLAY, JAMES, master of Edinburgh High School, a deed, 1750. [NRS.RD3.210.498]

BARCLAY, JOHN, a merchant in Edinburgh, a sasine, 1755. [NRS.RS27.146.107]

BARCLAY, PATRICK, son of Andrew Barclay and his wife Helen Lyon, a merchant from Edinburgh, settled in Virginia before 1745. [NRS.S/H.24.8.1745; AC8.659]

BARCLAY, WILLIAM, son of John Barclay a minister, appr. to John Aitoun a wright burgess of Edinburgh, 1732. [ERA]

BARCLAY, WILLIAM, a merchant burgess and guilds-brother of Edinburgh, 1763, apprentice to McCulloch and Tod burgesses and guildbrothers. [EBR]

BARCLAY, WILLIAM, a baker in Pleasance, Edinburgh, heir to his father William Barclay, a tailor in Canongate, 1767; also heir to his aunt Elspeth Barclay, widow of Thomas Aitken in Canongate, 1769. [NRS.S/H]

The People of Edinburgh, 1725-1775

BARR, ROBERT, son of Robert Barr a stabler, appr. to Alexander Armstrong a coppersmith burgess of Edinburgh, 1745. [ERA]; a burgess of Edinburgh, 1763. [EBR]

BARROWMAN, PETER, a stabler burgess of Edinburgh, 1762, husband of Margaret dau. of Walter Somervail in Portsburgh. [EBR]

BARROWMAN, WILLIAM, a baker in Canongate, heir to his cousin Margaret Forrester, dau. of James Forrester, a shipmaster in Burntisland, 1765. [NRS.S/H]

BARTLET, ALEXANDER, a master of Edinburgh High School, a burgess and guilds-brother of Edinburgh, 1762. [EBR]

BARTRAM, WILLIAM, appr. to Patrick Manderson a merchant burgess of Edinburgh, 1735. [ERA]

BATCHELOR, CHARLES, son of Charles Batchelor a barber burgess of Edinburgh, heir to his sister Janet Batchelor, 1764. [NRS.S/H]

BATHGATE, WILLIAM, a writer from Edinburgh, to Jamaica on 3 September 1736. [NRS.RH9.17.31]

BATHIE, DAVID, son of Robert Bathie a servant of Lady Mary Cunningham, appr. to Walter Brunton a saddler and belt-maker in Edinburgh, 1775-1781. [ERA]

BAULK, WILLIAM, son of William Baulk a sailor in Leith, appr. to Patrick Cargill a cutler burgess of Edinburgh, 1754. [ERA]

BAVERIDGE, GEORGE, son of George Baveridge a brewer in the Abbey of Holyrood, appr. to Andrew Newton and Andrew Henderson merchants in Edinburgh, 1742. [ERA]

BAVERIDGE, JAMES, son of George Baveridge a baxter in Portsburgh, Edinburgh, appr. to Richard Pollock a baxter in Edinburgh, 1742. [ERA]

BAXTER, GILBERT, a merchant burgess and guilds-brother of Edinburgh, 1766/1772. [EBR]

BAXTER, JOHN, son of Andrew Baxter in Edinburgh, appr. to David Somerville a merchant in Edinburgh, 1773-1782. [ERA]

BAXTER, WILLIAM, a baxter in North Leith, burgess of Canongate, 1726. [CBR]

BAYNE, ROBERT, son of John Bayne in Portsburgh, Edinburgh, appr. to George Forrest a barber wigmaker burgess of Edinburgh, 1753. [ERA]

BEATH, JOHN, a shoemaker in Edinburgh, heir to his mother Mary Wishart, wife of Andrew Beath a shoemaker there, 1776. [NRS.S/H]

BEATSON, ANDREW, a merchant burgess and guilds-brother of Edinburgh, 1761/1765, husband of Mary dau. of Adam Anderson a barber burgess. [EBR]

BEATSON, JOHN, a resident of Edinburgh and master of the Neptune of London, test., 1767, C.E. [NRS]

BEATSON, JOHN, a shipmaster in North Leith, 1773. [WED#8]

The People of Edinburgh, 1725-1775

BEATSON, WILLIAM, a shipmaster in Queen Street, Leith, 1773. [WED#8]

BEATT, DAVID, son of David Beatt a writing master, appr. to David Navey a merchant burgess of Edinburgh, 1731. [ERA]

BEGBIE, GEORGE, a cow-feeder in Canongate, a decreet, 1748. [NRS.CS16.1.80]

BEGBIE, GEORGE, a smith burgess and guilds-brother of Edinburgh, 1773, husband of Agnes dau. of William Armstrong a coppersmith burgess and guilds-brother. [EBR]

BEGBIE, JOSEPH, son of Patrick Begbie a hatmaker in Beggar-row, Edinburgh, appr. to David Anderson a hatmaker in Edinburgh, 1758-1765. [ERA]

BEGBIE, WILLIAM, son of Adam Begbie a tailor in Potter-row, Edinburgh, appr. to William Rankin a tailor in Edinburgh, 1778-1785. [ERA]

BEGG, WILLIAM, a merchant burgess and guilds-brother of Edinburgh, 1763. [EBR]

BEGRIE, JOHN, a grocer burgess of Edinburgh, 1775, husband of Ann dau. of Adam Henderson a burgess. [EBR]

BELL, ALEXANDER, a wigmaker burgess and guilds-brother of Edinburgh, 1767, husband of Jean dau. of George Gray a merchant burgess. [EBR]

BELL, ANDREW, from Edinburgh, a blacksmith in Beaufort, South Carolina, probate, 1753, S.C.

BELL, ANDREW, an engraver burgess of Edinburgh, 1761, son of John Bell a baxter burgess. [EBR]

BELL, ANDREW, in Edinburgh, a deed, 1773. [NRS.RD4.214/116]

BELL, ANDREW, son of Andrew Bell a smith in Canongate, appr. to Andrew Boog a cutler in Edinburgh, 1775-1781. [ERA]

BELL, BARTHOLEMEW, a skipper in Leith, 1729, son of William Bell a cooper in Leith, test., 1740, Comm. Edinburgh. [NRS.AC10.144.147]

BELL, BENJAMIN, a surgeon burgess of Edinburgh, 1773. [EBR]

BELL, GEORGE, a carpenter and sailor in Leith, husband of Anne Porteous, 1744. [SL#52]

BELL, HUGH, a brewer in Edinburgh, heir to his brother Bartholemew Bell a brewer there, 1761; also to his father John Bell, a brewer there, 1766; and to his mother Margaret Campbell, widow of John Bell a brewer there, 1778. [NRS.S/H]

BELL, ISOBEL, spouse to Alexander Philp a merchant in Leith later purser aboard HMS Thetis, test., 1757, C.E. [NRS]

BELL, JOHN, born 1753, a surgeon from Edinburgh, to Nevis in January 1774. [NRS.CE60.1.7]

BELL, JOHN, a bookseller and merchant burgess and guilds-brother of Edinburgh, 1762. [EBR]

The People of Edinburgh, 1725-1775

BELL, JOHN, a baker burgess of Edinburgh, 1770, former apprentice to Walter Colvil a baker burgess. [EBR]
BELL, NICOL, a coppersmith burgess of Edinburgh, 1776, son of Robert Bell a coppersmith. [EBR]
BELL, THOMAS, a candlemaker burgess of Edinburgh, 1774, former apprentice to John Harries a candlemaker burgess. [EBR]
BELL, WILLIAM, a cooper in Leith, 1733. [NRS.AC11.65]
BENNET, FRANCIS, a sailor in Leith, husband of Helen Jamieson, 1767. [SL#103]
BENNET, MAXWELL, a writer from Edinburgh, in Jamaica, a decreet, 1780. [NRS.CS16.1.179]
BENNET, PATRICK, a burgess of Edinburgh, 1766. [EBR]
BENNET, WILLIAM, a barber burgess of Edinburgh, 1778, son of John Bennet a stabler burgess. [EBR]
BENNY, DANIEL. In Edinburgh, a deed 1769. [NRS.RD3.232/226]
BENNY, JOHN, a distiller in Edinburgh, a burgess in 1747, a deed, 1750. [NRS.RD4.176/2.303][EBR]
BERRY, DAVID, a merchant in Edinburgh, a burgess and guilds-brother in 1717, a deed, 1749. [NRS.RD2.167.125][EBR]
BERRY, JAMES, a merchant burgess and guilds-brother of Edinburgh, 1765, son of David Berry a merchant burgess. [EBR]
BERRIE, WILLIAM, a watchmaker burgess of Canongate, 1726. [CBR]
BERRY, WILLIAM, a burgess and guilds-brother of Edinburgh, 1771, son of David Berry a merchant.[EBR]
BERTRAM, GILBERT, a merchant in Edinburgh, a deed, 1750. [NRS.RD2.167.439]
BEVERAGE, JAMES, a dyer in Edinburgh, 1729. [NRS.AC10.147]
BEVERIDGE, JAMES, a merchant in Edinburgh, a deed, 1750. [NRS.RD3.210.407]
BEVERLIE, ALEXANDER, a merchant burgess of Edinburgh, 1762, former apprentice to John Shaw a merchant burgess. [EBR]
BIGGAR, JOHN, a linen manufacturer burgess and guilds-brother of Edinburgh, 1761, son of Robert Biggar a merchant burgess and guilds-brother. [EBR]
BIGGAR, WALTER, a linen manufacturer burgess and guilds-brother of Edinburgh, 1761, son of Robert Biggar a merchant burgess and guilds-brother. [EBR]
BINNING, JOHN, from Edinburgh, in Boston, New England,1762. [SCS]
BISHOP, HELEN, relict of Patrick Halliday a skipper in Leith, test., 1774, C.E. [NRS]
BISSETT, ALEXANDER, son of David Bissett a waterman in Canongate, appr. to Francis Montgomery a barber in Edinburgh, 1763-1768. [ERA]

The People of Edinburgh, 1725-1775

BISSET, JAMES, a gardener in Edinburgh, a deed, 1750. [NRS.RD2.168.317]

BISSETT, MCQUEEN, son of David Bissett a waterman in Canongate, appr. to William Herriot a gunsmith in Edinburgh, 1762-1769. [ERA]

BLACK, JOHN, a meal-maker burgess of Canongate, husband of Lydia Dunbar, 1727. [CBR]

BLACK, JOHN, a shoemaker burgess of Edinburgh, 1770. [EBR]

BLACK, JOHN, son of William Black a porter, appr. to William Downie a watchmaker in Edinburgh, 1771-1778. [ERA]

BLACK, Dr JOSEPH, a burgess and guilds-brother of Edinburgh, 1766, [EBR]; a deed, 1773. [NRS.RD2.213/390]

BLACK, WILLIAM, son of Andrew Black a mason, appr. to Andrew Burn a mason in Edinburgh, 1757-1763. [ERA]

BLACKADDER, ADAM, son of John Blackadder of St Leonards, appr. to William Dempster a goldsmith and jeweller in Edinburgh, 1763-1770. [ERA]

BLACKBURN, JAMES, a merchant in Edinburgh, 1743. [NRS.AC11.155]

BLACKHALL, JOHN, an accountant burgess and guilds-brother of Edinburgh, 1764, former servant to Francis Farquharson. [EBR]

BLACKSTOCK, EDWARD, in North Leith, commander of HMS Prince William, test., 1740, Comm. Edinburgh. [NRS]

BLACKWOOD, ALEXANDER, son of Sir Robert Baird, a merchant in Edinburgh, a burgess and guilds-brother in 1723, a bond, 1749. [NRS.RD2.168.281][EBR]

BLAIR, ANDREW, sailor in Leith, husband of Margaret Greig, 1755. [SL#79]

BLAIR, ANDREW, son of Alexander Blair a wright, appr. to James Howden a clock and watchmaker in Edinburgh, 1775-1782. [ERA]

BLAIR, ARCHIBALD, son of John Blair an apothecary, a writer in Edinburgh, a burgess and guilds-brother in 1714, a decreet, 1746. [NRS.CS16.1.79][EBR]

BLAIR, CHARLES, a goldsmith burgess of Edinburgh, test., 1753, C.E. [NRS]

BLAIR, FRANCIS, a merchant burgess and guilds-brother of Edinburgh, 1776, former apprentice to Neil McVicar a merchant and linen manufacturer burgess and guilds-brother. [EBR]

BLAIR, GILBERT, skipper in Leith, 1742. [ECL#49]

BLAIR, JAMES, skipper in Leith, master of the Anne of Edinburgh, test., 1737, C.E. [NRS]

BLAIR, JAMES, a merchant in Edinburgh, 1732. [NRS.AC11.54]

BLAIR, JOHN, a merchant in Williamsburg, Virginia, son of Peter Blair a skinner in Edinburgh, a decreet, 1746. [NRS.CS16.1.79]

BLAIR, JOHN, a merchant in Edinburgh, a decreet, 1773. [NRS.CS16.1.154]

BLAIR, WILLIAM, a merchant in Edinburgh, heir to his grandmother Euphemia Nisbet, widow of David Blair a minister there, 1765. [NRS.S/H]

The People of Edinburgh, 1725-1775

BLYTH, JAMES, a wright burgess of Edinburgh, 1776, former apprentice to Alexander Penman a wright burgess. [EBR]

BLYTH, ROBERT, a merchant burgess and guilds-brother of Edinburgh, 1773, husband of Jean dau. of William Russell a merchant burgess and guilds-brother. [EBR]

BLYTH, WILLIAM a tailor in Leith, 1738. [NRS.AC7.43.493]

BOAG, JOHN, a mariner in Leith, husband of Elizabeth Loudoun, test., 1748, C.E. [NRS]

BOIG, JOHN, a sailor in Leith, 1735. [SL#39]

BODDIE, JAMES, in Edinburgh, a deed, 1763. [NRS.RD3.232/273]

BOGGIE, HUGH, son of Kenneth Boggie in Edinburgh, appr. to Thomas Donald a locksmith in Edinburgh, 1761-1768. [ERA]

BOGLE, PATRICK, a burgess and guilds-brother of Edinburgh, 1744. [EBR]

BONAR, ANDREW, a merchant in Edinburgh, 1750. [NRS.AC10.347]

BONTHRON, JAMES, a wright in Edinburgh, heir to his uncle David Bonthron, a shoemaker in Strathmiglo, 1769. [NRS.S/H]

BOOG, ANDREW, a cutler burgess of Edinburgh, 1779, son of Robert Boog a cutler burgess. [EBR]

BOOG, JOHN, a mariner in Leith, husband of Janet Ferrier, 1764. [SL#98]

BORTHWICK, ALEXANDER, a merchant burgess and guilds-brother, 1776. [EBR]

BORTHWICK, JOHN, a merchant from Edinburgh, a burgess and guilds-brother in 1756, in North America, decreets, 1770, 1772. [NRS.CS16.1.141/148][EBR]

BORTHWICK, JOSEPH, a skipper in Leith, 1759. [ECL#39]

BOSWELL, ALEXANDER, son of Alexander Boswell a merchant, a painter in Edinburgh, a burgess in 1719, a deed, 1750. [NRS.RD3.210.565][EBR]

BOSWELL, Dr JOHN, in Edinburgh, a deed, 1772. [NRS.RD4.213/204]

BOSWELL, THOMAS, a writer in Edinburgh, heir to his father George Boswell, a writer there, 1762. [NRS.S/H]; a deed, 1773; died 8 April 1776, his widow Elizabeth Balfour born 1743, died 20 June 1814. [NRS.RD2.214/2/381][Greyfriars MI, Edinburgh]

BOSWELL, THOMAS, a skipper in Rotten Row, Leith, 1773. [WED#8]

BOSWELL, WALTER, an appr. to Robert Reid a saddler, a saddler in Edinburgh, a burgess in 1713, a deed, 1749. [NRS.RD2.167.82][EBR]

BOWIE, JAMES, a painter burgess of Edinburgh, 1776. [EBR]

BOWIE, PATRICK, son of Archibald Bowie a minister at Monzie, a merchant in Edinburgh, a burgess and guilds-brother in 1743, a deed, 1750. [EBR] [NRS.RD4.176/2.22]

BOWIE, ROBERT, a brewer in the Yardheads of Leith, process of scandal, 1726. [NRS.CC8.6.218]

BOWMAN, JOHN, a sailor in Leith, 1739. [ECL#10]

The People of Edinburgh, 1725-1775

BOWMAN, THOMAS, son of William Bowman in Canonmills, appr. to Alexander Ritchie a skinner in Edinburgh, 1770-1775. [ERA]

BOYD, JAMES, a writer in Edinburgh, a deed, 1750. [NRS.RD2.167.229]

BOYD, JOHN, a mariner in Leith, husband of Ann Young, 1765. [SL#101]

BOYD, ROBERT, a writer in Edinburgh, a bond, 1723. [NRS.RD4.176/1.481]

BOYD, WILLIAM, a sailor in Leith, husband of Mary Wilson, 1751. [SL#69]

BRAIDWOOD, FRANCIS, a wright burgess and guilds-brother of Edinburgh, 1776, son of William Braidwood a candlemaker burgess. [EBR]

BRAIDWOOD, THOMAS, a teacher of book-keeping in Edinburgh, a decreet, 1774.[NRS.CS1.1.11]

BRAIDWOOD, WILLIAM, a candle-maker in Edinburgh, a burgess 1750, and his widow Helen Lithgow, a decreet, 1779. [NRS.CS16.1.175]

BRAND, JOHN, a clothier and dyer burgess of Edinburgh, 1770. [EBR]

BRANDON, JOHN, a dyer burgess of Edinburgh, 1762, son of Charles Brandon a dyer burgess. [EBR]

BRASH, JAMES, a mariner in Leith, husband of Jean Brash, test., 1771, C.E. [NRS]

BREAKENRIDGE, JOHN, son of John Breakenridge, a watchmaker in Portsburgh, Edinburgh, a decreet, 1781. [NRS.CS16.1.183]

BRIDGES, THOMAS, a merchant burgess and guilds-brother of Edinburgh, 1774, former appr. to Hugh Hamilton a merchant burgess. [EBR]

BROCK, THOMAS, a flesher burgess of Edinburgh, 1774. [EBR]

BRODIE, ALEXANDER, in Edinburgh, a deed, 1773. [NRS.RD3.232/202]; a baker burgess of Edinburgh, 1774, former appr. to James Craig a baker. [EBR]

BRODIE, FRANCIS, a wright burgess of Edinburgh, 1763, husband of Cecilia dau. of William Grant a writer burgess and guilds-brother. [EBR]

BRODIE, JOHN, a sailor in Leith, husband of Margaret Barton, 1738. [ECL#21]

BRODIE, JOHN, a mariner in Leith, husband of Euphan Glover, 1768. [SL#103]

BRODIE, WILLIAM, a wright burgess of Edinburgh, 1763, son of Francis Brodie a burgess and guilds-brother. [EBR]

BROMLEY, JOHN, a mariner in Leith, husband of Rachel Gibson, 1730. [SL#29]

BROWN, ALEXANDER, in Leith, a mariner aboard HMS Firm, husband of Ann Galbraith, 1762. [SL#92]

BROWN, CHARLES, a stabler in Edinburgh, a deed, 1750. [NRS.RD2.167.274]

BROWN, CHARLES, a writer in Edinburgh, a deed, 1750. [NRS.RD2.168.45]

BROWN, DAVID, son of Reverend John Brown, a merchant in Edinburgh, a burgess and guilds-brother in 1727, a deed,1750. [NRS.RD2.167.418][EBR]

BROWN, DAVID, son of David Brown a journeyman wright, appr. to James Cowan a watch-maker in Edinburgh, 1772-1780. [ERA]

BROWN, GEORGE, a sailor in Leith, test., 1774, C. E. [NRS]

The People of Edinburgh, 1725-1775

BROWN, HUGH, a journeyman goldsmith in Edinburgh, son of Roderick Brown turnkey of Edinburgh Tolbooth, test., 1763, C.E. [NRS]

BROWN, JAMES, an ale-seller in Pleasance, burgess of Canongate, 1725. [CBR]

BROWN, JAMES, in Edinburgh, a deed, 1750. [NRS.RD3.210.320]

BROWN, JOHN, a skipper in Leith, test., 1760, Comm. Edinburgh. [NRS]

BROWN, JOHN, son of James Brown a brushmaker, appr. to Robert Brown a founder in Edinburgh, 1773-1779. [ERA]

BROWN, JOHN, a shipmaster in North Leith, 1773. [WED#8]

BROWN, JOHN, son and heir of James Brown an Excise officer in Leith, 1773. [NRS.S/H]

BROWN, MATTHEW, son and heir of Mathew Brown a writer in Edinburgh, 1774. [NRS.S/H]

BROWN, NICOL, son of Nicol Brown a flesher, a flesher in Edinburgh, a deed, 1750, a burgess in 1751. [NRS.RD4.176/1.237][EBR]

BROWN, PATRICK, son of James Brown, a wigmaker in Edinburgh, a burgess in 1731, a bond, 1749. [NRS.RD2.168.281][EBR]

BROWN, PATRICK, heir to his father Malcolm Brown, a saddler burgess of Edinburgh, 1768. [NRS.S/H]

BROWN, RALPH, a skipper in North Leith, husband of Isobel Caldwell, test., 1735, C.E. [NRS]

BROWN, ROBERT, an Excise officer in Leith, heir to his brother William Brown an Excise officer there, 1771. [NRS.S/H]

BROWN, WILLIAM, a merchant in Leith, a deed, 1749. [NRS.RD4.176/1.165]

BROWN, WILLIAM, born 1733, a cooper from Edinburgh, to Virginia in April 1751. [CLRO/AIA]

BROWN, WILLIAM, born 1683, a minister in Edinburgh, died 23 March 1736, husband of Bridget Balfour. [Greyfriars MI, Edinburgh]

BRUCE, ALEXANDER, a merchant in Edinburgh, a deed, 1750. [NRS.RD4.176/1.17]

BRUCE, ALEXANDER, a vintner in Edinburgh, a tack, 1741. [NRS.RD3.210.561]

BRUCE, ALEXANDER, a wright burgess of Edinburgh, 1774, son of Alexander Bruce an upholsterer burgess. [EBR]

BRUCE, DAVID, from Edinburgh, a Moravian missionary in Pennsylvania, New York, and New Jersey, from 1740 to 1749, died in Sharon, Connecticut, on 9 July 1749. [CCMC]

BRUCE, EDWARD, a writer in Edinburgh, heir to his mother Janet Gibson or Bruce, dau. of Sir Edward Gibson of Kinnaird, 1776. [NRS.S/H]

BRUCE, JAMES, son of William Bruce a printer, appr. to Baillie Blinshall a saddler in Edinburgh, 1760-1767. [ERA]

The People of Edinburgh, 1725-1775

BRUCE, JANET, born 1757, a servant from Edinburgh, to Philadelphia, Pennsylvania, in May 1775. [TNA.T47.12]

BRUCE, JOHN, a merchant in Edinburgh, 1744. [NRS.AC11.227]

BRUCE, JOHN, a musician in Edinburgh, a deed, 1750. [NRS.RD2.167.347]

BRUCE, ROBERT, a founder burgess of Edinburgh, 1762, son of John Bruce a merchant burgess. [EBR]

BRUCE, ROBERT, a slater burgess of Edinburgh, 1769, husband of Elizabeth dau. of William Rendale a slater burgess. [EBR]

BRUCE, WILLIAM, son of William Bruce, a merchant in Edinburgh, a burgess and guilds-brother in 1747, a deed, 1750. [NRS.RD4.176/2.442][EBR]

BRUCE, WILLIAM, an upholsterer burgess and guilds-brother of Edinburgh, 1768/1775, husband of Agnes dau. of George Begbie a smith burgess. [EBR]

BRUNTON, JOHN, a merchant burgess and guilds-brother of Edinburgh, 1769, husband of Elizabeth dau. of James Fyfe a tailor burgess and guilds- brother. [EBR]

BRUNTON, PETER, son of Peter Brunton, an appr. to William Cowan a lorimer in Edinburgh, 1770-1776. [ERA]

BRYCE, WALTER, a saddler burgess of Edinburgh, 1772, former appr. of Thomas Cleland a saddler burgess. [EBR]

BRYCE, THOMAS, a merchant burgess and guilds-brother of Edinburgh, 1775. [EBR]

BRYDIE, ANDREW, a skipper in Leith, 1735. [NRS.AC10.209]

BRYMER, ALEXANDER, a baker in Leith, a deed, 1750. [NRS.RD4.176/2.262]

BRYMER, JOHN, a sailor in Leith, 1740. [ECL#22]

BRYMER, WILLIAM, a tailor burgess of Canongate, 1725. [CBR]

BRYSON, GAVIN, appr. to Patrick Stewart a barber and wig-maker, wigmaker in Edinburgh, a burgess in 1735, a guilds-brother in 1737, a deed, 1750. [NRS.RD4.176/2.195][EBR]

BRYSON, ROBERT, a shipmaster in Leith, 1735; master of the Ann of Edinburgh, to Boston, New England,1738; test., 1738, C.E. [NRS][NRS.AC7.43.493; AC10.211]

BRYSON, ROBERT, a baker burgess and guilds-brother of Edinburgh, 1777, son of Thomas Bryson a brewer burgess and guilds-brother. [EBR]

BRYSON, THOMAS, a brewer burgess and guilds-brother of Edinburgh, 1771. [EBR]

BUCHAN, ROBERT, a minister educated at Edinburgh University, to Virginia 1772. [EMA#17][FPA#310]

BUCHANAN, ARCHIBALD, born 1740, a pewterer from Edinburgh, to New York or Georgia in May 1775. [TNA.T47.12]

The People of Edinburgh, 1725-1775

BUCHANAN, DAVID, a barber burgess of Edinburgh, 1762, son of Walter Buchanan a barber burgess. [EBR]

BUCHANAN, THOMAS, a tailor in Edinburgh, son of T. Buchanan a writer there, heir to his uncle Duncan Buchanan, a merchant in London, 1761. [NRS.S/H]

BUCHANAN, WILLIAM, appr. to Peter Mitchell a goldsmith in Canongate, 1731-1736. [ERA]

BUCK, JOHN, a sailor in Leith, 1736; test., 1750, C.E. [NRS] [ECL#16]

BUCKLEY, FRANCIS, a merchant in Edinburgh, a burgess and guilds-brother in 1748, and his wife Janet Robertson, a sasine, 1757. [NRS.RS27.150.60][EBR]

BUIE, JOHN, a merchant in Edinburgh, a deed, 1738. [NRS.RD3.210.61]

BULL, ROBERT, a merchant in Leith, 1740. [NRS.AC10.277]; records 1741-1751. [NRS.CS228/H2/38; CS96.3823]

BULL, ROBERT, junior, a workman in the iron and wood works in Leith, son of R. Bull, a merchant in Leith, heir to his uncle James Wardrop, a merchant in Maryland, 1761; also to his grandfather John Wardrop, a wright in Edinburgh, 1762. [NRS.S/H]

BULL, ROBERT, proprietor of the Smith and Wright Manufactory at Leith, and his wife Margaret Cuming, a sasine, 1770. [NRS.RS27.187.123]

BUNCLE, GEORGE, a servant to Joseph Wardrope a carpenter in Edinburgh, from Leith to Savanna, Georgia, in March 1734. [ESG#65]

BURD, EDWARD, master of the Christian of Leith to Newfoundland, 1726; a merchant in Leith, 1737. [NRS.RH9.14.102; AC10.262]

BURD, JANET, born 1691, died 1775. [Greyfriars MI, Edinburgh]

BURN, JAMES, a writer in Edinburgh, a deed, 1749. [NRS.RD3.210.50]

BURN, JAMES, son of William Burn and his wife Janet Scotland, from Edinburgh, settled in Baltimore, Maryland, before 1782. [NRS.RD3.294.274]

BURN, ROBERT, a merchant burgess and guilds-brother of Edinburgh, 1776. [EBR]

BURN, WILLIAM, son of James Burn a wright, a merchant in Edinburgh, a burgess and guilds-brother in 1749, a deed, 1750. [NRS.RD2.168.334][EBR]

BURNET, ALEXANDER, from Edinburgh, to Fredericksburg, Virginia, in 1774. [TNA.T47.9.11]

BURNET, ROBERT, a skipper on The Shore, Leith, 1773. [WED#8]

BURNET, WILLIAM, a burgess and guilds-brother of Edinburgh, 1762.[EBR]

BURNS, JAMES, son of Edward Burns in Lisbon, Portugal, a merchant burgess and guilds-brother of Edinburgh, 1765. [EBR]

BURNS, JAMES, son of Robert Burns in Edinburgh, appr. to William Bruce an upholsterer in Edinburgh, 1775-1781. [ERA]

BURNS, PETER, a baker burgess of Edinburgh, 1771, husband of Mary dau. of Robert Letham a baker burgess. [EBR]

The People of Edinburgh, 1725-1775

BURRELL, ALEXANDER, son of Robert Burrell, a cordiner burgess of Canongate, 1729. [CBR]

BURTON, GEORGE, a merchant burgess and guilds-brother of Edinburgh, 1778. [EBR]

BURTON, ROBERT, a sailor in Leith, husband of Marion Crawford, 1744; master of the Hopewell of Leith wrecked on a voyage home from Rotterdam in October 1751; test., 1757, C.E. [NRS][SL#52][AJ#197]

BUTCHER, JOHN, a sailor in Leith, husband of Eliza Donaldson, 1733. [SL#36]

BUTCHER, WILLIAM, a gardener burgess of Canongate, 1726. [CBR]

BUTTER, CHARLES, a merchant in Edinburgh, a burgess in 1709, a deed, 1750. [NRS.RD4.176/2.402]; a decreet, 1780. [NRS.CS16.1.179][EBR]

BUTTER, ROBERT, son of Robert Butter in Edinburgh, appr. to John Craig a weaver and reed-maker in Edinburgh, 1774-1780. [ERA]

CAIRNS, ANDREW, a right burgess of Edinburgh, 1775. [EBR]

CAIRNS, JOHN, a burgess of Canongate, 1729. [CBR]

CAIRNS, ROBERT, son of Thomas Cairns a brewer in Leith, appr. to William Hay a merchant burgess of Edinburgh, 1722. [ERA]

CAIRNS, ROBERT, a brewer in Leith, sasines, 1766. [NRS.RS27.172/343, 173/363]

CAITCHEON, JOHN, a carver burgess of Edinburgh, 1763, husband of Helen dau. of Robert Gordon a baxter burgess and guilds-brother, [EBR]; a sculptor in Edinburgh, heir to his grandfather, portioner of Abbeyhill and Canongate, 1764. [NRS.S/H]

CAITHNESS, EDWARD, son of William Caithness in Leith, appr. to James Wood merchant burgess of Edinburgh, 1730; a merchant in Edinburgh, a burgess and guilds-brother in 1739, a decreet, 1757. [ERA] [NRS.CS16.1.99] [EBR]

CALDCLEUGH, ALEXANDER, son of Robert Caldcleugh, a carter in Leith, a sasine, 1768. [NRS.RS27.181.111]

CALDER, JOHN, a merchant burgess and guilds-brother of Edinburgh, 1771, son of Thomas Cameron a burgess and guilds-brother. [EBR]

CALDER, THOMAS, a mariner in Leith, husband of Katherine Innes, 1770. [SL#107]

CALDERSTONES, ROBERT, a merchant in North Leith, a burgess of Canongate, 1725. [CBR]

CALLENDAR, EDWARD, son of Edward Callendar a Writer to the Signet, appr. to William Ayton a goldsmith burgess of Edinburgh, 1735. [ERA]

CALLANDER, JOHN, a writer in Edinburgh, a deed, 1751. [NRS.RD4.177/2.285]

CALLANDER, WILLIAM, son of William Callander a baxter burgess, appr. to James Beaton a baxter burgess of Edinburgh, 1741. [ERA]

The People of Edinburgh, 1725-1775

CALDWELL, ISOBEL, spouse of Ralph Brown a skipper in Leith, test., 1738, C.E. [NRS]

CAMERON, FRANCIS, son of Daniel Cameron in Causewayside, Edinburgh, appr. to John Miller a hatter burgess, 1751. [ERA]

CAMERON, GEORGE, an engraver burgess of Edinburgh, 1762, son of Allan Cameron a chairmaster burgess. [EBR]

CAMERON, JAMES, a sailor in Leith, 1737. [SL#44]

CAMERON, JOHN, son of Daniel Cameron in Edinburgh, appr. to Thomas Henderson a founder in Edinburgh, 1766 to 1773. [ERA]

CAMERON, JOHN, a merchant burgess of Edinburgh, 1770. [EBR]

CAMERON, JOHN, a merchant burgess of Edinburgh, 1772, husband of Mary dau. of John Richardson a tanner burgess. [EBR]

CAMPBELL, ALEXANDER, son of John Campbell a city officer of Edinburgh, appr. to Roderick Chalmers a white iron-smith, 1768-1774. [ERA]

CAMPBELL, ARCHIBALD, son of Charles Campbell, appr. to Patrick Lindsay a merchant bailie of Edinburgh, 1725. [ERA]

CAMPBELL, ARCHIBALD, a writer in Edinburgh, a deed, 1751. [NRS.RD2.169.357]

CAMPBELL, ARCHIBALD, a merchant burgess of Edinburgh, 1766. [EBR]

CAMPBELL, COLIN, a skipper in Leith, 1739. [NRS.AC11.119]

CAMPBELL, COLIN, a merchant burgess of Edinburgh, 1766. [EBR]

CAMPBELL, DANIEL, a tailor burgess of Canongate, 1727. [CBR]

CAMPBELL, DAVID, son of Hugh Campbell a lint-dresser in Edinburgh, appr. to Robert Hunter a shoemaker in Edinburgh, 1757-1763. [ERA]

CAMPBELL, DUNCAN, a mariner in Leith, test., 1765, C.E. [NRS]

CAMPBELL, GABRIEL, son of Robert Campbell, a smith and farrier in Canongate, a sasine, 1768. [NRS.RS27.179.172]

CAMPBELL, JAMES, son of Reverend Colin Campbell, appr. to Alexander Monro a surgeon apothecary burgess of Edinburgh, 1727. [ERA]

CAMPBELL, JAMES, a merchant in Leith, a deed, 1751. [NRS.RD2.170.227]

CAMPBELL, JAMES, a goldsmith burgess of Edinburgh, tests., 1764 & 1772, C.E. [NRS.RS27.223/147]

CAMPBELL, JAMES, a merchant burgess of Edinburgh, 1775. [EBR]

CAMPBELL, JENNY, born 1759, a servant from Edinburgh, to Philadelphia, Pennsylvania, in May 1775. [TNA.T47.12]

CAMPBELL, JOHN, a mariner aboard the Leith Galley, test., 1752, C.E. [NRS]

CAMPBELL, JOHN, a merchant burgess of Edinburgh, 1762. [EBR]

CAMPBELL, JOHN, son-in-law of William Finlayson a journeyman mason, appr. to John Kinloch a smith in Edinburgh, 1768-1774. [ERA]

CAMPBELL, JOHN, an inn-keeper in Edinburgh, a sasine, 1770. [NRS.RS27.188.140]

CAMPBELL, MUNGO, in the West Indies, later in Edinburgh, a decreet, 1780. [NRS.CS16.1.181]

CAMPBELL, NEIL, a merchant burgess of Edinburgh, 1766. [EBR]

CAMPBELL, PETER, porter to the Royal Bank of Scotland, a burgess of Edinburgh, 1761, husband of Elizabeth dau. of John Donaldson a glover burgess. [EBR]

CAMPBELL, ROBERT, of Finab, a burgess and guilds-brother of Edinburgh, 1748. [EBR]

CAMPBELL, ROBERT, son of Robert Campbell a servant of Archibald Campbell a brewer, appr. to James Ferguson a coppersmith in Edinburgh, 1774-1780. [ERA]

CAMPBELL, SAMUEL, born in Edinburgh during 1738, died in New York on 17 April 1813. [SM.75.39][EEC.1813]

CAMPBELL, THOMAS, a merchant burgess and guilds-brother of Edinburgh, 1773, son of Archibald Campbell a brewer burgess and guilds-brother. [EBR]

CAMPBELL, WILLIAM, a writer in Edinburgh, heir to his father James Campbell of Lochend, 1763. [NRS.S/H]

CAMPBELL, WILLIAM, a writer in Edinburgh, heir to his father Patrick Campbell MD in Wigton, 1768. [NRS.S/H]

CANT, CATHERINE, born 1756, a servant from Edinburgh, to Philadelphia, Pennsylvania, in May 1775. [TNA.T47.12]

CANT, JAMES, a wright in Canongate, a sasine, 1768; released from Edinburgh Tolbooth for transportation to America in 1773. [NRS.RS27.181.218; HH11.28]

CARFRAE, GEORGE, a tanner burgess of Canongate, 1724, husband of Bessie, dau. of William Manners a burgess. [CBR]

CARFRAE, JAMES, a merchant burgess and guilds-brother of Edinburgh, 1774, former appr. to Robert Thomson a merchant burgess. [EBR]

CARFRAE, MARTIN, son of William Carfrae a journeyman locksmith, appr. to John Richardson a smith in Edinburgh, 1769-1775. [ERA]

CARFRAE, WILLIAM, a merchant burgess and guilds-brother of Edinburgh, 1772. [EBR]

CARGILL, PATRICK, a cutler in Canongate, a sasine, 1762. [NRS.RS27.160.322]

CARLE, JAMES, a sailor in Leith, 1736. [ECL#16]

CARLISLE, PETER, a sailor in Leith, husband of Elizabeth Butler, 1773. [SL#112]

CARMICHAEL, ANDREW, a writer in Edinburgh, a sasine, 1767. [NRS.RS27.178.82]

CARMICHAEL, DAVID, a merchant in Edinburgh, 1731. [NRS.AC10.176/177]

The People of Edinburgh, 1725-1775

CARMICHAEL, DAVID, a shoemaker burgess of Edinburgh, 1764, husband of Christian dau. of Thomas Dick a shoemaker burgess. [EBR]

CARMICHAEL, JAMES, son of James Carmichael a glover, appr. to Hugh Wilson a merchant burgess of Edinburgh, 1730. [ERA]

CARMICHAEL, JAMES, son of Robert Carmichael a journeyman printer, appr. to Yule and Duncan merchants in Edinburgh, 1766-1771. [ERA]

CARMICHAEL, JOHN, junior, a merchant in Edinburgh, and his wife Barbara Berry, a deed, 1743; trading with South Carolina in 1734, 1756, trading with Boston in 1744; a decreet, 1756. [NRS.RD4.177/1.479; AC7.49.14; AC9.1960; E504.15.2]

CARMICHAEL, JOHN, son of Robert Carmichael a printer, appr. to Thomas Hendry an ironsmith in Edinburgh, 1771-1777. [ERA]

CARMICHAEL, STEWART CATHARINE, (sic), heir to her father Stewart Carmichael, a merchant in Edinburgh, 1764. [NRS.S/H]

CARMICHAEL, THOMAS, a merchant burgess of Edinburgh, 1767, husband of Margaret dau. of Ludovick Couper a skinner burgess. [EBR]

CARMICHAEL, THOMAS, a merchant burgess and guilds-brother of Edinburgh, 1772, former appr. to William Morrison a merchant burgess. [EBR]

CARMICHAEL, WALTER, a merchant from Edinburgh, settled in Queen Anne County, Maryland, by 1767. [NRS.RD4.239.714/6][MSA.Wills.37.130]

CARMICHAEL, WILLIAM, son of John Carmichael a barber in Leith, appr. to Alexander Menzies a barber burgess of Edinburgh, 1742. [ERA]

CARNABIE, WILLIAM, son of John Carnabie, a plumber burgess of Canongate, 1725. [CBR]

CARNEGIE, PATRICK, a skipper in Port Glasgow, a burgess and guilds-brother of Edinburgh, 1750. [EBR]

CARNEGIE, PHILIP, son of John Carnegie, a vintner in Edinburgh, a sasine, 1764. [NRS.RS27.167.254]

CARNEGIE, THOMAS, a brewer in Canongate, 1769. [NRS.AC7.53]; a brewer burgess of Edinburgh, 1770, son of John Carnegie a merchant burgess. [EBR]

CARR, ISABELL, an indweller in Canongate, a sasine, 1765. [NRS.RS27.170.142]

CARRICK, MUNGO, a hosier in Edinburgh, a decreet, 1773. [NRS.CS16.1.154]

CARRUTHERS, JAMES, from Edinburgh, in Boston, New England, 1733. [SCS]

CARSE, ALEXANDER, a cutler burgess of Edinburgh, 1763, husband of Janet dau. of Andrew Wilson a smith burgess. [EBR]

CARSE, WILLIAM, a flesher burgess of Canongate, 1728. [CBR]

CARSE, WILLIAM, a skipper in Leith, 1746. [NRS.AC11.174]

CARSTAIRS, JOHN, a surgeon in Canongate, a sasine, 1765. [NRS.RS27.174.227]

CASSELLS, ANDREW, a shipmaster in Leith, sasines, 1767; in Bernard Street, Leith, 1773. [NRS.RS27.176.296/304][WED#16][NRS.GD226.18.251]

The People of Edinburgh, 1725-1775

CASSIE, ROBERT, son of Robert Cassie a vintner, appr. to John Moubray the younger, a wright burgess of Edinburgh, 1734. [ERA]

CATHCART, JAMES, a sailor in Leith, 1732. [SL#34]

CATHIE, JAMES, a shoemaker burgess of Canongate, 1727, a deed, 1751; a sasine, 1762. [NRS.RD4.177/1.185; RS27.160.260][CBR]

CATHIE, WILLIAM, a cordiner burgess of Canongate, 1727. [CBR]

CATTENACH, ANDREW, third son of John Cattenach, appr. to James Hamilton a wigmaker burgess of Edinburgh, 1728. [ERA]

CATTENACH, JOHN, son of John Cattenach in Edinburgh, appr. to William Stewart a merchant in Edinburgh, 1766-1771. [ERA]

CATTENACH, THOMAS, son of John Cattenach a printer, appr. to Thomas Heriot a merchant and Dean of Guild of Edinburgh, 1737. [ERA]

CAUVIN, JOSEPH, a writer in Edinburgh, son and heir of Louis Cauvin a teacher of French there, 1779. [NRS.S/H]

CHALMERS, ANDREW, a writer in Edinburgh, sasines, 1764. [NRS.RS27.164.135/141]

CHALMERS, EDWARD, a skipper in Leith, 1734.[ECL#51]; test., 1738, C.E. [NRS]

CHALMERS, GEORGE, a plumber burgess of Edinburgh, 1773, former appr. to Robert Selby a plumber burgess. [EBR]

CHALMERS, JAMES, son of Reverend James Chalmers, appr. to James Beveridge a litster burgess of Edinburgh, 1727. [ERA]

CHALMERS, JAMES, a merchant in Leith, 1730. [NRS.CH2.621.90]

CHALMERS, JAMES, a skipper in Leith, test., 1738, C.E. [NRS]

CHALMERS, JOHN, in North Leith, a burgess of Canongate, 1728. [CBR]

CHALMERS, JOHN, son of Charles Chalmers a Writer to the Signet, appr. to Roderick Chalmers a painter burgess of Edinburgh, 1731. [ERA]

CHALMERS, JOHN, a sailor in Leith, husband of M. Cook, 1747. [SL#56]

CHALMERS, JOHN, a smith in Potterow, Edinburgh, a deed, 1751. [NRS.RD2.169.240]

CHALMERS, JOHN, son of William Chalmers a merchant, appr. to James Gilliland a goldsmith in Edinburgh, 1765-1772. [ERA]

CHALMERS, PATRICK, son of Reverend Chalmers, appr. to Patrick Manderson a merchant, 1734. [ERA]

CHALMERS, PETER, a mariner in Leith, husband of Janet Brown, 1769. [SL#106]

CHALMERS, ROBERT, a distiller in Canongate, a deed, 1751. [NRS.RD2.170.269]

CHALMERS, ROBERT, a flesher in Canongate, heir to his mother Barbara Angus, wife of John Chalmers a flesher there, 1767. [NRS.S/H]

CHALMERS, RODERICK, a smith burgess of Edinburgh, 1768, son of John Chalmers a smith burgess. [EBR]

CHALMERS, THOMAS, a merchant in Leith, 1742. [NRS.AC11.152]

The People of Edinburgh, 1725-1775

CHALMERS, WILLIAM, a flesher burgess of Edinburgh, 1771, son of John Chalmers a flesher burgess. [EBR]

CHAPMAN, DANIEL, a merchant burgess of Edinburgh, 1765, son and heir of Andrew Chapman a mealmaker burgess there, 1770, later in America, a decreet, 1773. [NRS.S/H; CS16.1.154][EBR]

CHARLES, WILLIAM, a flesher in Musselburgh, a burgess of Edinburgh, 1773, husband of Grizel dau. of George Clark a merchant burgess. [EBR]

CHARTERIS, SAMUEL, a writer burgess and guilds-brother of Edinburgh, 1761. [EBR]

CHEAP, HUGH, a merchant trading between Leith and South Carolina, 1775. [NRS.E504.22]

CHEAP, JAMES, a merchant trading between Leith and South Carolina, 1775. [NRS.E504.22]

CHEAP, THOMAS, British Consul in Madeira, a burgess and guilds-brother of Edinburgh, 1763. [EBR]

CHEAP, W., in Edinburgh, a deed, 1773. [NRS.RD4.214/355]

CHESSNUT, ANTHONY, a wright burgess of Edinburgh, 1761. [EBR]

CHEYNE, CHARLES, son of James Cheyne a Writer to the Signet, appr. to Archibald Angus a merchant burgess of Edinburgh, 1735. [ERA]; a merchant in Edinburgh, inventories, 1761. [NRS.CS21.176.24 June]

CHEYNE, JOHN, a surgeon burgess and guilds-brother of Edinburgh, 1770, son of Robert Cheyne a merchant in Cupar a burgess and guilds-brother. [EBR]

CHEYNE, ROBERT, a merchant in Cupar, Fife, a burgess and guilds-brother of Edinburgh, 1762, son of John Cheyne a surgeon burgess and guilds-brother. [EBR]

CHEYNE, Miss, born 1749, eldest dau. of Charles Cheyne a merchant in Edinburgh, died in Lunenburg, Nova Scotia, 8 January 1821. [S.5.226]

CHISHOLM, JAMES, a surgeon in Edinburgh, a sasine, 1762. [NRS.RS27.160.145]

CHRISTALL, JOHN, a slater in Canongate, and his wife Elizabeth Ramsay, a sasine, 1762. [NRS.RS27.160.157]

CHRISTIE, ANN and ISABELL, dau.s of Robert Christie a currier in Leith, a deed, 1751. [NRS.RD4.177/2.373]

CHRISTIE, GEORGE, a sailor in Leith, husband of Rachel Dick, 1755. [SL#80]

CHRISTIE, JAMES, a shipmaster at Coalhill, Leith, 1773. [WED#16]

CHRISTIE, JAMES, a cork-cutter burgess and guilds-brother of Edinburgh, 1776, son of William Christie a merchant burgess and guilds-brother. [EBR]

CHRISTIE, JAMES, born in Edinburgh on 13 January 1750, son of John Christie and his wife Janet Clarkson, to Philadelphia, Pennsylvania, in 1775, an

The People of Edinburgh, 1725-1775

American Army officer from 1776 to 1783, a merchant in New York, died 31 March 1793. [ANY.I.160]

CHRISTIE, JOHN, from Edinburgh, transported to the colonies in November 1734. [NRS.JC3.19.173]

CHRYSTIE, WILLIAM, a wheelwright in Leith, a sasine, 1764. [NRS.RS27.164.16]

CHRISTIE, WILLIAM, a shoemaker burgess of Edinburgh, 1769. [EBR]

CLAPPERTON, ALEXANDER, a writer in Edinburgh, a decreet, 1774. [NRS.CS16.1.157]

CLAPPERTON, JAMES, a merchant burgess and guilds-brother of Edinburgh, 1763, son of William Clapperton a merchant burgess and guilds-brother. [EBR]

CLAPPERTON, WILLIAM, a merchant in Edinburgh, a burgess and guilds-brother in 1737, deeds, 1751. [NRS.RD2.169.5/111][EBR]

CLARK, ALEXANDER, born 1683, son of William Clark a wright, a merchant, died 1753, his wife Margaret Bouston, born 150, died 1709. [Greyfriars MI]

CLARK, ALEXANDER, son of Alexander Clark a glover, a stay-maker in Edinburgh, husband of Janet Holm, a burgess in 1741, a sasine, 1766; heir to his great grandfather John Holmes, a weaver in South Leith, 1768. [NRS.RS27.175.41; S/H]

CLARK, ALEXANDER, a waulker burgess of Edinburgh, 1777. [EBR]

CLARK, ANDREW, a brewer in Leith, a deed, 1751. [NRS.RD2.169.12]

CLARK, ANDREW, a gentleman from Leith, settled in Port Royal, Jamaica, before 1770. [NRS.RD4.211.55; RD4.208.945]

CLARK, DAVID, MD, a surgeon burgess of Edinburgh, 1778, son of David Clark a hard leather manufacturer. [EBR]

CLARK, JAMES, a shoemaker burgess of Edinburgh,1770, [EBR]; 1783, 1784. [NRS.AC7.59/61]

CLARK, JOHN, a doctor in Edinburgh, a deed, 1730. [NRS.RD4.177/2.2]

CLARK, ROBERT, a goldsmith and jeweller burgess and guilds-brother of Edinburgh, 1763, husband of Margaret dau. of Reverend James Hart in Edinburgh, a burgess and guilds-brother. [EBR]

CLARK, ROBERT, a joiner burgess and guilds-brother of Edinburgh, 1777, son of Robert Clark a merchant burgess and guilds-brother. [EBR]

CLARK, WILLIAM, born 1644, deacon of the wrights, died 1729. [Greyfriars MI]

CLARK, WILLIAM, a merchant burgess of Canongate, 1725. [CBR]

CLARK, WILLIAM, a tailor burgess of Canongate, 1728. [CBR]

CLARK, WILLIAM, son of Nathaniel Clark in Edinburgh, appr. to David Anderson a hatter in Edinburgh, 1760-1767. [ERA]

CLARK, ..., a wright from Edinburgh, and his wife Jean Campbell, in America, a decreet, 1780. [NRS.CS16.1.179]

CLARKSON, ALEXANDER, a stabler burgess of Edinburgh, 1761. [EBR]

The People of Edinburgh, 1725-1775

CLARKSON, JAMES, a baker burgess of Edinburgh, 1771, son of Thomas Clarkson a baker burgess. [EBR]

CLARKSON, WILLIAM, son of Alexander Clarkson in Edinburgh, appr. to James Young a barber and wig-maker, 1765-1771. [ERA]; a burgess of Edinburgh, 1768. [EBR]

CLAUSEN, JOHN, a baker in Edinburgh, 1737. [NRS.AC11.96]

CLEARIHUE, JOHN, a vintner in Edinburgh, a burgess and guilds-brother in 1759, a sasine, 1766. [NRS.RS27.173.116][EBR]

CLEGHORN, ALEXANDER, son of Robert Cleghorn a burgess, appr. to James Aitken a baxter burgess of Edinburgh, 1740. [ERA]

CLEGHORN, ALEXANDER, a baker burgess of Edinburgh, 1775, former appr. to Thomas Punton a baxter burgess. [EBR]

CLEGHORN, DAVID, a merchant in Edinburgh, a deed, 1751. [NRS.RD3.211.133]

CLEGHORN, DAVID, a brewer in Edinburgh, heir to his grandfather Alexander Cleghorn, a merchant there, 1766; also to his father Thomas Cleghorn, a merchant in Edinburgh, 1766. [NRS.S/H]

CLEGHORN, HUGH, a brewer in Edinburgh, a sasine, 1761. [NRS.RS27.157.110]

CLEGHORN, ROBERT, a baker burgess of Edinburgh, 1774, former appr. to Thomas Clarkson a baxter burgess. [EBR]; a merchant burgess and guilds-brother of Edinburgh, 1769. [EBR]

CLEGHORN, THOMAS, a merchant burgess and guilds-brother of Edinburgh, 1765. [EBR]

CLEGHORN, WILLIAM, son of James Cleghorn a brewer, appr. to Robert Scott the younger a merchant in Edinburgh, 1762-1767. [ERA]

CLEGHORN, WILLIAM, a bookbinder burgess of Edinburgh, 1774. [EBR]

CLEILAND, ROBERT, in Edinburgh, once of Carnbee, heir to his brother George Cleiland, a shipmaster in Pittenweem, 1760. [NRS.S/H]

CLELAND, CHRISTIAN, widow of James Crockat junior, a merchant in Edinburgh, a sasine, 1770. [NRS.RS27.187.56]

CLELLAND, JOHN, of Cleughead, a burgess of Canongate, 1729. [CBR]

CLELAND, JOHN, a clock and watchmaker burgess of Edinburgh, 1775, former appr. to Daniel Binny a clock and watchmaker burgess. [EBR]

CLELAND, ROBERT, a writer in Edinburgh, a bond, 1735. [NRS.RD2.169.352]

CLELLAND, THOMAS, son of Thomas Clelland a merchant in Jamaica, appr. to Thomas Clelland a saddler in Edinburgh, 1755. [ERA]

CLELLAND, WILLIAM, a vintner burgess of Canongate, 1728. [CBR]

CLEPHAN, AGNES, wife of Robert Dryburgh a ship carpenter in Leith, a sasine, 1765. [NRS.RS27.169.154]

CLEPHAN, DAVID, a skipper in Leith, 1757. [SL#88]

The People of Edinburgh, 1725-1775

CLERK, Captain ABRAHAM, a burgess and guilds-brother of Edinburgh, 1757. [EBR]

CLERK, ALEXANDER, son of Robert Clerk a journeyman smith, appr. to George Winter a barber and wigmaker burgess of Edinburgh, 1753. [ERA]

CLERK, FRANCIS, a wright burgess of Edinburgh, 1774, son of Andrew Clerk a wright burgess. [EBR]

CLERK, GILBERT, a writer in Edinburgh, 1737. [NRS.AC10.248]; records, 1740s. [NRS.CS229K.1.28]

CLERK, Captain HUGH, a merchant in Edinburgh, 1747; trading with South Carolina, 1745-1751. [NRS.AC11.175; AC8.723; GD18.5321; E504.22]

CLERK, JAMES, son of James Clerk an Excise officer, appr. to James Crawford a glazier burgess of Edinburgh, 1728. [ERA]

CLERK, JAMES, a wright burgess of Edinburgh, 1768, son of Andrew Clerk a wright burgess. [EBR]

CLERK, JOHN, a merchant in Glasgow, a burgess and guilds-brother of Edinburgh, 1763, former appr. to Andrew Simpson a merchant burgess and guilds-brother. [EBR]

CLERK, THOMAS, a merchant in London, heir to his father John Clerk MD in Edinburgh, 1760. [NRS.S/H]

CLERK, WILLIAM, a sailor in Leith, husband of Dorothea Deepie, 1732. [SL#34]

CLEUGH, ROBERT, son of Robert Cleugh a brewer, appr. to David Brown a merchant burgess of Edinburgh, 1728. [ERA]

CLINTON, JAMES, son of William Clinton a teacher of humanity in Edinburgh, appr. to John Wallace a surgeon burgess of Edinburgh, 1739. [ERA]

CLYDESDALE, ROBERT, son of Archibald Clydesdale, appr. to Alexander Brand a watch-maker in 1738, a watchmaker in Edinburgh, a burgess and guilds-brother in 1754, sasines, 1770. [ERA] [NRS.RS27.188/347; 189/129; 191/50] [EBR]

COACK, WILLIAM, a shoe-maker in Calton, Edinburgh, an indenture, 1749; appr. to Alexander Davidson a cordiner, a burgess, 1735. [EBR] [NRS.RD2.169.231]

COATES, WILLIAM, a sailor in Leith, husband of Catherine Hastie, 1767. [SL#106]

COCHRAN, ADAM, son of William Cochran in Pleasants, Edinburgh, appr. to James Cochran a candlemaker burgess of Edinburgh, 1740. [ERA]

COCHRANE, JAMES, a brewer burgess of Canongate, 1725. [CBR]

COCHRAN, JOHN, son of John Cochran a mason, appr. to James Willie a mason burgess of Edinburgh, 1737. [ERA]

COCHRAN, JOHN, son of Richard Cochran a journeyman wright, appr. to Alexander Aitchison a goldsmith burgess of Edinburgh, 1751. [ERA]

The People of Edinburgh, 1725-1775

COCHRANE, JOHN, son of William Cochrane a merchant, appr. to William Thomson a weaver in Edinburgh, 1762-1768. [ERA]; a burgess of Edinburgh, 1778. [EBR]

COCHRANE, ROBERT, a furniture painter from Edinburgh, bound for Charleston, South Carolina, aboard the Magdalene, Captain James McKenzie, in 1750. [NRS.AC10.323]

COCHRAN, THOMAS, son of Thomas Cochran in Edinburgh, appr. to George Watson a painter in Edinburgh, 1743. [ERA]

COCHRANE, WILLIAM, a merchant in Edinburgh, a burgess and guilds-brother in 1743, a deed, 1751. [NRS.RD3.211/1.430][EBR]

COCK, ARTHUR, a tailor in St Mary's Wynd, Edinburgh, a burgess in 1731, a deed, 1751. [NRS.RD2.169.247][EBR]

COCK, JAMES, son of Charles Cock a vintner in Bristo Street, Edinburgh, appr. to Charles Wallace a merchant in Edinburgh, 1772-1777. [ERA]

COCK, JOHN, a skinner burgess of Edinburgh, 1770, son of Robert Cock a skinner burgess. [EBR]

COCK, ROBERT, a skinner burgess of Edinburgh, 1769, former appr. to David Murray a skinner burgess. [EBR]

COCKBURN, ADAM, son of Patrick Cockburn an advocate, appr. to Robert Smith a surgeon apothecary in Edinburgh, 1747. [ERA]

COCKBURN, ANDREW, from Edinburgh, Captain in the Royal Navy, 1764. [NRS.S/H]

COCKBURN, ARCHIBALD, a merchant in Edinburgh, trading with Boston, New England, before 1739. [NRS.AC7.44.185]

COCKBURN, ARCHIBALD, of Cockpen, a burgess and guilds-brother of Edinburgh, 1765, son of Archibald Cockburn a merchant burgess and guilds-brother. [EBR]

COCKBURN, JAMES, a burgess of Canongate, 1729. [CBR]

COCKBURN, JAMES, son of Robert Cockburn a merchant in Canongate, appr. to Cleghorn and Livingston merchants in Edinburgh, 1749. [ERA]; a merchant burgess of Edinburgh, 1763. [EBR]

COCKBURN, JAMES, a hair merchant in Edinburgh, a decreet, 1779. [NRS.CS16.1.177]

COCKBURN, RICHARD, son of Richard Cockburn a hosier, appr. to Thomas Inglis an apothecary-druggist burgess of Edinburgh, 1731. [ERA]

COCKBURN, ROBERT, son of William Cockburn a gardener, a burgess of Canongate, 1729. [CBR]

COCKBURN, THOMAS, a merchant burgess and guilds-brother of Edinburgh, 1766, [EBR], a sasine, 1767. [NRS.RS27.178.161]

The People of Edinburgh, 1725-1775

COCKBURN, THOMAS, son of Robert Cockburn a merchant in Canongate, appr. to John Gibson a clock and watchmaker in Edinburgh, 1769-1775. [ERA]

COCKBURN, WILLIAM, a burgess of Canongate, 1729. [CBR]

COCKE, WILLIAM, appr. to Alexander Davidson a cordiner in Edinburgh, 1726. [ERA]

COCKE, WILLIAM, son of William Cocke in Edinburgh, appr. to Robert Gilchrist a cooper burgess of Edinburgh, 1743. [ERA]

COKE, WILLIAM, a book-seller in Leith, a decreet, 1774. [NRS.CS16.1.157]

COLQUHOUN, ROBERT, a merchant in Edinburgh, 1737. [NRS.AC11.101]

COLVILLE, CHARLES, son of Francis Colville a writer, appr. to Alexander Davidson a cordiner burgess of Edinburgh, 1736. [ERA]

COLVILLE, GEORGE, a horse hirer burgess of Canongate, 1728. [CBR]

COLVILLE, JAMES, son of Andrew Colville in Edinburgh, appr. to Alexander Drysdale a coppersmith burgess of Edinburgh, 1753. [ERA]

COLVIL, JOHN, a burgess of Edinburgh, 1761, son of Walter Colvil a baxter burgess. [EBR]

COLVILLE, ROBERT, son of Patrick Colville a merchant, appr. to John Yair a bookseller burgess and guilds-brother of Edinburgh, 1748. [ERA]

COLVIL, ROBERT, minister at Dysart, a burgess of Edinburgh, 1774, son of Walter Colvil a baxter burgess. [EBR]

COLVIN, JOHN, a candle-maker in Holyroodhouse Abbey, a sasine, 1769. [NRS.RS27.186.217]

COMB, ROBERT, son of Robert Comb a journeyman wright, appr. to Robert Kennedy a cooper in Edinburgh, 1757-1763. [ERA]

CONNELLY, JOHN, born 1716, a tailor from Edinburgh, to Jamaica in August 1736. [CLRO/AIA]

CONSTABLE, ALEXANDER, a mason in Leith, a sasine, 1763. [NRS.RS27.162.97]

CONSTABLE, HENRY, a mason in Leith, and his wife Dorothea Lamber, sasines, 1763, a deed, 1773. [NRS.RS27.162/97; 163/11; RD4.213/751]

COOK, ROBERT, son of Robert Cook in Leith mills, appr. to George Boswell a saddler burgess of Edinburgh, 1727. [ERA]

COOK, ROBERT, former appr. to Alexander Smith a cordiner, a burgess of Canongate, 1747. [CBR]

COOK, ROBERT, a skipper in Blackwall, London, son and heir of George Cook, a wigmaker in Leith, 1766. [NRS.S/H]

COOPER, ARCHIBALD, a shoemaker burgess of Edinburgh, 1776. [EBR]

COOPER, GEORGE, a skipper in Leith, husband of Jean Cooper, 1738. [ECL#57]

CORBETT, ALEXANDER, son of Captain Alexander Corbett, appr. to John Montgomery a wright burgess of Edinburgh, 1727. [ERA]

The People of Edinburgh, 1725-1775

CORBETT, EDWARD, born 1754, a merchant from Edinburgh, to Charleston, South Carolina, in October 1774. [NRS.T47.12; E504.22]
CORBETT, JAMES, a merchant burgess of Edinburgh, 1765. [EBR]
CORMACK, JAMES, a sailor in Leith, 1743; a pilot there, 1758. [ECL#28][SL#83]
CORMACK, ROBERT, a skipper in Leith, 1735. [NRS.AC10.210]
CORMACK, ROBERT, a merchant in Leith, 1732; a deed, 1750. [NRS.AC11.50; RD2.169.456]
CORNELL, GEORGE, a tailor burgess of Canongate, 1729. [CBR]
CORNER, GEORGE, a tailor in North Leith, a deed, 1751. [NRS.RD2.169.102]
CORSAR, THOMAS, son of Alexander Corsar a soldier in the City Guard of Edinburgh, appr. to Nathan Porteous a skinner in Edinburgh, 1749. [ERA]
COSH, WILLIAM, and his wife Esther Robson, in Edinburgh, a sasine, 1752. [NRS.RS27.141.229]
COULTER, WILLIAM, a hosier burgess of Edinburgh, 1778. [EBR]
COULTER, JOHN, a merchant in Edinburgh, trading with Virginia, 1727. [NRS.AC9.976]
COULTER, MICHAEL, a merchant in Edinburgh, trading with Virginia, 1727. [NRS.AC9.976]
COULTER, PATRICK, son of Alexander Coulter a pewterer burgess, appr. to John Scouller a coppersmith burgess, 1741. [ERA]
COUPAR, JAMES, son of Alexander Coupar a journeyman flesher, appr. to Thomas Cumming a flesher in Edinburgh, 1766-1771. [ERA]
COUPER, JOHN, son of John Couper a beadle, a burgess of Canongate, 1733. [CBR]
COUPER, JOHN, son of James Couper in Edinburgh, appr. to William McVicar in Edinburgh, 1741. [ERA]
COUPER, ROBERT, son of John Couper a gentleman, appr. to Robert Drummond a barber wigmaker burgess of Edinburgh, 1728. [ERA]
COUPAR, THOMAS, a boatbuilder in Leith, later a carpenter aboard <u>HMS Siam</u>, test., 1787, C.E. [NRS]
COUSINS, THOMAS, a boatman in Leith, test., 1763, C.E. [NRS]
COUTTS, JAMES, son of David Coutts a brewer's servant in Canongate, appr. to Andrew Newton a freeman weaver of Edinburgh, 1741. [ERA]
COUTTS, JOHN, son of Patrick Coutts a merchant, a merchant in Edinburgh, a burgess and guilds-brother in 1721; 1731; a deed, 1750. [NRS.AC10.176/177; RD4.177/2.575][EBR]
COVENTRY, or JOHNSTON, or MCGILL, ANNE, a thief from Edinburgh, transported to the colonies in December 1743. [EBR.BC.3.74][NRS.HH11.22]
COVENTRY, JOHN, a sailor in Leith, husband of Margaret Kilgour, 1741. [SL#47]

The People of Edinburgh, 1725-1775

COVENTRIE, JOHN, son of David Coventrie a shoemaker in Potterrow, Edinburgh, appr. to John Jamieson a merchant burgess of Edinburgh, 1748. [ERA]

COVERLIE, WILLIAM, son of Thomas Coverlie, appr. to Robert Monson a barber wigmaker in Edinburgh, 1751. [ERA]

COWAN, CHARLES, in Leith, a bond, 1773. [NRS.RD3.232/549]

COWAN, JAMES, a skipper in Leith, 1740. [ECL#10]; test., 1755, C.E. [NRS]

COWAN, JAMES, a watchmaker burgess and guilds-brother of Edinburgh, 1768, son of James or George Cowan a wright burgess. [EBR]

COWAN, JAMES, a candlemaker burgess of Edinburgh, 1777, son of James Cowan a butcher in Musselburgh. [EBR]

COWAN, THOMAS, a flesher burgess of Edinburgh, 1773, son of John Cowan, a flesher in Musselburgh, a burgess. [EBR]

COWAN, WILLIAM, son of James Cowan in Pleasance, Edinburgh, appr. to Adam Cockburn a lorimer burgess of Edinburgh, 1742. [ERA]; a founder burgess, 1777. [EBR]

COWAN, WILLIAM, a merchant burgess and guilds-brother of Edinburgh, 1774, former appr. to Francis Marshall a merchant burgess and guilds-brother. [EBR]

COX, ROBERT, a burgess and guilds-brother of Edinburgh, 1763. [EBR]

CRAICH, SAMUEL, son of Patrick Craich a salt-officer, appr. to Alexander Weir a mason burgess of Edinburgh, 1732. [ERA]

CRAIG, ALEXANDER, appr. to Richard Moreson a barber burgess of Edinburgh, 1734. [ERA]

CRAIG, GEORGE, a sailor in Leith, husband of May Edmonston, 1745, [SL#53]; a deed, 1750, a shipmaster in Leith, 1762. [NRS.RD2.169.243][SL#93]

CRAIG, HUGH, a merchant in Edinburgh, 1740. [NRS.AC11.130]

CRAIG, JAMES, son of Adam Craig, a musician in Edinburgh, a deed, 1746. [NRS.RD3.211/1.483]

CRAIG, JAMES, an architect burgess and guilds-brother of Edinburgh, 1767. [EBR]

CRAIG, JOHN, a weaver and reed-maker burgess of Edinburgh, 1765, husband of Margaret dau. of Robert Dickson a weaver burgess. [EBR]

CRAIG, ROBERT, son of James Craig a music-master, appr. to William Jameson a goldsmith jeweller burgess of Edinburgh, 1729. [ERA]

CRAIG, THOMAS, a sailor in Leith, 1753. [SL#75]

CRAIG, WILLIAM, a wright burgess of Edinburgh, 1774, son of William Craig a wright burgess. [EBR]

CRAIGIE, THOMAS, a stay and habit-maker burgess of Edinburgh, 1763. [EBR]

CRAIK, HENRY, a tailor burgess of Canongate, 1727. [CBR]

The People of Edinburgh, 1725-1775

CRANSTON, ROBERT, son of John Cranston, appr. to William Auld a locksmith burgess of Edinburgh, 1744. [ERA]

CRAW, GEORGE, a smith burgess of Canongate, 1732. [CBR]

CRAW, WILLIAM, a saddler burgess of Edinburgh, 1775, son of James Craw a brewer burgess and guilds-brother. [EBR]

CRAWFORD, AGNES, relict of Robert Gordon a sailor in Leith, heir to her brother James Crawford, a brazier in Canongate, 1766; a sasine, 1768. [NRS.RS27.181.53; S/H]

CRAWFORD, CHARLES, a coppersmith burgess of Canongate, 1726. [CBR]

CRAWFORD, CHRISTIAN, spouse of John Stouppart a skipper in North Leith, test., 1741, C.E. [NRS]

CRAWFORD, GIDEON, a book-seller in Edinburgh, a guildsbrother in 1737, a bond, 1750. [NRS.RD4.177/1.179][EBR]

CRAWFORD, JAMES, son of Hugh Crawford a land-waiter at Leith, appr. to John Ferguson a merchant and late Baillie of Edinburgh, 1729. [ERA]

CRAWFORD, JANE, widow of James Turnbull a weaver in Canonmills, heir to her brother James Crawford, a brazier in Canongate, 1766. [NRS.S/H]

CRAWFORD, JOHN, a coppersmith in Leith, a deed, 1751. [NRS.RD2.170.53]

CRAWFORD, JOHN, a merchant in Edinburgh, later master of the Ranger, 1769, [NRS.S/H]; skipper in Coalhill, Leith, 1773; heir to his brother Charles Crawford a wright there, 1774. [WED#16][NRS.S/H]

CRAWFORD, Mrs MARY, in Leith, heir to her brother Thomas Mearns, son of Alexander Mearns a merchant in Leith, 1764. [NRS.S/H]

CRAWFORD, PATRICK, a merchant in Edinburgh, a burgess and guilds-brother of Edinburgh, 1735; 1748; a sasine, 1764. [NRS.AC11.183; RS27.165.100][EBR]

CRAWFORD, PATRICK, Lord Conservator of the Scots Priviledges at Campvere, Holland, a burgess and guilds-brother of Edinburgh, 1770. [EBR]

CRAWFORD, PATRICK GEORGE, a burgess and guilds-brother of Edinburgh, 1770. [EBR]

CRAWFORD, ROBERT, a sailor in Leith, husband of Anne Drummond, 1732. [SL#32]

CRAWFORD, WILLIAM, an ale-seller in North Leith, a burgess of Canongate, 1725. [CBR]

CRAWFORD, WILLIAM, a skipper in North Leith, test., 1727, C.E. [NRS]

CRAWFORD, WILLIAM, son of John Crawford a maltster, appr. to James Stirling a merchant burgess of Edinburgh, 1738. [ERA]

CRAWFORD, WILLIAM, a baxter burgess and guilds-brother of Edinburgh, 1762, son of Alexander Crawford a baxter burgess and guilds-brother. [EBR]

CRAWFORD, WILLIAM, a merchant in Leith, a burgess and guilds-brother of Edinburgh, 1776, former appr. to Mansfield, Hunter and Company. [EBR]

The People of Edinburgh, 1725-1775

CRAWFORD, WILLIAM, a smith burgess of Edinburgh, 1778, husband of Jean dau. of Josiah Williamson a merchant burgess. [EBR]

CREE, ROBERT, a wright on Abbeyhill, Edinburgh, later a carpenter aboard the Heriot of London, test., 1778, C.E. [NRS]

CREIGHTON, WILLIAM, born 1757, a merchant from Edinburgh, to Jamaica in July 1775. [TNA.T47.12]

CRICHTON, ALEXANDER, son of Patrick Crichton, a coach-maker in Edinburgh, a burgess and guilds-brother in 1759, a sasine, 1761; a decreet, 1778. [NRS.RS27.158.302; CS16.1.173][EBR]

CRICHTON, JAMES, a writer in Edinburgh, a deed, 1751. [NRS.RD3.211.92]

CRICHTON, THOMAS, a surgeon in Canongate, and his wife Helen Ramsay, a deed, 1750. [NRS.RD4.177/1.56]

CROCKATT, CHARLES, a merchant in Edinburgh, trading with Charleston, South Carolina, decreets, 1738, 1739. [NRS.AC7.43.213; CS16.1.69]

CROCKATT, CHARLES, a mariner in Leith, test., 1775, C.E. [NRS]

CROCKATT, JAMES, in Charleston, South Carolina, a burgess and guilds-brother of Edinburgh, 1749, son of Charles Crockatt a merchant and bailie. [EBR]

CROCKAT, JOHN, a slater in Leith, a sasine, 1770; a bond, 1773. [NRS.RS27.188.245; RD3.232/562]

CROCKATT, THOMAS, a sailor in Leith, 1763. [ECL#41]

CROMAR, GEORGE, a gardener, and his wife Margaret Scott, in Summerhall on the Walkside of Leith, a sasine, 1769. [NRS.RS27.186.31]

CROMBIE, JAMES, a sailor in Leith, 1736. [ECL#16]

CROMBIE, THOMAS, son of John Crombie miller at the Water of Leith, appr. to John Fairholm a skinner burgess and deacon of the skinners of Edinburgh, 1748. [ERA]; a burgess of Edinburgh, 1761. [EBR]

CROOK, JOHN, son of Edward Crook in Edinburgh, appr. to George Aitkin a locksmith burgess of Edinburgh, 1728. [ERA]

CROOK, ROBERT, son of Clement Crook of St Kitts, West Indies, appr. to James McKay a coppersmith burgess of Edinburgh, 1753. [ERA]

CROOKBONE, BERNARD, son of George Crookbone in Suron, appr. to Bernard Ross a skinner burgess of Edinburgh, 1706; a glover, a burgess of Edinburgh, 1739. [ERA][EBR]

CROOKBONE, JOHN, son of Bernard Crookbone a vintner in Edinburgh, an indenture, 1748. [NRS.RD4.177/1.407]; cf John Crookbane, born in Scotland 1736, a silversmith in Fredericksburg, Virginia and a militiaman of the Virginia Regiment, 1756. [VMHB,1/2]

CROOKBONE, THOMAS, son of George Crookbone, appr. to Alexander Gray a wigmaker burgess of Edinburgh, 1728. [ERA]

CROOKS, JOHN, a mason in Edinburgh, a sasine, 1769. [NRS.RS27.185.358]

The People of Edinburgh, 1725-1775

CROOKS, THOMAS, a baker burgess of Edinburgh, 1768, son of William Crooks a baker burgess. [EBR]

CROSBIE, ANDREW, an advocate burgess and guilds-brother of Edinburgh, 1766. [EBR]

CROUDEN, WILLIAM, a mariner in Leith, husband of Mary Lowry, 1741; master of the Margaret and Mary of Leith, 1748; a skipper in Leith, 1761. [SL#48][NRS.AC10.332; GD226.18.228]

CROUDEN, WILLIAM, a sailor, son of William Crouden a skipper in Leith, husband of Isobel Mitchell, 1759. [SL#85]

CRUICKSHANKS, JOHN, son of John Cruickshanks a brewer, appr. to John Bell a merchant burgess of Edinburgh, 1730. [ERA]

CRUIKSHANK, PATRICK, late of St Vincent, his wife Margaret Davidson born 1748, died 1779, their dau. Catherine died 1779. [Greyfriars MI, Edinburgh]

CRUICKSHANKS, WILLIAM, a candle-maker in Canongate, a deed, 1751; a sasine, 1769. [NRS.RD3.211/1.261; RS27.182.300]

CRUNDELL, WILLIAM, son of James Crundell a brewer in Leith, appr. to John Fyfe a merchant in Edinburgh, 1767-1772. [ERA]

CRUSSO, JOHN, a periwig-maker in Edinburgh, 1746. [NRS.AC10.317]

CULBERTSON, WILLIAM, a sailor in Leith, husband of Janet Ross, 1747. [SL#56]

CULLEN, WALTER, born 1755, a merchant from Edinburgh, to Jamaica in July 1775. [TNA.T47.12]

CULTAR, EDWIN, a writer in Edinburgh, a bond, 1730. [NRS.RD3.211/1.259]

CUMING, CHARLES, son of Peter Cuming a whip-maker, appr. to Walter Brunton a saddler in Edinburgh, 1772-1778. [ERA]

CUMING, JAMES, jr., a merchant in Edinburgh, 1730. [NRS.AC10.157]

CUMING, JAMES, son of Robert Cuming a flesher, a flesher in Edinburgh, a burgess in 1735, a deed, 1751. [NRS.RD2.169.284][EBR]

CUMING, JAMES, son of Thomas Cuming a sentinel of Edinburgh, appr. to William Nimmo a weaver burgess of Edinburgh, 1740. [ERA]

CUMING, JAMES, son of James Cuming a writing master, appr. to Robert Nories a painter burgess of Edinburgh, 1747. [ERA]

CUMING, PATRICK, a merchant in Edinburgh, 1730. [NRS.AC10.157]

CUMING, ROBERT, a mariner in Leith, son of Robert Cuming a flesher in Edinburgh, a deed, 1751; heir to his mother Alison Ritchie, wife of Robert Cumming a flesher in Edinburgh, 1763. [NRS.RD4.177/2.278] [NRS.S/H]

The People of Edinburgh, 1725-1775

CUMING, THOMAS, son of Robert Cuming a shipmaster in Leith, appr. to James Hewatt a goldsmith in Edinburgh, 1761-1768. [ERA]

CUMING, WILLIAM, a merchant in Edinburgh, 1730. [NRS.AC10.157]

CUMING, WILLIAM, a merchant in Edinburgh, a sasine, 1763. [NRS.RS27.161.297]

CUNDELL, JAMES, a brewer in Leith, a sasine, 1769; heir to his brother James Cundell a cooper in London, 1775. [NRS.RS27.179.178; S/H]

CUNNINGHAM, DAVID, a baker in Edinburgh, and his wife Elizabeth Kirkland, a sasine, 1768. [NRS.RS27.180.272]

CUNNINGHAM, ESTHER, dau. of George Cunningham a surgeon in Edinburgh, a decreet, 1769. [NRS.CS16.1.134]

CUNNINGHAM, GEORGE, son of Robert Cunningham, appr. to Andrew Baillie a smith burgess of Edinburgh, 1729. [ERA]

CUNNINGHAM, GEORGE, son of Reverend Cunningham, appr. to John Kennedy a surgeon apothecary burgess of Edinburgh, 1734. [ERA]

CUNNINGHAM, Dr HENRY, a physician from Edinburgh, in East Florida, decreets, 1769/1770. [NRS.CS16.1.134/141]; probate 1771 Georgia

CUNNINGHAM, JANET, spouse of Robert McKenzie a skipper in Leith, test., 1752, C.E. [NRS]

CUNNINGHAM, JOHN, son of Patrick Cunningham a minister, appr. to John Walker a skinner burgess of Edinburgh, 1727. [ERA]

CUNNINGHAM, JOHN, a merchant in Edinburgh, 1742. [NRS.AC11.150]

CUNNINGHAM, JOHN, a sailor in Leith, husband of Jean Sinclair, 1749. [SL#61]

CUNNINGHAM, JOHN, a distiller in Leith, husband of Marion Smellie, a sasine, 1756. [NRS.RS27.147.443]

CUNNINGHAM, JOHN, son of James Cunningham the elder a baker, appr. to James Sprott a tanner and currier in Edinburgh, 1774-1780. [ERA]

CUNNINGHAM, NINIAN, a writer in Edinburgh, a deed, 1750. [NRS.RD2.169.94]

CUNNINGHAM, PATRICK, son of John Cunningham a brewer, appr. to James Burn a wright burgess of Edinburgh, 1739. [ERA]

CURRIE, JAMES, son of William Currie a wright at the Windmill, appr. to George Forrest a barber and wig-maker in Edinburgh, 1756-1762. [ERA]

CURRIE, JAMES, a skipper at Leith Bidge, 1773. [WED#16]

CURRIE, NICOL, a skipper on The Shore, Leith, 1773; test. 1786, Comm. Edinburgh. [NRS][WED#16]

CURRIE, ROBERT, a merchant in Edinburgh, a sasine, 1761. [NRS.RS27.157.450]

CURRIE, WILLIAM, settled in South Carolina, 1772, a merchant and a Loyalist there, in Edinburgh by 1784. [TNA.AO12.51.65. etc]

CUTHBERT, MARY, born 1756, a servant from Edinburgh, to Philadelphia, Pennsylvania, in May 1775. [TNA.T47.12]

The People of Edinburgh, 1725-1775

CUTHBERTSON, PETER, a goldsmith in Canongate, test., 1756, C.E. [NRS]
DAFFION, JOHN, son of William Daffion a hatter, appr. to Robert Salton a glazier in Edinburgh, 1771-1777. [ERA]
DALE, JAMES, son of John Dale a wigmaker, appr. to James Deans a merchant burgess and guilds-brother of Edinburgh, 1741. [ERA]
DALGAIRNS, JOHN, a cartwright in Edinburgh, heir to his father John Dalgairns, a merchant in Meigle, 1764. [NRS.S/H]
DALLAS, ALEXANDER, a silk dyer in Edinburgh, a decreet, 1769. [NRS.CS16.1.138]
DALLAS, STEWART, son of James Dallas, appr. to Robert Dallas a wright burgess of Edinburgh, 1729. [ERA]
DALLAS, HENRIETTA, dau. of W. Dallas, a shipmaster in Leith, heir to her grandfather George Thomson, a shipmaster there, 1769. [NRS.S/H]
DALLAS, JOHN, a sailor in Leith, husband of Janet Kinnaird, 1759. [SL#86]
DALLAS, WALTER, born 1690s, a merchant from Edinburgh, settled in Annapolis, Maryland, died there before 1772. [NRS.CS16.1.95/99]
DALLAS, WILLIAM, a skipper in Leith, 1740. [ECL#9]
DALMAHOY, ADAM, son of John Dalmahoy a harness-maker in Canongate, appr. to James Miller a skinner in Edinburgh, 1775-1780. [ERA]
DALMAHOY, MALCOLM, son of John Dalmahoy a shoemaker in Canongate, appr. to William Deas a painter in Edinburgh, 1776-1782. [ERA]
DALRYMPLE, DAVID, the younger of Hails, a burgess and guilds-brother of Edinburgh, 1747. [EBR]
DALTON, ROBERT, born 1732, a midshipman, married Margaret Riddel in Leith 1762; a skipper in Leith who died 8 September 1780. [SL#92][South Leith MI]
DALZIEL, ..., a minister from Edinburgh, to Warwick, Bermuda, in 1779. [F.7.660]
DANIELL, JOHN, a sailor in Leith, son of James Daniell a skipper there, test., 1739, C.E. [NRS.S/H.1737]
DARLING, JAMES, a smith burgess of Canongate, 1725. [CBR]
DAVIDSON, ALEXANDER, son of Alexander Davidson, a shoemaker from Canongate, transported to the colonies in March 1747. [P.2.144]
DAVIDSON, CATHERINE, wife of W. Paton a brewer in Leith, heir to her brother James Davidson, a sailor in Kingston, Jamaica, 1764. [NRS.S/H]
DAVIDSON, DAVID, a mariner in Leith, husband of Johan Pattoun, 1768. [SL#105]
DAVIDSON, HENRY, a solicitor burgess and guilds-brother of Edinburgh, 1771. [EBR]
DAVIDSON, THOMAS, a skipper in Leith, test., 1787, C.E. [NRS]
DAVIDSON, WALTER, a saddler burgess of Canongate, 1725. [CBR]

The People of Edinburgh, 1725-1775

DAVIDSON, WILLIAM, son of William Davidson a journeyman glover, appr. to William How a skinner burgess of Edinburgh. [ERA]

DAVIDSON, WILLIAM, son of William Davidson in Edinburgh, appr. to James Fairholm a wigmaker in Edinburgh, 1766-1771. [ERA]

DAVIE, ADAM, a goldsmith burgess and guilds-brother of Edinburgh, 1761, son of William Davie a goldsmith burgess and guilds-brother. [EBR]

DAWES, GEORGE, son of General Charles Dawes in Jamaica, appr. to Dr George Young a surgeon apothecary in Edinburgh, 1754. [ERA]

DAWSON, ALEXANDER, son of William Dawson professor of Hebrew at Edinburgh University, appr. to Robert Hamilton a merchant in Edinburgh, 1760-1766. [ERA]

DAWSON, WILLIAM, a merchant burgess of Edinburgh, 1764, husband of Elizabeth, dau. of William Pillans a stabler burgess and guilds-brother. [EBR]

DEAS, DAVID, a ropemaker in Leith, 1729. [NRS.AC10.145]

DEAS, Captain DAVID, a merchant in Leith, 1733. [NRS.AC10.195]

DEAS, DAVID, a skipper in Leith, 1736. [ECL#48]

DEAS, DAVID, born 1722, son of David Deas and Catherine Dundas in Leith, a merchant from Leith, settled in Charleston, South Carolina, 1738, a burgess and guilds-brother of Edinburgh in 1764, died in Charleston in 1775. [NRS.RD3.224.27; 224/1.630; CS16.1.165/170; E504.22][SM.37.637]

DEAS, JOHN, born 1735, son of David Deas, a skipper in Leith, and his wife Catherine Dundas, to South Carolina in 1749, a burgess and guilds-brother of Edinburgh in 1769, a merchant, died in Charleston in 1790, probate, 1790, South Carolina. [EBR][TNA.AO12.73.129]

DEAS, ROBERT, son of David Deas a shipmaster in Leith, a merchant in Charleston, South Carolina, a decreet, 1755. [NRS.CS16.1.95]

DEAS, WILLIAM, a waulker burgess of Edinburgh, 1762, son of William Deas a waulker burgess. [EBR]

DEAS, WILLIAM, a landscape artist in South Carolina, a burgess and guilds-brother of Edinburgh, 1769. [EBR]

DEMPSTER, JAMES, a jeweller burgess and guilds-brother of Edinburgh, 1776, son of William Dempster a jeweller burgess and guildsbrother. [EBR]

DEMPSTER, LILLY, born 1759, a servant from Edinburgh, to Philadelphia, Pennsylvania, in May 1775. [TNA.T47.12]

DEMPSTER, THOMAS, son of John Dempster a brewer's servant, appr. to David Freebairn a barber burgess of Edinburgh, 1737. [ERA]

DENHAM, JOHN, a baker burgess of Edinburgh, 1776, former appr. to George Hardie a baker burgess. [EBR]

DENHOLM, ELIZABETH, from Edinburgh, wife of George Gordon, settled in Hanover, Jamaica, before 1753. [NRS.S/H]

The People of Edinburgh, 1725-1775

DENHOLM, JOHN, a clothier burgess of Edinburgh, 1770. [EBR]
DENHOLM, ROBERT, a skipper in Leith, test., 1767, C.E. [NRS]
DENNET, ANN, relict of Thomas Howison a skipper in Leith, test., 1757, C.E. [NRS]
DENOVAN, THOMAS, son of Henry Denovan in Piccardy, Edinburgh, appr. to Thomas Henry a white-ironsmith in Edinburgh, 1768-1774. [ERA]
DEWAR, AGNES, dau. of T. Dewar a brewer in Edinburgh, heir to her grandfather John Lyon, a tailor in Aberdeen, 1765. [NRS.S/H]
DEWAR, ANDREW, from Leith, in Boston, New England, 1746. [SCS]
DEWAR, FORREST, a surgeon burgess and guilds-brother of Edinburgh, 1772, son of John Dewar a merchant burgess and guilds-brother. [EBR]
DEWAR, GEORGE, a merchant burgess and guilds-brother of Edinburgh, 1774, son of John Dick a merchant burgess and guilds-brother. [EBR]
DEWAR, JAMES, appr. to James Wight a litster in Edinburgh, 1726. [ERA]
DEWAR, JAMES, a merchant in Edinburgh, a decreet, 1781. [NRS.CS16.1.183]
DEWAR, ROBERT, appr. to John Angus a merchant in Edinburgh, 1726. [ERA]
DEWAR, ROBERT, son of William Dewar, a merchant from Edinburgh, settled in Antigua and St Eustatia before 1768. [NRS.S/H. 1768/1772; RS27.180.276; RGS.110.95; CS16.1.173]
DICK, ANDREW, son of John Dick a brewer, appr. to Andrew Currie a weaver burgess of Edinburgh, 1735. [ERA]
DICK, DAVID, son of David Dick a surgeon, appr. to Aeneas Taush a tailor burgess of Edinburgh, 1729. [ERA]
DICK, DAVID, a brewer burgess and guilds-brother of Edinburgh, 1777, son of James Dick a brewer burgess and guilds-brother. [EBR]
DICK, JAMES, a skipper in Leith, test., 1772, C.E. [NRS]
DICK, JAMES, born 1706, a merchant from Edinburgh, to Maryland in 1734, settled in London Town on the South River, died 1782 in Lewistown, Maryland. [NYGaz.11.11.1782][MSA.All Hallows church register#56]
DICK, JOHN, a mariner aboard the Janet and Sarah, test., 1735, C.E. [NRS]
DICK, JOHN, junior, a skipper in Leith, test., 1774, C.E. [NRS]
DICK, JOHN, a skipper in Leith, 1742, husband of Margaret Jollie, 1771, resident at Precious Close, Leith, 1773; father of Robert and Margaret, test., 1774, C.E. [NRS.AC11.154A][SL#73/108][WED#22]
DICK, Sir JOHN, H.M.Consul at Leghorn, Italy, a burgess and guilds-brother of Edinburgh, 1768. [EBR]
DICK, THOMAS, son of Robert Dick, a merchant from Edinburgh, settled in Annapolis, Maryland, before 1758. [NRS.S/H]
DICK, WILLIAM, appr. to Robert Bennet a wright in Edinburgh, 1726. [ERA]

The People of Edinburgh, 1725-1775

DICK, WILLIAM, son of John Dick a carpet weaver, appr. to James Thomson a merchant burgess of Edinburgh, 1748. [ERA]

DICK, WILLIAM, a merchant burgess and guilds-brother of Edinburgh, 1761, former appr. to James Thomson a merchant burgess and guilds-brother. [EBR]

DICKIE, ALEXANDER, a watchmaker burgess of Edinburgh, 1778, husband of Marianne dau. of John English a merchant burgess and guilds-brother, 1778. [EBR]

DICKIE, JANE, widow of William Gray, a writer in Edinburgh, heir to her brother John Dickie a Writer to the Signet, 1768. [NRS.S/H]

DICKIE, JOHN, a merchant in Edinburgh, 1731. [NRS.AC11.48]

DICKIESON, ALEXANDER, a glazier burgess and guilds-brother of Edinburgh, 1767, husband of Elizabeth dau. of Alexander Clark a merchant burgess and guilds-brother. [EBR]

DICKSON, ALEXANDER, son of Alexander Dickson, appr. to George Thomson a glazier in Edinburgh, 1733. [ERA]

DICKSON, ALEXANDER, a mariner in Leith, a burgess and guilds-brother of Edinburgh, 1773, husband of Grizel dau. of James Shand a burgess and guilds-brother. [EBR]

DICKSON, ANDREW, born 1746, a laborer from Edinburgh, to New York in April 1775. [TNA.T47.12]

DICKSON, JAMES, a bookseller burgess and guilds-brother of Edinburgh, 1772/1777. [EBR]

DICKSON, RICHARD, a sailor in Leith, 1742. [ECL#11]

DICKSON, THOMAS, appr. to James Donaldson a merchant in Edinburgh, 1727. [ERA]

DICKSON, WILLIAM, son of David Dickson an Excise officer, appr. to James Brown a freeman weaver of Edinburgh, 1741. [ERA]

DIEUMAS, PETER, son of Peter Dieumas, appr. to George Drummond a white-iron smith burgess of Edinburgh, 1742. [ERA]

DINWIDDIE, ROBERT, late Governor of Virginia, a burgess and guilds-brother of Edinburgh, 1758. [EBR]

DOAK, JAMES, son of James Doak a journeyman wright, appr. to Ralph Dundas a merchant burgess and guilds-brother of Edinburgh, 1750. [ERA]

DOAK, ROBERT, son of Hugh Doak a wright, appr. to John Muir His Majesty's cutler in Edinburgh, 1730. [ERA]

DOBIE, JAMES, a weaver burgess of Edinburgh, 1768, husband of .... dau. of John Allan a weaver burgess. [EBR]

DOBIE, JOHN, son of George Dobie a brewer, appr. to Thomas Hendry a white iron smith in Edinburgh, 1771-1777. [ERA]

The People of Edinburgh, 1725-1775

DOBIE, RICHARD, born in Liberton, Edinburgh, during 1730, a merchant in Montreal, died there 23 March 1805. [Gentleman's Magazine#75.773]

DOBIE, ROBERT, son of Thomas Dobie a horse hirer, appr. to Alexander Fairbairn a locksmith in Edinburgh, 1740. [ERA]

DOBIE, ROBERT, son of George Dobie a stabler, appr. to John Fraser a white-ironsmith in Edinburgh, 1772-1778. [ERA]

DODDS, DANIEL, a vintner burgess of Edinburgh, 1777. [EBR]

DODDS, PATRICK, a wright in Canongate, 1742. [NRS.AC11.154A]

DODS, RUTHERFORD, son of Peter Dods a smith at the Glassworks, appr. to Thomas Sibbald a smith in Edinburgh, 1765-1772. [ERA]

DOIG, ELIZABETH, wife of Alexander Scott a merchant in Edinburgh, heir to her father David Doig of Cookstown who died in August 1763, 1764. [NRS.S/H]

DOIG, GEORGE, son of David Doig a baker, appr. to George Bell a cordiner burgess of Edinburgh, 1730. [ERA]

DOIG, JAMES, of Antigua, a burgess and guilds-brother of Edinburgh, 1757. [EBR]

DON, JAMES, a merchant, possibly from Edinburgh, settled in Maryland before 1760. [NRS.CS16.1.107; CS17.1.2]

DON, JOHN, born 1707, a printer in Edinburgh, died 18 May 1784. [St Cuthbert's MI, Edinburgh]

DON, JOHN, born in Edinburgh during 1771, died in Augusta, Georgia, 10 August 1810. [Augusta Chronicle, 11 August 1810]

DONALD, JAMES, a druggist burgess of Edinburgh, 1772. [EBR]

DONALD, THOMAS, a smith burgess and guilds-brother of Edinburgh, 1761, husband of Elizabeth dau. of Robert Simpson. [EBR]

DONALDSON, ALEXANDER, in Edinburgh, a deed, 1773. [NRS.RD4.213/371]

DONALDSON, JAMES, born 1697, a wright from Edinburgh, transported to Virginia in 1747; landed at Port North Potomac, Maryland, on 5 August 1747. [P.2.158][TNA.T1.328]

DONALDSON, JAMES, son of James Donaldson an Excise officer, appr. to Archibald Robertson a merchant burgess of Edinburgh, 1736. [ERA]

DONALDSON, JOHN, a sailor in Leith, husband of Christian Donaldson, 1765. [SL#300]

DONALDSON, MARY, dau. of Ludovic Donaldson a writer in Edinburgh, heir to her uncle James Donaldson, a merchant in Turriff, 1762. [NRS.S/H]

The People of Edinburgh, 1725-1775

DONALDSON, NICOL, heir to his father James Donaldson, a merchant in Edinburgh, 1762. [NRS.S/H]

DONALDSON, PETER, born 1740, a mason from Edinburgh, to Dominica in December 1773. [TNA.T47.9.11]

DONALDSON, ROBERT, a shoemaker in Calton, heir to his grandmother Isabella Tweedale, wife of W. Galway a skinner in Edinburgh, 1769. [NRS.S/H]

DONALDSON, WILLIAM, a barber and wigmaker burgess of Edinburgh, 1762, husband of Mary dau. of James Smitton a barber & wigmaker burgess, 1762. [EBR]

DORRACH, PATRICK, son of John Dorrach in Edinburgh, appr. to William Wilson a cordiner burgess of Edinburgh, 1750. [ERA]

DOT, DAVID, a wright in Edinburgh, heir to his aunt Christian Dot, widow of James Wilson a teacher in Collessie, 1767. [NRS.S/H]

DOUGAL, JOHN, son of John Dougal servant to James Flint a merchant, appr. to William Cargill late deacon of the weavers in Edinburgh, 1730. [ERA]

DOUGLAS, ADAM, a tobacconist burgess of Edinburgh, 1777. [EBR]

DOUGLAS, ADOLPHUS, son of Alexander Douglas a brewer in Leith, appr. to Thomas Craig a merchant burgess of Edinburgh, 1736. [ERA]

DOUGLAS, ALEXANDER, son of John Douglas a wright, appr. to James Yorkston a cutler burgess of Edinburgh, 1749. [ERA]

DOUGLAS, ALEXANDER, a skipper in Leith, test., 1776, C.E. [NRS]

DOUGLAS, ANDREW, son of John Douglas a wright, appr. to Thomas Crawford a glazier burgess of Edinburgh, 1728. [ERA]

DOUGLAS, ANDREW, son of John Douglas in Edinburgh, appr. to Alexander Easton a cordiner burgess of Edinburgh, 1736. [ERA]

DOUGLAS, CHARLES, a burgess of Canongate, 1728. [CBR]

DOUGLAS, DANIEL, a vintner burgess of Edinburgh, 1777. [EBR]

DOUGLAS, JOHN, son of Andrew Douglas in Leith, appr. to Robert Oliphant a hatter burgess of Edinburgh, 1750. [ERA]; a burgess of Edinburgh, 1761. [EBR]

DOUGLAS, ROBERT, a ship's carpenter in Leith, son of David Douglas a sailor in South Leith, 1738. [NRS.S/H]

DOUGLAS, ROBERT, appr. to James Brown a weaver burgess of Edinburgh, 1747. [ERA]

DOUGLAS, ROBERT, a merchant in Leith, 1748. [NRS.AC10.339]

DOUGLAS, RYNOLD, a burgess of Edinburgh, 1763, husband of Joan dau. of Thomas Short a wright burgess. [EBR]

DOUGLAS, THOMAS, son of Thomas Douglas a merchant, appr. to John Brown a cordiner burgess of Edinburgh, 1741. [ERA]

DOUGLAS, WILLIAM, son of David Douglas in Canongate, appr. to James Rutherford a goldsmith burgess of Edinburgh, 1748. [ERA]

The People of Edinburgh, 1725-1775

DOUGLAS, WILLIAM, a merchant in Leith, a burgess and guilds-brother of Edinburgh, 1775, former appr. to Alexander Hunter a merchant burgess and guilds-brother. [EBR]
DOULL, JAMES, son of James Doull, a surgeon from Edinburgh, settled in Maryland before 1751. [NRS.RD4.172.158/525]
DOW, ALEXANDER, a merchant burgess and guilds-brother of Edinburgh, 1771. [EBR]
DOW, WILLIAM, a skinner burgess of Edinburgh, 1766, husband of Janet dau. of Alexander Brown a skinner burgess. [EBR]
DOWIE, JOHN, a vintner burgess of Edinburgh, 1778. [EBR]
DOWNIE, DAVID, son of John Downie a watchmaker, appr. to William Gilchrist deacon of the goldsmiths of Edinburgh, 1753. [ERA]; a burgess of Edinburgh, 1776. [EBR]
DOWNIE, JAMES, in Edinburgh, once a sailor in Newcastle, heir to his grandfather James Bowie a wright in Edinburgh, 1771. [NRS.S/H]
DOWNIE, WILLIAM, son of John Downie a watchmaker near Edinburgh, appr. to James Geddes a watchmaker burgess of Edinburgh, 1745. [ERA]; a burgess of Edinburgh, 1767. [EBR]
DRUMMOND, Dr ARCHIBALD, eldest son of George Drummond late Provost of Edinburgh, a burgess and guilds-brother of Edinburgh, 1767. [EBR]
DRUMMOND, GEORGE, son of Thomas Drummond, appr. to John Antonius a wright in Edinburgh, 1729. [ERA]
DRUMMOND, JAMES, a merchant in Edinburgh, a decreet, 1748. [NRS.CS16.1.80]
DRUMMOND, JOHN, a cooper from Leith, to Brunswick, North Carolina, in June 1775. [TNA.T47.12]
DRUMMOND, PETER, a flesher in Canongate, husband of Janet Pedden, a sasine, 1755. [NRS.RS27.145.223]
DRUMMOND, WILLIAM, son of William Drummond an Excise officer, appr. to Simeon Fraser a white-iron smith in Edinburgh, 1728. [ERA]
DRYBURGH, DAVID, a sailor in Leith, husband of Marion Walker, 1747. [SL#58]
DRYBURGH, DAVID, a skipper in Leith, test., 1761, C.E. [NRS]
DRYBURGH, DAVID, a sailor in Leith, test., 1767, C.E. [NRS]
DRYBURGH, ROBERT, a ship-builder in Leith, husband of Agnes Barron, a sasine, 1751; a decreet, 1777. [NRS.RS27.138.81; CS16.1.171]
DRYBURGH, ROBERT, a carpenter in Leith, a burgess and guilds-brother of Edinburgh, 1769, husband of Mary dau. of Robert McLellan a merchant burgess and guilds-brother. [EBR]
DRYSDALE, JOHN, a burgess and guilds-brother of Edinburgh, 1765. [EBR]
DUDGEON, ALEXANDER, a brewer burgess of Edinburgh, 1770. [EBR]

The People of Edinburgh, 1725-1775

DUDGEON, ROBERT, a baker burgess of Edinburgh, 1775, former appr. to Alexander Steven a baker burgess. [EBR]

DUDGEON, WALTER, son of Alexander Dudgeon in Edinburgh, appr. to Robert Grierson a locksmith in Edinburgh, 1777-1784. [ERA]

DUFF, JOHN, son of Alexander Duff in Edinburgh, appr. to Archibald Richardson a bookbinder burgess of Edinburgh, 1748. [ERA]

DUFF, JOHN, a chairmaster burgess of Edinburgh, 1768. [EBR]

DUFFIE, ALEXANDER, a burgess of Canongate, 1729. [CBR]

DUGUID, PETER, a merchant burgess of Edinburgh, 1773, son of George Duguid a hatter burgess. [EBR]

DUN, ABIGAIL, dau. of John Dun a writer in Edinburgh, a decreet, 1760. [NRS.CS16.1.107]

DUN, WILLIAM, son of James Dun a tailor, appr. to Thomas Clelland a saddler burgess of Edinburgh, 1754. [ERA]

DUNBAR, GEORGE, a merchant from Edinburgh, to New York before 1782, a deed, 1782, and a decreet, 1783. [NRS.RD2.235.17; CS17.1.2]

DUNBAR, JOHN, a merchant burgess of Edinburgh, 1763. [EBR]

DUNBAR, WILLIAM, son of William Dunbar a weaver in Canongate, appr. to Thomas Spence a weaver in Edinburgh, 1756-1762. [ERA]

DUNBAR, WILLIAM, a barber and wig-maker from Edinburgh, husband of [1] Penelope McEwan, [2] Katherine Burnet, was transported to the colonies in August 1763. [NRS.RH2.4.255]

DUNBAR, WILLIAM, a weaver burgess of Edinburgh, 1770, former appr. to Thomas Spence a weaver burgess. [EBR]

DUNCAN, ALEXANDER, son of Charles Duncan, a merchant from Edinburgh, emigrated to the colonies before 1758, a partner in the firm Duncan, Schaw and Sutherland in Wilmington, North Carolina, died there 1767. [REB.1758.60] [St James church register, Wilmington][NRS.CS16.1.117]

DUNCAN, ALEXANDER, a glover burgess of Edinburgh, 1762, husband of John Howden a cooper burgess. [EBR]

DUNCAN, ALEXANDER, depute town clerk of Edinburgh, a burgess and guildsbrother of Edinburgh, 1763. [EBR]

DUNCAN, HENRY, a waulker burgess of Edinburgh, 1775, son of Peter Duncan a waulker burgess. [EBR]

DUNCAN, JAMES, from Leith, in Boston, New England, 1734. [SCS]

DUNCAN, PETER, a baker burgess of Edinburgh, 1774, former appr. of Adam Keir a baker burgess. [EBR]

DUNCAN, ROBERT, a cooper burgess of Edinburgh, 1768, former appr. to Andrew Syme a cooper burgess. [EBR]

The People of Edinburgh, 1725-1775

DUNCAN, WILLIAM, a sailor in Leith, husband of Christian Moyes, 1755. [SL#78]

DUNCAN, WILLIAM, a tailor burgess of Edinburgh, 1774, son of John Duncan a cramer burgess. [EBR]

DUNDAS, CHARLES, a burgess and guilds-brother of Edinburgh, 1763. [EBR]

DUNDAS, HUGH, a skipper in Leith, tests., 1740/1743, Comm. Edinburgh, [NRS]; husband of Elizabeth Borthwick, test., 1739, C.E, [NRS]; parents of Hugh and Janet by 1735, [NRS.GD226.18.204]; Janet a merchant in Edinburgh, test., 1777, C.E. [NRS]

DUNDAS, JANET, a merchant in Edinburgh, dau. of Hugh Dundas a skipper in Leith, test., 1777, C.E. [NRS]

DUNDAS, JOHN, a skipper in Leith, husband of Janet Wilkie, 1731. [SL#30]

DUNDAS, JOHN, a Writer to the Signet, Clerk of Edinburgh, a burgess and guilds-brother of Edinburgh, 1776, husband of Catherine dau. of Robert Smith a surgeon burgess and guilds-brother. [EBR]

DUNDAS, LAURENCE, a merchant in Edinburgh, 1742/1743. [NRS.AC10.305; AC11.226]

DUNDAS, THOMAS, jr., a merchant in Edinburgh, trustee of the Edinburgh Shipping Company, 1747. [NRS.AC10.328]

DUNLOP, THOMAS, a wright in Edinburgh, account book, 1736-1747. [NRS.CS238/Misc.27]

DUNNET, JOHN, a cooper in Leith, 1738,1750. [NRS.AC11.111/190]

DUNNETT, THOMAS, a cooper in Leith, 1738. [NRS.AC11.111]

DUNOON, DAVID, a saddler in Canongate, 1728. [NRS.AC11.36]

DUNSIRE, ANDREW, a mariner in Leith, husband of Margaret Fotheringham, 1761. [SL#91]

EASON, WILLIAM, son of James Eason a surgeon's servant, appr. to David Rannie a barber wigmaker burgess of Edinburgh, 1726. [ERA]

EASON, WILLIAM, born 1718, a tanner burgess of Edinburgh, died 23 June 1785, and his wife Christian Gilchrist, born 1698, died 6 May 1762. [St Cuthbert's MI, Edinburgh]

EATON, THOMAS, born 1746, a chapman from Edinburgh, to Philadelphia, Pennsylvania, in August 1774. [TNA.T47.12]

EDGAR, JOHN, a sailor in Leith, husband of Janet Simpson, 1774. [SL#110]

EDIE, DONALD, a shipmaster in Leith, husband of Hannah Pillans, 1752, [SL#71]; a decreet, 1763, 1767. [NRS.CS16.1.115; AC7.52]

EDMOND, DAVID, son of John Edmond a journeyman wright, appr. to James Wemyss a goldsmith burgess and guilds-brother of Edinburgh, 1755. [ERA]

EDMOND, JOHN, son of John Edmond a journeyman wright, appr. to James Wemyss a goldsmith burgess and guilds-brother of Edinburgh, 1752. [ERA]

The People of Edinburgh, 1725-1775

EDMONSTONE, ARCHIBALD, a skipper in Leith, father of John and Sophia, test., 1763, C.E. [NRS]

EDWARD, ALEXANDER, son of John Edward a soap-boiler burgess, a burgess of Canongate, 1725. [CBR]

EDWARD, JOHN, a sailor in Leith, husband of Margaret Leech, 1735. [SL#38]

EDWARD, JOHN, son of Thomas Edward, appr. to William Moriss a glass grinder in Edinburgh, 1738. [ERA]

EISILMAN, ARCHIBALD, son of Alexander Eisilman a porter, appr. to William Thomson a weaver in Edinburgh, 1772-1779. [ERA]

ELDER, WILLIAM, a stabler in Canongate, 1747. [NRS.AC11.150]

ELLIOT, ALEXANDER, a baker in Edinburgh, 1746/1747. [NRS.AC10.326; AC11.170]

ELSTON, JOHN, a writer in Edinburgh, 1778. [NRS.AC7.56]

ENGLEHART, CASPER, a jeweller in Edinburgh, admitted as a burgess of St Andrews in 1763. [St ABR]

ERSKINE, GEORGE, appr. to James Handyside a candlemaker in Edinburgh, 1726. [ERA]

ERSKINE, JOHN, from Edinburgh, in Boston, New England, 1740. [SCS]

ERSKINE, THOMAS, a brewer burgess of Canongate, 1729. [CBR]

ESPLIN, JOHN, son of James Esplin a tanner, appr. to Francis Newton a merchant burgess of Edinburgh, 1730. [ERA]

EWART, JAMES, of the Royal Bank of Scotland in Edinburgh, 1763. [NRS.CS25. Misc.]

EWART, JEAN, a coal-bearer from Edinburgh, transported to Maryland in 1771. [NRS.JC27.10.3]

EWING, GEORGE, born 1754, a carpenter from Edinburgh, to Dominica in December 1773. [TNA.T47.9.11]

FAIRBAIRN, GEORGE, a baxter burgess of Edinburgh, 1768, former appr. to Henry Hardie a baxter burgess. [EBR]

FAIRFOULL, WALTER, son of Thomas Fairfoull, appr. to Thomas Forrest a glazier burgess of Edinburgh, 1740. [ERA]

FAIRHOLM, ADAM, a merchant in Edinburgh, a decreet, 1744. [NRS.CS16.1.75]

FAIRHOLM, JAMES, a barber and wigmaker burgess of Edinburgh, 1762, former appr. of Adam Anderson and Robert Morison barbers and wigmakers burgesses. [EBR]

FAIRHOLM, THOMAS, a merchant from Edinburgh, in Tobago, decreets, 1744, 1776, 1779. [NRS.CS16.1.75/170/175]

FAIRHOLM, THOMAS, a merchant in Edinburgh, factor for the Swedish East India Company, 1741; trustee of the Edinburgh Shipping Company, 1747. [NRS.AC10.290/328]

The People of Edinburgh, 1725-1775

FAIRWEATHER, JAMES, a skipper in Leith, test., 1750, C.E. [NRS]

FALCONER, GEORGE, appr. to James Falconer a silver-turner burgess of Edinburgh, 1726. [ERA]

FALCONER, MARION, wife of William Marshall a skipper in Leith, heir to her mother Jean Baird, wife of John Falconer a skipper in Bo'ness, 1776. [NRS.S/H]

FALLA, WILLIAM, son of William Falla a tailor in Canongate, appr. to Thomas Henderson a founder in Edinburgh, 1764-1771. [ERA]

FARMER, PETER, a skipper, Burgess Close, Leith, 1773. [WED#27]

FARQUHAR, ALEXANDER, born 1713, from Edinburgh, to Pennsylvania in August 1728. [CLRO/AIA]

FARQUHAR, FRANCIS, a skipper in Leith, master of the <u>Catherine of Leith</u>, 1739; husband of Betty Gilmore, 1769; test., 1778, C.E. [ECL.44] [NRS.AC11.121]

FARQUHAR, JAMES, a merchant in Edinburgh, 1739. [NRS.AC11.121]

FARQUHAR, JOHN, a writer and merchant from Edinburgh, settled in Spanish Town, Jamaica, test., 1767, C.E. [NRS.CC8.8.120]

FARQUHAR, ROBERT, a master of Edinburgh High School, a burgess and guilds-brother of Edinburgh, 1762. [EBR]

FARQUHAR, THOMAS, a merchant from Edinburgh, later in Virginia, 1782. [NRS.CS17.1.1/97]

FARQUHARSON, ALEXANDER, son of Charles Farquharson a writer, appr. to John Dalgleish a watch and clockmaker in Edinburgh, 1749. [ERA]; a burgess of Edinburgh, 1764. [EBR]

FARQUHARSON, DANIEL, son of James Farquharson, appr. to Daniel Wright a wright burgess of Edinburgh, 1738. [ERA]

FARQUHARSON, DAVID, a skinner burgess of Edinburgh, 1762, appr. to Alexander Ogilvy a skinner burgess. [EBR]

FARQUHARSON, DONALD, a merchant burgess of Edinburgh, 1770. [EBR]

FARQUHARSON, LEWIS, son of Lewis Farquharson a writer, appr. to John Welsh a goldsmith in Edinburgh, 1761-1768. [ERA]

FARQUHARSON, PETER, a merchant burgess of Edinburgh, 1765. [EBR]

FARQUHARSON, THOMAS, son of Charles Farquharson, appr. to George Boswell a saddler in Edinburgh, 1748. [ERA]

FEDDES, JOHN, son of Robert Feddes a gardener, appr. to Peter Spalding a goldsmith in Edinburgh, 1761-1768. [ERA]

FENTON, ISABELLA, widow of Paul Husband a merchant in Edinburgh, heir to her father Thomas Fenton a merchant there, 1771. [NRS.S/H]

FERGUS, JOHN, son of John Fergus a merchant burgess, appr. to Charles Bruce a wright burgess of Edinburgh, 1741. [ERA]

The People of Edinburgh, 1725-1775

FERGUSON, ADAM, professor of moral philosophy, a burgess and guilds-brother of Edinburgh, 1766. [EBR]

FERGUSON, ALEXANDER, a watchmaker in Cupar and a freeman in Edinburgh, a burgess of Edinburgh, 1775, son of John Ferguson a tailor burgess. [EBR]

FERGUSON, ALEXANDER, a dyer and bonnetmaker burgess of Edinburgh, 1777, former appr. to Andrew Crombie a dyer. [EBR]

FERGUSON, ANTHONY, a merchant burgess and guilds-brother of Edinburgh, 1762, former appr. to .... Haliburton a merchant burgess. [EBR]

FERGUSON, DAVID, son of David Ferguson a barber and wigmaker in Leith, appr. to Walter Gibson a surgeon in Leith, 1755. [ERA]

FERGUSON, DUNCAN, son of John Ferguson a porter, appr. to John Lauder a coppersmith in Edinburgh, 1767-1773. [ERA]

FERGUSON, GEORGE, son of John Ferguson, appr. to John Muir a cutler burgess of Edinburgh, 1729. [ERA]

FERGUSON, JAMES, a merchant burgess of Edinburgh, 1770. [EBR]

FERGUSON, JOHN, a coppersmith burgess of Edinburgh, 1763, son of James Ferguson a coppersmith burgess. [EBR]

FERGUSON, JOHN, a sailor in Leith, husband of Helen Kay, 1764. [SL#98]

FERGUSON, JOHN, a sailor in Leith, 1768, 'engaged in the Greenland fishery', husband of Isabel Henderson, 1771. [ECL#43/45/60]

FERGUSON, MARGARET, wife of John Stevenson a skipper in Leith, heir to her father David Ferguson a barber there, 1775. [NRS.S/H]

FERGUSON, THOMAS, son of Thomas Ferguson, appr. to John Bruce a merchant in Edinburgh, 1728. [ERA]

FERGUSON, THOMAS, a coppersmith burgess of Edinburgh, 1767, son of James Ferguson a coppersmith burgess. [EBR]

FERGUSON, WALTER, a candlemaker burgess of Edinburgh, 1772, former appr. to William Braidwood a candlemaker. [EBR]

FERRIER, WALTER, a tanner burgess and guilds-brother of Edinburgh, 1774; son of David Ferrier a stabler burgess and guilds-brother. [EBR]

FINLAY, DAVID, a barber and wigmaker burgess of Edinburgh, 1775. [EBR]

FINLAY, GEORGE, a merchant in Edinburgh, 1784. [NRS.AC7.61]

FINLAY, ROBERT, son of James Finlay in Edinburgh, appr. to James Somerville a goldsmith in Edinburgh, 1759-1766. [ERA]

FINLAY, ROBERT, tacksman of customs at Edinburgh fruit market, a burgess and guilds-brother of Edinburgh, 1776. [EBR]

FINLAYSON, DUNCAN, a merchant in Edinburgh, husband of Lillias Thomson, a sasine, 1754. [NRS.RS27.144.277]

FINNY, ALEXANDER, a wright in Portsburgh, Edinburgh, a decreet, 1776. [NRS.CS16.1.168]

The People of Edinburgh, 1725-1775

FISHER, WILLIAM, son of James Fisher a miller at Canonmills, appr. to Archibald Howie late deacon of the weavers of Edinburgh, 1732. [ERA]
FISHER, WILLIAM, son of Robert Fisher servant to James Rattray a brewer, appr. to Andrew Newton a weaver in Edinburgh, 1764-1770. [ERA]
FITTES, WILLIAM, a merchant burgess and guilds-brother of Edinburgh, 1771, son of William Fittes a merchant burgess and guilds-brother. [EBR]
FITTES, WILLIAM, a merchant burgess of Edinburgh, 1774, son of John Fittes a merchant burgess and guilds-brother, and as a former appr. to William Taylor a merchant burgess and guilds-brother. [EBR]
FLEMING, DAVID, a merchant in Edinburgh, heir to his brother William Fleming a brewer there, 1769. [NRS.S/H]
FLEMING, DAVID, a merchant from Edinburgh, in South Carolina, a decreet, 1773. [NRS.CS1.1.103/154]
FLEMING, JAMES, a skipper in Leith, 1743. [ECL#28]
FLEMING, JOHN, from Edinburgh, in Boston, New England, 1764. [SCS]
FLEMING, ROBERT, a printer and book-seller in Edinburgh, heir to his father Robert Fleming a book-seller and printer there, 1771. [NRS.S/H]
FLEMING, WILLIAM, a brewer burgess of Canongate, 1726. [CBR]
FLEMING, WILLIAM, a journeyman mason burgess of Edinburgh, 1764, husband of Helen dau. of James Henderson a workman burgess. [EBR]
FLEMING, WILLIAM, a merchant burgess of Edinburgh, 1762, former appr. to James Miller a merchant burgess, [EBR]; in North Back of Canongate, once a merchant in Edinburgh, son and heir of William Fleming a brewer at Craigend, 1775. [NRS.S/H]
FLINT, JAMES, a brewer baillie of Edinburgh, 1746. [NRS.AC10.323]
FLUCKER, HANNAH, dau. of Thomas Flucker, late of Boston, New England, now in Edinburgh, test., 1787, C.E. [NRS.CC8.5.22]
FOORD, ALEXANDER, a merchant burgess of Edinburgh, 1764. [EBR]
FOORD, ROBERT, a merchant burgess and guilds-brother of Edinburgh, 1777, former appr. to Robert Scott a merchant burgess and guildsbrother. [EBR]
FOOT, ROBERT, son of James Foot a porter in the Weigh-house, appr. to Archibald Stratoun a watchmaker burgess of Edinburgh, 1755. [ERA]
FORBES, ALEXANDER, a printer from Edinburgh, in Boston, New England, 1767. [SCS]
FORBES, ARTHUR, appr. to James Witherspoon a weaver in Edinburgh, 1757-1763. [ERA]
FORBES, DAVID, son of Reverend Arthur Forbes at the Port of Menteith, a burgess of Canongate, 1731. [CBR]
FORBES, JAMES, a merchant in Edinburgh, husband of Ann Robertson, a sasine, 1757. [NRS.RS27.148.438]

The People of Edinburgh, 1725-1775

FORBES, JAMES, a flax-dresser in Edinburgh, heir to his father James Forbes a flax-dresser there, 1773. [NRS.S/H]

FORBES, JOHN, a skipper in Bo'ness, a burgess of Edinburgh, 1767, husband of Jean dau. of John Mitchell HM Customs Surveyor at Thurso, a burgess. [EBR]

FORBES, JOHN, judge advocate of Grenada, a burgess and guilds-brother of Edinburgh, 1771. [EBR]

FORBES, Sir WILLIAM, appr. to Coutts Brothers and Company merchants in Edinburgh, 1766-1771. [ERA]; a burgess and guilds-brother, 1766. [EBR]

FORD, JOHN, a skipper at Coalhill, Leith, 1773. [WED#27]

FORDYCE, CHARLES, from Edinburgh, Captain of the 14th Regiment of Foot, died in Virginia, probate 1777 PCC

FORREST, ALLAN, a stocking weaver burgess of Edinburgh, 1762, son of James Forrest a felt-maker burgess. [EBR]

FORREST, ANDREW, a merchant in Edinburgh, heir to his uncle Andrew, son of James Junkenson a burgess of Biggar, 1772; also to his father John Forrest a merchant in Edinburgh, 1778. [NRS.S/H]

FOREST, ARTHUR, from Edinburgh, in Boston, New England, 1739. [SCS]

FORREST, GEORGE, son of Richard Forrest a shoemaker, appr. to James Smiton a barber burgess of Edinburgh, 1744. [ERA]

FORREST, JOHN, a merchant in Edinburgh, 1742, trustee of the Edinburgh Shipping Company, 1747. [NRS.AC10.305/328]

FORREST, JOHN, a merchant burgess and guilds-brother of Edinburgh, 1767, son of John Forrest a burgess and guilds-brother. [EBR]

FORREST, WILLIAM, a weaver burgess of Edinburgh, 1771, husband of Halket dau. of deacon David Thomson a weaver burgess. [EBR]

FORREST, WILLIAM, a merchant burgess of Edinburgh, 1776, husband of Elizabeth dau. of James McKay a coppersmith burgess and guilds-brother. [EBR]

FORRESTER, DAVID, in North Leith, a smith burgess of Canongate, 1727. [CBR]

FORRESTER, DAVID, a merchant burgess of Edinburgh, 1774. [EBR]

FORRESTER, PETER, a merchant burgess and guilds-brother of Edinburgh, 1771. [EBR]

FORRESTER, ROBERT, a skipper at Coalhill, Leith, 1773, [WED#27]; master of the Elizabeth and Peggy of Leith, test., 1774, C.E. [NRS]

FORRESTER, WILLIAM, skipper at New Quay, Leith, 1773. [WED#27]

FORSYTH, ANDREW, a sailor in Leith, 1769. [SL#106]

FORSYTH, EDWARD, son of John Forsyth a silk weaver in Canongate, appr. to Robert Dewar a glazier in Edinburgh, 1756-1775. [ERA]

FORSYTH, JAMES, a bookbinder burgess of Edinburgh, 1764. [EBR]

The People of Edinburgh, 1725-1775

FORTUNE, GEORGE, a merchant burgess of Edinburgh, 1773, son of Thomas Fortune a tanner burgess. [EBR]

FORTUNE, JOHN, a vintner in Old Ship Close, Edinburgh, a burgess of Edinburgh, 1772. [EBR]

FORTUNE, THOMAS, son of Thomas Fortune a merchant's servant, appr. to William Tod senior, a merchant in Edinburgh, 1734. [ERA]

FOTHERINGHAM, EUGEN, a skipper in Leith, son of Thomas Fotheringham of Powrie, test., 1732, C.E. [NRS]

FOTHERINGHAM, JOHN, a mariner in Leith, husband of Anne Leslie, 1761. [SL#91]

FOWLER, ANDREW, a skipper in Leith, test., 1755, C.E. [NRS]

FRAME, RICHARD, a mason burgess of Edinburgh, 1761, former appr. to John Ronaldson a mason burgess. [EBR]

FRANCIS, DAVID, son of Hew Francis a supervisor of H.M. Excise, appr. to George Young a surgeon apothecary burgess of Edinburgh, 1731. [ERA]

FRANKLIN, BENJAMIN, of Philadelphia, Pennsylvania, a burgess and guilds-brother of Edinburgh, 1759. [EBR]

FRANKLIN, WILLIAM, son of Benjamin Franklin of Philadelphia, a burgess and guildsbrother of Edinburgh, 1759. [EBR]

FRASER, ADAM, a mariner in Leith, husband of L. Donaldson, 1762. [SL#92]

FRASER, ALEXANDER, son of Hugh Fraser a drawer in the Tolbooth, appr. to George Watson a painter burgess of Edinburgh, 1726. [ERA]

FRASER, ALEXANDER, from Edinburgh, in Boston, New England,1746. [SCS]

FRASER, ALEXANDER, an Excise Office clerk, a burgess and guilds-brother of Edinburgh, 1777, husband of Geils dau. of William Henderson a merchant burgess and guilds-brother. [EBR]

FRASER, DANIEL, a sailor in Leith, husband of Janet Kelman, 1742. [SL#51]

FRASER, JOHN, son of John Fraser a vintner, appr. to George Watson a painter burgess of Edinburgh, 1736. [ERA]

FRASER, JOHN, son of Gabriel Fraser a gauger in Leith, appr. to William Gray a bookbinder burgess of Edinburgh, 1744. [ERA]

FRASER, JOHN, a sailor in Leith, 1755. [ECL#36]

FRASER, JOHN, a Writer to the Signet, a burgess and guilds-brother of Edinburgh, 1762, husband of Jean dau. of David Brown a merchant. [EBR]

FRASER, JOHN, son of Alexander Fraser a clerk in the Excise Office, appr. to Patrick Inglis a merchant in Edinburgh, 1773-1778. [ERA]

FRASER, JOHN, a carpenter in Leith, test., 1779, C.E. [NAS]

FRASER, SIMON, a white-iron smith burgess and guilds-brother of Edinburgh, 1764, grandson of Daniel Dalrymple a wright burgess and guilds-brother. [EBR]

The People of Edinburgh, 1725-1775

FRASER, WILLIAM, a white-iron smith burgess and guilds-brother of Edinburgh, 1765, son of Simon Fraser a white-iron smith burgess and guilds-brother. [EBR]

FREEBAIRN, CHARLES, a wright burgess and guilds-brother of Edinburgh, 1761. [EBR]

FREEBAIRN, JAMES, a merchant in Edinburgh, 1739. [NRS.AC11.125]

FRENCH, JAMES, a master of Edinburgh High School, a burgess and guilds-brother of Edinburgh, 1762. [EBR]

FRIGG, Captain THOMAS, a burgess and guilds-brother of Edinburgh, 1763. [EBR]

FULLERTON, WILLIAM, late of Calcutta, Bengal, a burgess and guilds-brother of Edinburgh, 1763. [EBR]

FULTON, WILLIAM, son of Archibald Fulton in Leith, appr. to George Gray a barber wigmaker burgess of Edinburgh, 1726. [ERA]

FYFE, JAMES, a merchant burgess and guilds-brother of Edinburgh, 1772, son of James Fyfe a merchant burgess and guilds-brother. [EBR]

FYFFE, JOHN, a merchant and guilds-brother of Edinburgh, 1763. [EBR]

FYFE, ROBERT, a mariner in Leith, husband of Margaret Clark, 1762. [SL#92]

FYFE, WILLIAM, son of Peter Fyfe a vintner, appr. to Peter Forrester a merchant in Edinburgh, 1773-1778. [ERA]

GAIRDNER, GEORGE, an ironmonger and brazier in London, a burgess and guilds-brother of Edinburgh, 1774, son of Thomas Gairdner a merchant burgess and guilds-brother. [EBR]

GAIRDNER, JAMES, born 1761 in Edinburgh, son of Andrew Gairdner, a merchant, and his wife Rebecca Penman, to Charleston, South Carolina, in 1780, a cotton planter in Georgia, died 1830. [NRS.S/H][St Cuthbert's OPR]

GALBREATH, WILLIAM, a sailor in Leith, husband of Catherine Young, 1742. [SL#48]

GALBRAITH, WILLIAM, a barber and wigmaker burgess of Edinburgh, 1764, son of William Galbraith a barber and wigmaker burgess. [EBR]

GALL, JOHN, son of Duncan Gall a journeyman tailor, appr. to William Cowan a lorimer in Edinburgh, 1763-1770. [ERA]

GALL, JOSEPH, a weaver burgess of Edinburgh, 1773, former appr. to Patrick Bowie a weaver burgess. [EBR]

GALLAN, JOHN, a sailor in Leith, 1764. [ECL#41]

GALLOWAY, JOHN, a merchant burgess and guilds-brother of Edinburgh, 1777, son of Alexander Galloway a stabler. [EBR]

GALT, JOHN, a merchant in Edinburgh, trading with South Carolina, a decreet, 1775. [NRS.CS16.1.165]

The People of Edinburgh, 1725-1775

GARDEN, ALEXANDER, born 1685 in Edinburgh, minister of St Phillip's in Charleston, South Carolina, from 1726 until 1748, died 1756, probate, 1756, South Carolina.

GARDEN, FRANCIS, HM solicitor in Scotland, a burgess and guilds-brother, 1761. [EBR]

GARDINER, ALEXANDER, son of Alexander Gardiner a schoolmaster in Canongate, appr. to William Aiton a goldsmith burgess of Edinburgh, 1744. [ERA]

GARDINER, ANDREW, a merchant burgess and guilds-brother of Edinburgh, 1767, son of James Gardiner a merchant burgess and guilds-brother. [EBR]

GARDINER, Captain GEORGE, a burgess and guilds-brother of Edinburgh, 1762. [EBR]

GARDINER, GEORGE, son of George Gardiner an examiner and accountant of the Salt and Fishery Accounts in the Customs House, appr. to James Hay a surgeon in Edinburgh, 1760-1765. [ERA]

GARDINER, JOHN, an appr. merchant in Edinburgh, released from Edinburgh Tolbooth for transportation to America in 1744. [NRS.HH11.22]

GARDINER, JOHN, a peuterer burgess of Edinburgh, 1764, husband of Elizabeth dau. of Robert Brown a peuterer burgess. [EBR]

GARDINER, JOHN, a merchant burgess and guilds-brother of Edinburgh, 1769, son of George Gardiner a clerk in the Customs House at Leith, [EBR]

GARDINER, ROBERT, a smith and farrier burgess of Edinburgh, 1767, son of James Gardiner a smith and farrier burgess. [EBR]

GARDINER, WILLIAM, a dyer burgess and guilds-brother of Edinburgh, 1770, son of William Gardiner a dyer burgess and guilds-brother. [EBR]

GARDNER, EBENEZER, a merchant and manufacturer burgess and guilds-brother of Edinburgh, 1767, son of James Gardner a merchant burgess and guilds-brother; deceased, and his widow Margaret Lithgow, a decreet, 1779. [EBR][NRS.CS16.1.175]

GARDNER, JAMES, a sailor in Leith, husband of Margaret Sinclair, 1769. [SL#108]

GARDNER, JAMES, a coppersmith burgess of Edinburgh, 1762, son of James Gardner a merchant burgess. [EBR]

GARDNER, JAMES, a smith and farrier burgess of Edinburgh, 1775, son of Alexander Gardner a smith burgess. [EBR]

GARDNER, JOHN, son of John Gardner a shoemaker in St Ninian's Row, Edinburgh, appr. to James Sutherland a founder in Edinburgh, 1768-1774. [ERA]

GARDNER, RICHARD, born 1723, of HM Customs in Edinburgh, died 1788. [Greyfriars MI]

The People of Edinburgh, 1725-1775

GARDNER, THOMAS, a merchant in Edinburgh, 1748. [NRS.AC10.339]

GARNER, THOMAS, a sailor in Leith, husband of Ann Thomson, 1765. [SL#100]

GARNOCK, GEORGE, from Edinburgh, transported to the colonies in March 1768. [AJ#1056]

GAY, JOHN, a burgess and guilds-brother of Edinburgh, 1761. [EBR]

GEDD, JAMES, son of William Gedd, a printer from Edinburgh, settled in Jamaica after 1746. [P.2.222]

GED, WILLIAM, son of William Ged, a merchant from Edinburgh, died 4 January 1767 in St James, Jamaica. [SM.29.389]

GEDDES, CHARLES, born 1749 in Edinburgh, son of James Geddes, a watchmaker from Edinburgh, in Boston, New England, 1774, later in New York, died in Halifax, Nova Scotia, 27 September 1810. [SCS][NRS.RD2.232.86][EA#4926]

GEDDES, JAMES, son of James Geddes of Rachan an advocate, appr. to William Hog and Son merchants in Edinburgh, 1759-1764. [ERA]; a burgess and guilds-brother of Edinburgh, 1772. [EBR]

GELLATLY, WILLIAM, son of John Gellatly a merchant in Arbroath, appr. to William Cuming a merchant burgess of Edinburgh, 1712, [ERA]; a merchant in Edinburgh, 1733, 1742. [NRS.AC10.299; AC11.68]

GEMMEL, WILLIAM, a merchant burgess and guilds-brother of Edinburgh, 1761. [EBR]

GENTLEMAN, JOHN, husband of Janet, dau. of Thomas Allardice a merchant burgess, was admitted as a stabler burgess of Edinburgh, 1729. [EBR]

GEORGE, JAMES, son of Andrew George a vintner in Leith, appr. to David Freebairn a barber burgess of Edinburgh, 1732. [ERA]

GIB, ADAM, minister of the Associate Congregation, born 1714, died 1788. [Greyfriars MI, Edinburgh]

GIB, HUGH, appr. to Patrick Crocket a wright in Edinburgh, 1727. [ERA]; a burgess of Edinburgh, 1762. [EBR]

GIBB, JOHN, a merchant burgess and guilds-brother of Edinburgh, 1776.[EBR]

GIBB, Dr ROBERT, a physician from Edinburgh, to Georgetown, South Carolina, in 1754, a planter, a Loyalist in 1776, died in South Carolina, 1777. [TNA.AO.12.51.99]

GIBB, THOMAS, a skipper in Leith, test., 1738, C.E. [NRS]

GIBB, WILLIAM, a bookseller burgess and guilds-brother of Edinburgh, 1764, husband of Anne dau. of Gideon Crawford a bookseller burgess and guildsbrother. [EBR]

GIBSON, HENRY, a midshipman aboard HMS Emerald, married Mary Alison, in Edinburgh, 1768. [SL#101]

The People of Edinburgh, 1725-1775

GIBSON, JAMES, son of William Gibson a merchant, appr. to John Jack a slater burgess of Edinburgh, 1725. [ERA]

GIBSON, JAMES, from Edinburgh, in Boston, New England, 1734. [SCS]

GIBSON, JAMES, a mariner in Leith, husband of Janet Blaiketer, 1764. [SL#97]

GIBSON, JAMES, a stabler burgess of Edinburgh, 1764. [EBR]

GIBSON, JAMES, a skipper in Leith, test., 1768, C.E. [NRS]

GIBSON, JAMES, a surgeon burgess of Edinburgh, 1770, son of James Gibson a slater burgess. [EBR]

GIBSON, JOHN, son of James Gibson a stabler in Grassmarket, Edinburgh, appr. to David Binny a clock and watchmaker in Edinburgh, 1761-1767. [ERA]; a burgess of Edinburgh, 1767. [EBR]

GIBSON, ROBERT, a sailor in Leith, husband of Isabel Smith, 1739. [SL#43]

GIBSON, THOMAS, son of Thomas Gibson a sailor in Leith, appr. to Thomas Whitlaw a saddler burgess of Edinburgh, 1736. [ERA]

GIFFORD, THOMAS, a smith and farrier in Edinburgh, husband of Lillias Stirling, a sasine, 1751. [NRS.RS27.138.114]

GILCHRIST, JOHN, a master of Edinburgh High School, a burgess and guilds-brother of Edinburgh, 1762. [EBR]

GILCHRIST, JOHN, a merchant burgess and guilds-brother of Edinburgh, 1770, husband of Margaret dau. of Robert Mushet a merchant burgess and guilds-brother. [EBR]

GILCHRIST, WALTER, son of Thomas Gilchrist a tailor in Canongate, appr. to John Brown a merchant burgess of Edinburgh, 1748. [ERA]

GILCHRIST, WILLIAM, a blacksmith from Edinburgh, transported to the colonies in March 1741. [SM.3.143]

GILCHRIST, WILLIAM, a skinner burgess of Edinburgh, 1762, former appr. to David Scott a skinner burgess. [EBR]

GILCHRIST, WILLIAM, brother of William Gilchrist (sic), appr. to James Thomson a skinner in Edinburgh, 1768-1774. [ERA]

GILES, ARTHUR, a wright burgess of Edinburgh, 1768, former appr. to Charles Butter a wright burgess. [EBR]

GILES, WILLIAM, son and heir of John Giles a brewer in Leith, 1775. [NRS.S/H]

GILLESPIE, ANDREW, appr. to John Shaw a merchant and upholsterer in Edinburgh, 1760-1767. [ERA]; a burgess and guilds-brother of Edinburgh, 1763. [EBR]

GILLESPIE, JAMES, a merchant burgess of Edinburgh, 1765. [EBR]

GILLESPIE, WILLIAM, a merchant burgess and guilds-brother of Edinburgh, 1769, son of William Gillespie a merchant burgess and guilds-brother. [EBR]

GILLIES, JOHN, a sailor in Leith, husband of Eliza Baxter, 1732. [SL#35]

GILLIES, JOHN, a skipper in Leith, test., 1736, C.E.

The People of Edinburgh, 1725-1775

GILMORE, ROBERT, a ropemaker in Bristo, Edinburgh, a burgess of Edinburgh, father of Peter, 1761. [EBR]

GILMOUR, JOHN, a merchant burgess of Edinburgh, 1777. [EBR]

GILMOUR, ROBERT, a barber and wigmaker burgess of Edinburgh, 1776, former appr. to Daniel McKinnon a freeman burgess, wigmaker and hairdresser. [EBR]

GLADSTONES, THOMAS, a merchant burgess of Edinburgh, 1777, husband of Helen dau. of Walter Neilson a merchant burgess. [EBR]

GLANCE, DAVID, born 1705, a groom from Edinburgh, to Jamaica in 1724. [CLRO/AIA]

GLENDINNING, ROBERT, son of William Glendinning a stabler, appr. to Peter Forrester a merchant in Edinburgh, 1771-1776. [ERA]

GLOAG, JOHN, a merchant in Edinburgh, trading with Antigua in 1779. [NRS.CS16.1.175]

GLOVER, JAMES, a candle-maker burgess of Canongate, 1729. [CBR]

GLOVER, JOHN, son of James Glover a servant of Andrew Pringle a Senator of the College of Justice, an appr. to Thomas Laing an edge-tool maker in Edinburgh, 1769-1775. [ERA]

GOOD, WILLIAM, born 1721, died 1773. [Greyfriars MI, Edinburgh]

GOODALL, JOHN, son of James Goodall a wright in Canongate, appr. to Gilbert Auchenleck a cutler in Edinburgh, 1773-1780. [ERA]

GORDON, CUTHBERT, a manufacturer in Leith, a decreet, 1778. [NRS.CS16.1.173]

GORDON, CHARLES, son of Dr Charles Gordon in Jamaica, appr. to Thomas Carmichael a merchant in Edinburgh, 1772-1777. [ERA]

GORDON, HUGH, a goldsmith in Edinburgh, and his wife Rachel Robertson, a sasine, 1755. [NRS.RS27.144.410]

GORDON, JOHN, son of Alexander Gordon deputy clerk of the Admiralty, appr. to Robert Selkirk a merchant burgess of Edinburgh, 1741. [ERA]

GORDON, JOHN, a merchant in Edinburgh, 1742. [NRS.AC10.305]

GORDON, MARGARET, born 1747, a spinner from Edinburgh, to Antigua in October 1774. [TNA.T47.12]

GORDON, ROBERT, a sailor in Leith, died before 1766. [NRS.S/H]

GORDON, ROBERT, a goldsmith in Edinburgh, test., 1767, C.E. [NRS]

GORDON, THOMAS, a sailor in Leith, husband of Elizabeth Riddel, 1745. [SL#53]

GORDON, THOMAS, a skipper in South Leith, test., 1751, C.E. [NRS]

GORDON, THOMAS, born 1751, a bleacher from Edinburgh, to Maryland in March 1774. [TNA.T47.9/11]

The People of Edinburgh, 1725-1775

GORDON, WILLIAM, son of William Gordon in Edinburgh, appr. to John Howden a cooper burgess of Edinburgh, 1738. [ERA]
GORDON, WILLIAM, in Jamaica, a burgess and guilds-brother of Edinburgh, 1743. [EBR]
GOW, WILLIAM, son of William Gow a stabler, appr. to Robert Clydesdale a clock and watch-maker in Edinburgh, 1776-1783. [ERA]
GOWANS, WILLIAM, a wright in Drumseugh, died 21 February 1749, husband of Allison Mackie. [St Cuthbert's MI]
GRAHAM, ANDREW, son of Daniel Graham a writer, appr. to Alexander Reid a freeman tailor of the 'Canongate of Edinburgh', 1733. [ERA]
GRAHAM, ARCHIBALD, a sailor in Leith, husband of Mary Cairns, 1764. [SL#97]
GRAHAM, JOHN and WILLIAM, wine-coopers in Leith, 1750; a decreet, 1767. [NRS.AC10.354; CS16.1.130]
GRANT, ALEXANDER, a writer in Edinburgh, a decreet, 1781. [NRS.CS16.1.183]
GRANT, ANDREW, a merchant from Edinburgh, settled in Ogychee, Georgia, in 1734. [TNA.CO5.670.108][NRS.RD2.171.33]
GRANT, ANDREW, a merchant from Edinburgh, in Grenada, 1781. [NRS.CS16.1.183]
GRANT, DAVID, former appr. to David Denoon a saddler burgess, a burgess of Canongate, 1725. [CBR]
GRANT, DUNCAN, a merchant in Antigua, a burgess of Edinburgh, 1760. [EBR]
GRANT, GEORGE, a merchant in Jamaica, son of John Grant a merchant in Leith, 1768. [NRS.GD29.2167]
GRANT, JAMES, son of John Grant a Writer to the Signet, appr. to George Chalmers a merchant in Edinburgh, 1751. [ERA]
GRANT, JAMES, son of William Grant a wire-sieve maker in Edinburgh Castle, appr. to William Dunbar a barber and wigmaker in Edinburgh, 1753. [ERA]
GRANT, JOHN, a merchant in Leith, a burgess and guilds-brother of Edinburgh, 1772, husband of Elizabeth dau. of Alexander Whyte a merchant burgess and guilds-brother. [EBR]
GRANT, LEWIS, a merchant burgess and guilds-brother of Edinburgh, 1777, husband of Janet, dau. of Thomas Hill a merchant burgess and guilds-brother. [EBR]
GRANT, NATHANIEL, a printer burgess of Edinburgh, 1774, husband of Helen dau. of George Lind a merchant burgess and guilds-brother. [EBR]
GRANT, PATRICK, born 1733, a book-keeper from Edinburgh, to Jamaica in December 1750. [CLRO/AIA]
GRANT, ROBERT, a wigmaker burgess of Canongate, husband of ....Ross, 1728. [CBR]

The People of Edinburgh, 1725-1775

GRANT, THOMAS, a goldsmith in Edinburgh, spouse of Isobel Barclay, a sasine, 1778. [NRS.RS27.242.221]

GRANT, WILLIAM, a writer in Edinburgh, 1730. [NRS.AC10.157]

GRANT, WILLIAM, son of John Grant a Writer to the Signet, appr. to George Chalmers a merchant in Edinburgh, 1755. [ERA]

GRANT, WILLIAM, a tailor burgess of Edinburgh, 1763, son of Patrick Gray a merchant burgess. [EBR]

GRAY, ALEXANDER, son of Alexander Gray, appr. to Robert Lauder a baxter burgess of Edinburgh, 1742. [ERA]

GRAY, ALEXANDER, son of William Gray in Edinburgh, appr. to Thomas Grant a bowyer burgess of Edinburgh, 1751. [ERA]

GRAY, ANDREW, a merchant burgess and guilds-brother of Edinburgh, 1766. [EBR]

GRAY, DAVID, a merchant burgess and guilds-brother of Edinburgh, 1767, son of John Gray a merchant burgess and guilds-brother. [EBR]

GRAY, GEORGE, a merchant burgess of Edinburgh, 1761, son of John Gray a wigmaker burgess. [EBR]

GRAY, HUGH, a merchant burgess and guilds-brother of Edinburgh, 1768, son of George Gray a merchant burgess and guilds-brother. [EBR]

GRAY, JAMES, from Leith, transported to the colonies in July 1737. [NRS.JC27]

GRAY, JAMES, a burgess of Edinburgh, 1764, son of David Gray, and former appr. to David Bibby a watchmaker burgess. [EBR]

GRAY, JAMES, a skipper in Rotten Row, Leith, 1773; 1785. [WED#33][NRS.GD226.18.248]

GRAY, JAMES, a clock and watchmaker burgess of Edinburgh, 1775, former appr. to Daniel Binney a clock and watchmaker. [EBR]

GRAY, JOHN, born 1701, a clerk and writer from Edinburgh, to Antigua in August 1728. [CLRO/AIA]

GRAY, JOHN, son of Robert Gray a gardener, appr. to Adam Anderson a barber wigmaker burgess of Edinburgh, 1726. [ERA]

GRAY, JOHN, son of Alexander Gray a gardener, appr. to Williamson and Fish, merchant burgesses of Edinburgh, 1749. [ERA]

GRAY, JOHN, a baxter burgess and guilds-brother of Edinburgh, 1770, son of John Gray a merchant in Currie, a burgess and guilds-brother. [EBR]

GRAY, JOHN, a barber burgess and guilds-brother of Edinburgh, 1775, son of John Gray a merchant burgess and guilds-brother. [EBR]

GRAY, ROBERT, born 1672, a gardener and feuat at Fountainbridge, died 8 May 1735; his wife Helen, born 1677, died 12 May 1743, parents of John, born 1722, died 6 May 1728. [St Cuthbert's MI]

GRAY, ROBERT, a skipper in Leith, test., 1727, C.E. [NRS]

The People of Edinburgh, 1725-1775

GRAY, ROBERT, a merchant burgess of Edinburgh, 1770, former appr. to John McLean and William Morrison merchant burgesses and guilds-brethren. [EBR]

GRAY, THOMAS, a baker burgess and guilds-brother of Edinburgh, 1768, son of George Gray a merchant burgess and guilds-brother. [EBR]

GRAY, WILLIAM, appr. to William Daes a waulker in Edinburgh, 1747. [ERA]

GRAY, WILLIAM, a carrier in Edinburgh, heir to his niece Hannah, dau. of James Gray a carrier in Edinburgh, 1775. [NRS.S/H]

GREENHILL, DAVID, a candle-maker burgess of Canongate, son of John Greenhill a coachmaster burgess of Canongate, 1733. [CBR]

GREENLEES, JAMES, in Edinburgh, heir to his grandfather James Beveridge a merchant there, 1779. [NRS.S/H]

GREENLEES, MARY, dau. of John Greenlees a merchant in Virginia, and wife of John Monro a merchant in Edinburgh, a decreet, 1782. [NRS.CS17.1.1]

GREENLEES, ROBERT, an Excise officer in Leith, husband of Mary Robertson, a sasine, 1752. [NRS.RS27.148.361]

GREGORY, Dr JOHN, professor of medicine at Edinburgh University, a burgess and guilds-brother of Edinburgh, 1766. [EBR]

GREGORY, JOHN, master of the Moncrieff of Leith, test., 1781, C.E. [NRS]

GREIG, ADAM, son of Thomas Greig a wright in Portsburgh, Edinburgh, appr. to Thomas Gifford a blacksmith farrier burgess of Edinburgh, 1736. [ERA]

GREIG, ALEXANDER, son of William Greig a tailor burgess, appr. to John Esplin a merchant burgess of Edinburgh, 1741. [ERA]

GREIG, DAVID, appr. to Robert Low a goldsmith burgess of Edinburgh, 1747. [ERA]

GREIG, DAVID, a merchant burgess of Edinburgh, 1767. [EBR]

GREIG, ISABEL, wife of Thomas Angus a sailor in Leith, heir to her father Robert Greig a sailor in Kinghorn, 1778. [NRS.S/H]

GREIG, JAMES, son of James Greig a merchant, appr. to James Stewart a barber burgess of Edinburgh, 1734. [ERA]

GREIG, JAMES, born in Edinburgh during 1767, a baker and confectioner in New York from 1796 until his death there on 20 December 1804. [ANY.I.362]

GREIG, JENNY, born 1751, from Edinburgh, to Philadelphia, Pennsylvania, in May 1775. [TNA.T47.12]

GREIRSON, DAVID, a merchant burgess of Edinburgh, 1764. [EBR]

GREIRSON, ROBERT, a smith burgess of Edinburgh, 1769, former appr. to William Richardson a smith burgess. [EBR]

GREYM, ANDREW, son of Thomas Greym the macer of the Court of Session, appr. to William Hepburn a surgeon apothecary in Edinburgh, 1744. [ERA]

GRIEVE, ANN, born 1758, from Edinburgh, to New York in April 1775. [TNA.T47.12]

The People of Edinburgh, 1725-1775

GRIEVE, JOHN, son of Alexander Grieve a journeyman wright, appr. to James Maxwell a cordiner burgess of Edinburgh, 172. [ERA]

GRIEVE, ROBERT, a glazier burgess of Edinburgh, 1775, former appr. to William Govan a glazier burgess. [EBR]

GRIFFITH, GABRIEL, son of Gabriel Griffith, appr. to Alexander Anderson, a coppersmith burgess of Edinburgh, 1728. [ERA]

GRIGSON, JAMES, a merchant in Edinburgh, 1743. [NRS.AC11.155]

GRINDLAY, GEORGE, born 1742, a merchant burgess and guilds-brother of Edinburgh, 1764, husband of Marion dau. of William Bruce a merchant burgess and guilds-brother, died 1800.[EBR] [Greyfriars MI, Edinburgh]

GROAT, JAMES, a skipper in Leith, test., 1730, C.E. [NRS]

GUILLEN, CHARLES, a shoemaker in Portsburgh, a burgess and guilds-brother of Edinburgh, 1775, husband of Ann dau. of William Gillespie a merchant burgess and guilds-brother. [EBR]

GULBENS, JAMES, an ale-seller burgess of Canongate, 1726. [CBR]

GUTHRIE, WILLIAM, son of Reverend Harry Guthrie and his wife Rachel Milne, from Edinburgh, settled in St Elizabeth, Jamaica, before 1774. [NRS.RD3.733.387]

HADDAWAY, JOHN, son of Thomas Haddaway a brewer in Leith, appr. to Walter Gibson a surgeon apothecary in Edinburgh, 1742. [ERA]

HADDOW, GEORGE, son of Robert Haddow, appr. to Thomas Crawford a glazier burgess of Edinburgh, 1738. [ERA]

HADLEY, HENRY, a burgess and guilds-brother of Edinburgh, 1747. [EBR]

HAGGART, JAMES, son of James Haggart a sergeant of the City Guard of Edinburgh, appr. to Robert Drummond a barber wigmaker burgess of Edinburgh, 1751. [ERA]

HAGUE, RALPH, born 1749, a painter, from Edinburgh, to Maryland in October 1774. [TNA.T47.9/11]

HAIG, JAMES, son of David Haig a farmer and brewer in Lasswade, appr. to Mansfield, Hunter & Co in Edinburgh, 1765-1770, a merchant in Edinburgh, trading with Jamaica, a decreet, 1780. [ERA][NRS.CS16.1.179; CS17.1.2]

HAIGS, WILLIAM, son of Charles Haigs a baxter, appr. to Thomas Rutherford a baxter burgess and guilds-brother of Edinburgh, 1732. [ERA]

HAITLIE, HECTOR, son of John Haitlie a chamberlain, appr. to David Kello a cordiner burgess of Edinburgh, 1733. [ERA]

HALDANE, PATRICK, son of John Haldane, appr. to John Murray a surgeon apothecary in Edinburgh, 1731-1733. [ERA]

HALKERSTON, JOHN, son of John Halkerston a gardener in Canongate, appr. to James Yorkstoun a cutler burgess of Edinburgh, 1747. [ERA]

The People of Edinburgh, 1725-1775

HALKET, Colonel PATRICK, a burgess and guilds-brother of Edinburgh, 1747. [EBR]
HALL, CHARLES, son of James Hall a horse hirer, appr. to Arthur Erskine a blacksmith burgess of Edinburgh, 1734. [ERA]
HALL, JOHN, a writer in Edinburgh, a decreet, 1780. [NRS.CS16.1.179]
HALL, ROBERT, son of John Hall a weaver in Canongate, appr. to Patrick Robertson a goldsmith in Edinburgh, 1772-1779. [ERA]
HALL, THOMAS, a watch-maker burgess of Canongate, 1729. [CBR]
HALL, THOMAS, son of William Hall a merchant, appr. to John Houden a cooper burgess of Edinburgh, 1742. [ERA]
HALLIDAY, ADAM, jr., a baker in Leith, 1741. [NRS.AC10.291]
HALLIDAY, JAMES, son of Adam Halliday a baxter in Leith, appr. to Hugh Shiels a barber burgess of Edinburgh, 1744. [ERA]
HALLIDAY, JEAN, wife of George Home a writer in Edinburgh, a decreet, 1774. [NRS.CS16.1.164]
HALLIDAY, PATRICK, a mariner in Leith, test., 1755, C.E. [NRS]
HALLIDAY, WILLIAM, a skipper in Leith, master of the Seaflower of Leith, 1741. [NRS.AC10.291]
HALYBURTON, ANDREW, from Edinburgh, in Boston, New England, 1722. [SCS]
HALIBURTON, GAVIN, son of Andrew Haliburton a Writer to the Signet, appr. to Patrick Crighton saddler burgess of Edinburgh, 1731. [ERA]
HALIBURTON, GILBERT, a merchant in Edinburgh, 1737. [NRS.AC10.248]
HALYBURTON, JOHN, appr. to John Coutts a merchant in Edinburgh, 1724, [ERA]; senior, a merchant in Edinburgh, 1742. [NRS.AC10.297]
HAMILTON, ALEXANDER, son of Captain Alexander Hamilton, appr. to David Maitland a merchant burgess of Edinburgh, 1735. [ERA]
HAMILTON, ALEXANDER, from Edinburgh, in Boston, New England, 1744. [SCS]
HAMILTON, ARCHIBALD, a merchant in Edinburgh, 1740. [NRS.AC7.45.666]
HAMILTON, ARTHUR, a burgess and guilds-brother of Edinburgh, 1747. [EBR]
HAMILTON, DAVID, a street-caddy from Edinburgh, transported to the colonies in 1733. [EBR.BC2]
HAMILTON, DAVID, son of William Hamilton a sailor in Leith, appr. to John Moir a merchant in Edinburgh, 1766-1771. [ERA]
HAMILTON, HUGH, a merchant in Edinburgh, trading with Jamaica, 1772. [NRS.CS16.1.151]
HAMILTON, JAMES, appr. to John Smith goldsmith in Canongate, 1765. [ERA]
HAMILTON, JAMES, a skinner from Leith, transported to the colonies in March 1767. [SM.29.221][NRS.JC27.D35][AJ#1001]
HAMILTON, JAMES, a skipper, The Shore, Leith, 1773; test., 1787, C.E. [WED#36][NRS]

The People of Edinburgh, 1725-1775

HAMILTON, JOHN, son of Professor William Hamilton and his wife Mary, from Edinburgh, to Maryland before 1755. [NLS#6506]

HAMILTON, ROBERT, a merchant in Edinburgh, a decreet, 1761. [NRS.CS16.1.107]

HAMILTON, ROBERT, son of Gavin Hamilton late bailie of Edinburgh, was appointed as master of Perth Academy, 1770. [NRS.B59.24.6.21]

HAMILTON, WILLIAM, an ale-seller burgess of Canongate, 1725. [CBR]

HAMILTON, WILLIAM, born 1717, a cooper from Leith, to Jamaica in November 1736. [CLRO/AIA]

HARDIE, ANDREW, born 1711, a baxter burgess of Edinburgh, died 3 February 1756. [St Cuthbert's MI, Edinburgh]

HARDIE, JAMES, son of George Hardie a baker, appr. to James Methven a painter in Edinburgh, 1772-1778. [ERA]

HARDIE, JOHN, a skipper in North Leith, 1773. [WED#36]

HARRISON, ROBERT, son of George Harrison in Edinburgh, appr. to John Skirving a clock and watch-maker in Edinburgh, 1776-1783. [ERA]

HARROWER, JOHN, a weaver burgess of Canongate, 1733. [CBR]

HART, JOHN, son of John Hart, a wright burgess of Canongate, 1729. [CBR]

HART, JOHN, a wright in Canongate, 1741. [NRS.AC11.134]

HART, JOHN, son of William Hart a cap maker, appr. to Andrew Currie deacon of the weavers of Edinburgh, 1745. [ERA]

HART, SAMUEL, from Edinburgh, in Boston, New England,1743. [SCS]

HAY, ALEXANDER, son of James Hay a Writer to the Signet, appr. to Martin Eccles a surgeon apothecary burgess of Edinburgh, 1755. [ERA]

HAY, ANDREW, son of Gilbert Hay in Edinburgh, appr. to John Hamilton the deacon of the cordiners in Edinburgh, 1747. [ERA]

HAY, HENRIETTA, widow of Thomas Murray a shipmaster in Leith, a decreet, 1763. [NRS.CS16.1.117]

HAY, HENRY, a skipper in Leith, 1753. [NRS.RS18.13.301]

HAY, JAMES, born 1758, a joiner from Leith, to Philadelphia, Pennsylvania, in May 1775. [TNA.T47.12]

HAY, JOHN, a skipper in Leith, 1730. [NRS.AC10.175]

HAY, JOHN, son of Hugh Hay a salt officer, appr. to William Lizars a baxter burgess of Edinburgh, 1730. [ERA]

HAY, LEWIS, a merchant in Edinburgh,trading with Charleston, South Carolina, a decreet, 1764. [NRS.CS16.1.120]

HAY, MICHAEL, son of Thomas Hay a writer, appr. to Alexander Edminson a goldsmith burgess of Edinburgh, 1733. [ERA]

HAY, ROBERT, a cooper from Edinburgh, to Georgia in 1737. [SPC.43.513] [TNA.CO5.670.331]

The People of Edinburgh, 1725-1775

HECTOR, JOHN, son of William Hector a tailor, appr. to Alexander Gardiner a goldsmith in Edinburgh, 1769-1776. [ERA]

HENDERSON, ANDREW, son of George Henderson a tenant in Edinburgh, appr. to Francis Newton a merchant in Edinburgh, 1733. [ERA]

HENDERSON, ANDREW, son of Andrew Henderson a journeyman weaver, appr. to Ebenezer Gardiner a weaver in Edinburgh, 1772-1777. [ERA]

HENDERSON, GEORGE, son of Thomas Henderson a merchant, appr. to William Gray a bookbinder burgess of Edinburgh, 1731. [ERA]

HENDERSON, JAMES, an ale-seller burgess of Canongate, 1726. [CBR]

HENDERSON, JAMES, a chairman from Edinburgh, transported to the colonies in 1733. [EBR.BC.2]

HENDERSON, JAMES, son of Alexander Henderson in Edinburgh, appr. to James Campbell a jeweller burgess of Edinburgh, 1743. [ERA]

HENDERSON, JAMES, son of James Henderson a weaver, appr. to William Thomson a weaver in Edinburgh, 1762-..... [ERA]

HENDERSON, JOHN, a saddler from Edinburgh, settled in Jamaica before 1755, died in Edinburgh, test., 1756, C.E. [NRS.CC8.8.116]

HENDERSON, MICHAEL, son of James Henderson a smith, appr. to Edward Lothian a goldsmith in Edinburgh, 1759-1766. [ERA]

HENDERSON, ROBERT, son of John Henderson in Pleasance, Edinburgh, appr. to George Winter a barber and wig-maker in Edinburgh, 1765-1772. [ERA]

HENDERSON, THOMAS, son of Thomas Henderson a merchant, appr. to James McEwen a merchant burgess of Edinburgh, 1729. [ERA]

HENDERSON, WILLIAM, a carter in Orangefield, Edinburgh, a decreet, 1767. [NRS.CS16.1.130]

HENDRY, ALEXANDER, born 1745, a saddler from Edinburgh, to New York in May 1775. [TNA.T47.12]

HEPBURN, THOMAS, a merchant in Edinburgh, heir to his grand-father Thomas Fenton a merchant bailie there, 1771. [NRS.S/H]

HERON, ROBERT, son of William Henderson a journeyman skinner, appr. to Robert Somervell a skinner burgess of Edinburgh, 1736. [ERA]

HERRIOT, JOHN, a shoemaker in Leith, heir to his brother George Herriot a baker there, 1773. [NRS.S/H]

HIGHT, JOHN, a weaver burgess of Canongate, 1726. [CBR]

HILL, JAMES, from Edinburgh, a Lieutenant of the Royal Navy, 1772. [NRS.S/H]

HILL, JOHN, a goldsmith in Potterrow, Edinburgh, test., 1773, C.E. [NRS]

HODGE, ROBERT, born in Edinburgh during 1746, emigrated to Philadelphia, Pennsylvania, in 1770, a book-seller in New York, died 23 August 1813. [ANY.I.170]

The People of Edinburgh, 1725-1775

HOG, GEORGE, son of George Hog, appr. to George Jolly a barber wigmaker in Edinburgh, 1736. [ERA]

HOG, JOHN, son of Patrick Hog in Edinburgh, appr. to James McEwen a barber wigmaker burgess of Edinburgh, 1725. [ERA]

HOG, JOHN, son of Robert Hog, appr. to James Donaldson a barber burgess of Edinburgh, 1729. [ERA]

HOG, JOHN, son of Major Hog, appr. to John Crawford a wright burgess of Edinburgh, 1730. [ERA]

HOG, ROBERT, son of Robert Hog a stabler in Portsburgh, Edinburgh, appr. to James Burton a tanner burgess of Edinburgh, 1741. [ERA]

HOGG, WILLIAM, jr., a merchant in Edinburgh, 1730. [NRS.AC10.162]

HOG, WILLIAM, a merchant in Edinburgh, 1736; a decreet, 1763. [NRS.AC10.228; CS16.1.115]

HOME, DAVID, son of David Home Depure Clerk of Session, appr. to Henry Robertson an apothecary burgess of Edinburgh, 1727. [ERA]

HOME, JAMES, son of Ninian Home a wright, appr. to Robert Moubray a wright burgess of Edinburgh, 1731. [ERA]

HOME, JAMES, a skipper in Leith, test., 1776, C.E. [NRS]

HOME, JAMES, on the Mosquito Shore of Central America, son of James Home a skipper in Leith, test., 1785, C.E. [NRS]

HOME, ROBERT, son of Ninian Home a wright, appr. to Robert Moubray a wright burgess of Edinburgh, 1728. [ERA]

HOME, ROBERT, son of Alexander Home the Collector of Excise, appr. to William and Andrew Petrie merchants in Edinburgh, 1762-1767. [ERA]

HONEY, DAVID, a shoemaker in Canongate, husband of Helen Wallace, a sasine, 1755. [NRS.RS27.146.159]

HOOD, WALTER, son of Alexander Hood a brewer, appr. to Robert Russell a merchant burgess of Edinburgh, 1739. [ERA]

HORNE, SOPHIA, from Edinburgh, settled in New Jersey before 1747. [East Jersey Deeds, liber E, folio 101]

HORNER, JOHN, son of Francis Horner a merchant, appr. to Patrick Inglis a merchant in Edinburgh, 1776-1781. [ERA]

HOWISON, GEORGE, a skipper in Leith, test., 1776, C.E. [NRS]

HOWISON, JOHN, son of William Howison, appr. to William Mitchell a surgeon apothecary in Edinburgh, 1732. [ERA]

HOWISON, THOMAS, a skipper in Leith, 1736; test., 1750, C.E. [NRS.AC11.92]

HUDDLESTON, HUGH, a merchant from Canongate, settled in Jamaica, test., 1763, C.E. [NRS.CC8.8.119]

HULL, RICHARD, a merchant in Philadelphia, Pennsylvania, a burgess and guilds-brother of Edinburgh, 1744. [EBR]

The People of Edinburgh, 1725-1775

HUME, WILLIAM, son of William Wright, appr. to William Murray a merchant burgess and guilds-brother of Edinburgh, 1754. [ERA]

HUNTER, ANDREW, a merchant in Leith, letter books of Hunter and Smith merchants in Leith, 1774-1777. [NRS.CS96.1986]

HUNTER, DAVID, son of David Hunter, appr. to Thomas Gairdner a merchant burgess of Edinburgh, 1736. [ERA]

HUNTER, HENRY, son of William Hunter a slater in Canongate, appr. to William Kendall a slater in Edinburgh, 1759-1765. [ERA]

HUNTER, JAMES, tobacconist in Leith, process of scandal, 1739. [NRS.CC8.6.286]

HUNTER, JAMES, son of William Hunter a fermorer, appr. to Alexander Davidon a cordiner burgess of Edinburgh, 1740. [ERA]

HUNTER, JAMES, son of John Hunter of Brownhill, appr. to Coutts and Company merchants in Edinburgh, 1763-1771. [ERA]

HUNTER, JAMES, son of James Hunter, a merchant from Edinburgh, settled at Smithyfield, on the James River, Virginia, later in Southampton County, before 1773. [NAS.RD2.256.112; RS27.238.226; TNA.AO13.30.616]

HUNTER, or STEWART, JEAN, a tailor's servant from Edinburgh, transported to Virginia in 1773. [NRS.JC27.10.3]

HUNTER, JOHN, a druggist in Edinburgh, heir to his uncle Robert Gardine a writer there, 1770. [NRS.S/H]

HUNTER, LAUCHLAN, son of Robert Hunter in Edinburgh, appr. to Samuel Graham a bookbinder burgess of Edinburgh, 1729. [ERA]

HUNTER, PATRICK, a carpenter from Leith, to Cape Fear, North Carolina, in October 1752. [NRS.RD4.178.365]

HUNTER, PETER, son of David Hunter a baker in the Abbey (of Holyrood), appr. to Hugh Couden a baker in Edinburgh, 1761-1766. [ERA]

HUNTER, ROBERT, of Barbados, a burgess and guilds-brother of Edinburgh, 1743. [EBR]

HUNTER, WILLIAM, son of Alexander Hunter, appr. to William Hog a merchant burgess of Edinburgh, 1740. [ERA]

HUTCHISON, Colonel ALEXANDER, a burgess of Canongate, 1725. [CBR]

HUTCHISON, GEORGE, son of George Hutchison a journeyman mason, appr. to Turnbull and Aitchison watchmakers in Edinburgh, 1770-1776. [ERA]

HUTCHISON, PETER, a cow-feeder burgess of Canongate, 1728. [CBR]

HUTCHISON, WILLIAM, a burgess of Canongate, 1732. [CBR]

HUTCHISON, WILLIAM, son of Robert Hutchison a wright, appr. to William Newton boxmaster of the weavers of Edinburgh, 1736. [ERA]

HUTTON, ALEXANDER, 'one of the boys of George Watson's Hospital', appr. to William Morrison, 1771-1774. [ERA]

The People of Edinburgh, 1725-1775

HUTTON, JAMES, son of George Hutton, a tailor burgess of Canongate, 1732. [CBR]

HUTTON, JAMES, a tobacconist in Leith, 1738. [NRS.AC7.43.493]

HUTTON, JAMES, a merchant in Leith, accountant and manager of the Leith Ropery Company, 1769. [NRS.AC7.53]

HUTTON, JOHN, a skipper in Leith, 1736; a merchant in Leith, 1746; trading between Leith and South Carolina, 1775. [NRS.AC10.233/316; E504.22]

HUTTON, ROBERT, son of John Hutton a skipper in Leith, appr. to William Cuming a merchant in Edinburgh, 1749. [ERA]

INGLIS, ALEXANDER, son of Alexander Inglis a perfumer, appr. to Robert Wight a merchant burgess of Edinburgh, 1745. [ERA]

INGLIS, ALEXANDER, a goldsmith in St Kitts, son of Robert Inglis, a goldsmith in Edinburgh, and his wife Janet Cleghorn, test., 1752, C.E. [NRS]

INGLIS, CHARLES, son of George Inglis coachman to ..... Rigg of Morton, appr. to William Mitchell a skinner in Edinburgh, 1763-1769. [ERA]

INGLIS, ISOBEL, a pewterer in Edinburgh, 1736. [NRS.AC11.92]

INGLIS, JAMES, jr., a merchant in Edinburgh, trading with Grenada, Boston, Philadelphia, Wilmington, and Charleston, 1763-1780. [NRS.CS96.2004-6, 2249, 2250, 2258; CS238.J5.69]

INGLIS, JOHN, a jeweller in London, son of Robert Inglis, a goldsmith in Edinburgh, and his wife Janet Cleghorn, test., 1752, C.E. [NRS]

INGLIS, THOMAS, son of Hugh Inglis a wig-maker, appr. to Foggo and Galloway merchants in Edinburgh, 1767-1772. [ERA]

INGLIS, WALTER, son of William Inglis a gardener at the Water of Leith, appr. to Baillie Blinshall a saddler in Edinburgh, 1771-1778. [ERA]

INNES, ALEXANDER, son of Hugh Innes a minister, appr. to Adam Lindsay a surgeon apothecary burgess of Edinburgh, 1729. [ERA]

INNES, ALEXANDER, a merchant in Leith, and his wife Jean Ainslie, a sasine, 1760. [NRS.RS27.156.35]

INNES, EDWARD, a baxter burgess of Edinburgh, 1761, son of Edward Innes a baxter burgess. [EBR]

INNES, ROBERT, a skipper in Leith, 1758, dead by 1773, husband of Janet Fraser. [NRS.GD22.18.222/241]

INNES, WILLIAM, a baxter burgess of Edinburgh, 1766, son of Edward Innes a baxter burgess. [EBR]

IRELAND, JAMES, junior, son of James Ireland a writer in Edinburgh, released from Edinburgh Tolbooth for transportation to America in 1764. [NRS.HH11.27]

IRONS, ALEXANDER, son of John Irons a sergeant in Edinburgh Castle, appr. to William Herriot a gunsmith in Edinburgh, 1768-1774. [ERA]

The People of Edinburgh, 1725-1775

IRVING, ROBERT, son of Robert Irving a wright in Canongate, appr. to Benjamin Coutts a goldsmith burgess of Edinburgh, 1755. [ERA]
IZETT, JAMES, a hatmaker burgess of Edinburgh, 1772, son of John Izett a candlemaker burgess. [EBR]
JACK, ADAM, a slater in Stirling, a burgess of Canongate, 1731. [CBR]
JACK, DAVID, schoolmaster at Dunbar, a burgess of Canongate, 1731. [CBR]
JACKSON, JAMES, a merchant burgess and guilds-brother of Edinburgh, 1772, appr. to Archibald Gilchrist a merchant burgess and guilds-brother. [EBR]
JACKSON, WILLIAM, a baker in Musselburgh, a burgess and guilds-brother of Edinburgh, 1772, former appr. to Henry Hardie a baker burgess and guilds-brother. [EBR]
JACKSON, WILLIAM, a writer in Edinburgh, a decreet, 1772. [NRS.CS16.1.151]
JAFFRAY, JOHN, a merchant burgess and guilds-brother of Edinburgh, 1771, former appr. to Thomas Smith a merchant burgess and guilds-brother. [EBR]
JAMIESON, ALEXANDER, a shoemaker burgess of Edinburgh, 1777, husband of Helen dau. of George Brown a flesher burgess. [EBR]
JAMIESON, GAVIN, a sailor in Leith, process of scandal, 1738. [NRS.CC8.6.278]
JAMIESON, JAMES, a carpenter in Leith, 1737. [NRS.AC10.247]
JAMIESON, JOHN, cashier to the South Leith Ropery, 1744. [NRS.AC11.163]
JAMIESON, JOHN, a sailor in Leith, husband of Mary Seaman, 1743, [SL.49]; test., 1751, C.E. [NRS]
JAMIESON, JOHN, a merchant in Leith, a burgess and guilds-brother of Edinburgh, 1764, former appr. to Alexander Brown a merchant burgess and guilds-brother. [EBR]
JAMIESON, RICHARD, son of James Jamieson a journeyman baxter in Edinburgh, appr. to John Drysdale a shoemaker in Edinburgh, 1749. [ERA]
JAMIESON, ROBERT, son of James Jamieson a shipbuilder in Leith, appr. to William Tod jr. a merchant in Edinburgh, 1750. [ERA]; a burgess and guilds-brother of Edinburgh, 1764. [EBR]
JAMIESON, WILLIAM, son of Thomas Jamieson a skinner burgess, appr. to Richard Murray a merchant burgess of Edinburgh, 1743. [ERA]
JAMIESON, WILLIAM, a merchant from Edinburgh, settled in Virginia before 1778; in Charleston, a decreet, 1783. [NRS. CS16.1.173/178; CS17.1.2]
JEFFREY, ALEXANDER, a merchant from Edinburgh, died 1768, probate 1769, Accomack County, Virginia.
JEFFREY, JAMES, son of William Jeffrey a tailor, appr. to James Norrie a painter burgess of Edinburgh, 1738. [ERA]
JEFFREY, WILLIAM, son of William Jeffrey a staymaker in Potterrow, Edinburgh, appr. to William Ayton a goldsmith in Edinburgh, 1751. [ERA]

The People of Edinburgh, 1725-1775

JERMENT, RICHARD, a shipmaster in Leith, husband of Isobel Wardrop, a sasine, 1756. [NRS.RS27.148.84]

JONES, THOMAS, a burgess and guilds-brother of Edinburgh, 1766. [EBR]

JOHNSTON, CHARLES, son of William Johnston a druggist, appr. to George Young a surgeon burgess of Edinburgh, 1734. [ERA]

JOHNSTON, HUGH, son of William Johnston a mason, appr. to Charles Mack a mason in Edinburgh, 1766-1772. [ERA]; a burgess of Edinburgh, 1772. [EBR]

JOHNSTON, JOHN, a merchant burgess of Edinburgh, 1766, husband of Margaret dau. of James Paterson a tailor burgess. [EBR]

JOHNSTON, LEWIS, a merchant from Edinburgh, son of James Johnston, emigrated before 1756 to St Kitts and later Georgia, died there, probate 1798 PCC. [NRS.S/H.1756]

JOHNSTON, ROBERT, an ale-seller in Pleasance, a burgess of Canongate, 1725. [CBR]

JOHNSTON, ROBERT, a farmer in Duddingston, a burgess and guilds-brother of Edinburgh, 1763, husband of Christian dau. of Robert Duncan a burgess and guilds-brother. [EBR]

JOHNSTON, ROBERT, son of John Johnston a schoolmaster, appr. to Alexander Smyth a barber burgess of Edinburgh, 1732. [ERA]; a barber burgess of Edinburgh, 1775, husband of Elizabeth dau. of William Watson a smith and farrier in Musselburgh, a burgess. [EBR]

JOHNSTON, WILLIAM, son of William Johnston a journeyman flesher, appr. to John Malice a flesher burgess and freeman of Edinburgh, 1733. [ERA]

JOHNSTON, WILLIAM, a barber and wigmaker burgess of Edinburgh, 1772, husband of Ann dau. of William Thomson a merchant burgess. [EBR]

JOLLY, ANDREW, a tailor burgess and guilds-brother of Edinburgh, 1764, son of James Jolly a tailor burgess and guilds-brother. [EBR]

JOLLY, GEORGE, a tailor burgess and guilds-brother of Edinburgh, 1778, son of Walter Jolly a tailor burgess and guilds-brother. [EBR]

JOLLIE, JOHN, a merchant in Edinburgh, 1742/1743. [NRS.AC10.305; AC11.226]

JOLLIE, MARTIN, son of James Jollie, a tailor burgess of Edinburgh, and his wife Mary McNaught, a land agent in East Florida, and a Member of HM Council in East Florida, 1767-1776; died in Antigua Street, Edinburgh, on 16 December 1806. ['East Florida as a British Province 1763-1784, f.43, Gainesville, 1964] [TNA.CO5.55.141][PC.Col.V.564][APC.Col.1766-1783, #564][SM.69.78]

JOLLY, WALTER, son of Walter Jolly a tailor, appr. to Lamb and Seyth upholsterers in Edinburgh, 1773-1778. [ERA]

JONES, Dr HUGH, a physician from Edinburgh, in Jamaica, husband of Janet Mein, a decreet, 1782. [NRS.CS17.1.1]

The People of Edinburgh, 1725-1775

KAY, CHARLES, son of Reverend Dr George Kay a minister in Edinburgh, appr. to Robert Walker a surgeon apothecary in Edinburgh, 1765-1770. [ERA]

KAY, JAMES, son of John Kay in Edinburgh, appr. to John Gibson a clock and watch-maker in Edinburgh, 1771-1778. [ERA]

KAY, ROBERT, a skipper in South Leith, test., 1726, C.E. [NRS]

KEDDIE, ALEXANDER, a candlemaker burgess of Edinburgh, 1766, former appr. to Alexander Noble a candlemaker burgess. [EBR]

KEDDIE, THOMAS, a candlemaker burgess of Edinburgh, 1761, former appr. to William Gardner a candlemaker burgess. [EBR]

KEDDIE, THOMAS, son of Thomas Keddie a baker in Portsburgh, Edinburgh, appr. to Patrick Bowie a weaver in Edinburgh, 1763-1771. [ERA]

KEDDIE, THOMAS, a tanner burgess of Edinburgh, 1765, former appr. to John Esplin a tanner burgess. [EBR]

KEIR, WILLIAM, appr. to John Coutts a merchant in Edinburgh, 1743. [NRS.AC11.158]

KELLIE, ALEXANDER, a skipper in Edinburgh, heir to his brother James Kellie in Dunbar, 1778. [NRS.S/H]

KELLO, JOHN, son of John Kello in Edinburgh, appr. to Simon Frazer a white ironsmith in Edinburgh, 1761-1767. [ERA]; a burgess of Edinburgh, 1770. [EBR]

KELLOCH, MARGARET, widow of Alexander Gibson a skipper in Leith, 1728. [SL#25]

KELTIE, JOHN, a wigmaker burgess of Edinburgh, 1772, son of Robert Keltie a gardener burgess. [EBR]

KELTIE, ROBERT, a gardener burgess of Edinburgh, 1772, husband of Rachael dau. of Robert Tod a wright burgess. [EBR]

KEMP, GAVIN, a merchant in Leith, 1784. [NRS.AC7.61]

KENDALL, WILLIAM, son of John Kendall a skipper, appr. to John Watson a sklaiter burgess of Edinburgh, 1731. [ERA]

KENNEDY, ALEXANDER, son of James Kennedy a cooper in Portsburgh, Edinburgh, appr. to Andrew Syme a cooper burgess of Edinburgh, 1752. [ERA]

KENNEDY, DAVID, a wright burgess and guilds-brother of Edinburgh, 1768, husband of Elizabeth dau. of William Armstrong a coppersmith burgess and guilds-brother. [EBR]

KENNEDY, ROBERT, a burgess and guilds-brother of Edinburgh, 1767, son of George Kennedy of Romanno a burgess and guilds-brother, and husband of Elizabeth dau. of David son of William Alves, a Writer to the Signet and a burgess and guilds-brother. [EBR]

KENNEDY, THOMAS, a skinner burgess of Edinburgh, 1768, husband of Nelly dau. of David Donaldson a skinner burgess. [EBR]

The People of Edinburgh, 1725-1775

KENNIBROUGH, ROBERT, a glazier burgess of Edinburgh, 1771, former appr. to Robert Dewar a glazier burgess. [EBR]

KERR, ANDREW, son of John Kerr in Edinburgh, appr. to Samuel Graham a bookbinder burgess of Edinburgh, 1736. [ERA]

KERR, DANIEL, a goldsmith burgess of Edinburgh, 1764. [EBR]

KERR, GEORGE, son of John Kerr a tailor, appr. to John Fraser a white ironsmith in Edinburgh, 1765-1771. [ERA]

KERR, JAMES, a wright burgess of Edinburgh, 1763, son of James Kerr a tailor. [EBR]

KERR, ROBERT, son of Robert Kerr a painter, appr. to John Spence a painter in Edinburgh, 1771-1777. [ERA]

KERR, ROBERT, a merchant in Leith, a burgess and guilds-brother of Edinburgh, 1775, husband of Jean dau. of Patrick Murray a goldsmith. [EBR]

KERR, THOMAS, son of John Kerr a tailor in Canongatehead, appr. to James Thomson a barber in Edinburgh, 1765-1770. [ERA]; a wigmaker burgess of Edinburgh, 1764 (sic). [EBR]

KERR, THOMAS, a tailor burgess of Edinburgh, 1768. [EBR]

KERR, WILLIAM, son of William Kerr a candlemaker in Canongate, appr. to Laurence Oliphant a goldsmith burgess of Edinburgh, 1750. [ERA]; a burgess of Edinburgh, 1761. [EBR]

KERR, WILLIAM, a merchant in Leith, a burgess and guilds-brother of Edinburgh, 1775, son of Robert Kerr a merchant in Leith, a burgess and guilds-brother. [EBR]

KETTLE, DAVID, son of John Kettle a merchant, appr. to John Edmondstone a goldsmith in Edinburgh, 1762-1769. [ERA]

KETTLE, WILLIAM, son of John Kettle a merchant in Leith, appr. to James Duff a clock and watch-maker in Edinburgh, 1759-1765. [ERA]

KEY, THOMAS, a goldsmith burgess of Edinburgh, test., 1753, C.E. [NRS]

KID, JOHN, a wine merchant in Edinburgh, heir to his brother James Kid, son of James Kid a minister in Queensferry, 1777. [NRS.S/H]

KINCAID, ALEXANDER, HM printer and stationer, a burgess and guilds-brother of Edinburgh, 1776, son of Alexander Kincaid HM printer and stationer, a burgess and guilds-brother. [EBR]

KINCAID, JOHN, son of John Kincaid of Kincaid, appr. to Alexander Kincaid a goldsmith burgess of Edinburgh, 1728, [ERA]; a goldsmith burgess of Edinburgh, test., 1729, C.E. [NRS]

KINCAID, JOHN, of Virginia, a burgess and guilds-brother of Edinburgh, 1743. [EBR]

KING, GEORGE, a weaver burgess of Edinburgh, 1761, husband of Elizabeth dau. of William Gillespie a merchant burgess. [EBR]

The People of Edinburgh, 1725-1775

KING, PATRICK, born 1750, a wright from Edinburgh, to New York in April 1775. [TNA.T47.12]

KINLOCH, JOHN, a white-iron smith burgess of Edinburgh, 1765, son of John Kinnear a candlemaker burgess. [EBR]

KINNEAR, GEORGE, a merchant burgess and guilds-brother of Edinburgh, 1779, son of Thomas Kinnear a merchant. [EBR]

KINNIBURGH, WILLIAM, a candlemaker burgess of Edinburgh, 1769, former appr. to James McCoull a candlemaker burgess. [EBR]

KINROSS, CHARLES, son of Charles Kinross a Customs officer, appr. to George Winter a barber and wigmaker in Edinburgh, 1763-1770. [ERA]

KIRK, DAVID, a brewer at Coalhill, North Leith, a burgess of Canongate, 1733. [CBR]

KIRKLAND, BARBARA, widow of Daniel Bryden a wright in Edinburgh, heir to George Bryden, son of Charles Bryden of Whelphill, 1773. [NRS.S/H]

KIRKPATRICK, GILBERT, son of Gilbert Kirkpatrick a waggoner, appr. to Norman McPherson a watchmaker, 1767-1774. [ERA]

KIRKWOOD, ANDREW, son of Alexander Kirkwood a schoolmaster, appr. to James Smith a cordiner burgess of Edinburgh, 1730. [ERA]

KIRKWOOD, ROBERT, a skipper in Leith, test., 1751, C.E. [NRS]

KITCHEN, ANDREW, son of Andrew Kitchen in Leith, appr. to John Malcolm a barber in Edinburgh, 1768-1773. [ERA]

KNIGHT, ALEXANDER, a sailor in Leith, 'at the Greenland fishery' 1773. [ECL.46]

KNOX, JAMES, son of Hugh Knox, from Causewayside, Edinburgh, transported to the colonies in 1751. [NRS.B59.26.11.15.11]

KNOX, JOHN, son of David Knox in Edinburgh, settled in New York before 1750. [NRS.S/H.1750]

KNOX, Dr ROBERT, a burgess and guilds-brother of Edinburgh, 1764, son of .... Knox a surgeon burgess and guilds-brother. [EBR]

LACHLAN, JOSEPH, a merchant burgess and guilds-brother of Edinburgh, 1763. [EBR]

LACKY, JAMES, born 1731, a weaver from Edinburgh, transported to the Leeward Islands in 1747, landed on Martinique. [P.2.328][TNA.SP36.102]

LAIDLAW, ALEXANDER, a mealmaker in Leith, a bond, 1772. [NRS.CS967.110.7]

LAIDLAW, ALEXANDER, a white-iron smith burgess of Edinburgh, 1777, former appr. to Andrew Cockburn a whire-iron smith burgess. [EBR]

LAIDLAY, ROBERT, a candlemaker burgess of Edinburgh, 1775, former appr. to James Watson a candlemaker burgess. [EBR]

LAING, GEORGE, a barber and wigmaker burgess of Edinburgh, 1773, former appr. to James Smeton a barber burgess. [EBR]

The People of Edinburgh, 1725-1775

LAING, ROBERT, a saddler burgess of Edinburgh, 1778, former appr. of William Anderson a saddler burgess. [EBR]

LAING, THOMAS, an edge toolmaker burgess of Edinburgh, 1768. [EBR]

LAING, WILLIAM, a merchant burgess and guilds-brother of Edinburgh, 1777, husband of Sarah dau. of David Mathieson a wright burgess and guilds-brother. [EBR]

LAMB, ANDREW, a candlemaker burgess of Edinburgh, 1762, son of John Lamb a wright burgess. [EBR]

LAMB, GAVIN, son of Andrew Lamb a tailor, appr. to Alexander Learmont a tanner burgess of Edinburgh, 1735. [ERA]

LAMB, GEORGE, son of George Lamb a wright in Potterrow, Edinburgh, appr. to Robert Boig a cutler in Edinburgh, 1748. [ERA]

LAMB, GEORGE, a merchant burgess of Edinburgh, 1762. [EBR]

LAMB, JAMES, born 1722, a watch-maker from Edinburgh, transported to the Leeward Islands in 1747, landed on Martinique. [P.2.330][TNA.SP36.102]

LAMB, JOHN, in North Leith, a burgess of Canongate, 1733. [CBR]

LAMB, PATRICK, son of George Lamb a wright in Potterrow, Edinburgh, appr. to William Eizat a wright burgess of Edinburgh, 1745. [ERA]

LAMB, WILLIAM, a merchant burgess and guilds-brother of Edinburgh, 1768, former appr. of James Caddell a merchant burgess and guilds-brother. [EBR]

LAMONT, JANET, born 1757, from Edinburgh, to New York in April 1775. [TNA.T47.12]

LAMONT, JOHN, a merchant burgess and guilds-brother of Edinburgh, 1734, by right of his wife Euphan, dau. of Robert Yilton a merchant burgess and guildsbrother. [EBR]

LAMPO, SAMUEL, from Yorkshire, a skipper in Leith, master of the Prince Charles of Lorain, guilty of scuttling his vessel off Cumberland in May 1751, transported to America. [NRS.E173.J2.3/1; AC3.82]

LANDELS, JOHN, a skipper in North Leith, 1773. [WED.45]

LANDELLS, RICHARD, son of William Landells a farmer, appr. to William Ranken a wright burgess of Edinburgh, 1727. [ERA]

LANDER, JOHN, born 1755, a husbandman from Edinburgh, to Philadelphia, Pennsylvania, in October 1774. [TNA.T47.9/11]

LANG, ALEXANDER, an ale-seller burgess of Canongate, 1726. [CBR]

LANGLANDS, ALEXANDER, a waulker burgess of Edinburgh, 1768, husband of Isobell dau. of Andrew Forrest a waulker burgess. [EBR]

LANGLANDS, JOHN, a sailor, son and heir of George Langlands, a surgeon in Edinburgh, and his wife Anne Marshall, 1764. [NRS.S/H]

LANGLY, BENJAMIN, a burgess and guilds-brother of Edinburgh, 1762. [EBR]

The People of Edinburgh, 1725-1775

LAUCHLAN, JOHN, son of Robert Lauchlan, a wright burgess of Canongate, 1729. [CBR]

LAUDER, ALEXANDER, a merchant burgess and guilds-brother of Edinburgh, 1767. [EBR]

LAUDER, ANDREW, a candlemaker burgess of Edinburgh, 1773, former appr. to James McCoull a candlemaker burgess. [EBR]

LAUDER, COLIN, a surgeon burgess and guilds-brother of Edinburgh, 1772, son of George Law a surgeon burgess and guilds-brother. [EBR]

LAUDER, FRANCIS, son of John Lauder a coppersmith, appr. to Walter Hog a merchant burgess of Edinburgh, 1729. [ERA]

LAUDER, JAMES, second son of Alexander Lauder a writer, appr. to John Cleland a merchant in Edinburgh, 1743. [ERA]

LAUNIE, WILLIAM, an upholsterer burgess of Edinburgh, 1777, son of William Launie an apholsterer burgess and guilds-brother. [EBR]

LAURIE, ANDREW, son of Andrew Laurie precentor in the New Church, appr. to Robert Bull a merchant in Edinburgh, 1739. [ERA]

LAURIE, GILBERT, a chemist and druggist in Edinburgh, a decreet, 1756. [NRS.CS16.1.98]

LAWRIE, JAMES, born 1714, a tanner in Portsburgh, Edinburgh, died 17 February 1762. [St Cuthbert's MI, Edinburgh]

LAURIE, JOHN, son of John Laurie a flesher in Leith, appr. to Thomas Robertson deacon of the fleshers in Edinburgh, 1735. [ERA]

LAURIE, JOHN, son of Andrew Laurie precentor in the New Church, appr. to David Brown a freeman weaver in Edinburgh, 1737. [ERA]

LAWRIE, JOSEPH, born 1712, a tanner in Portsburgh and a burgess of Edinburgh, died 4 March 1746. His wife Margaret McLellan, born 1726, died 4 March 174, parents of Thomas. [St Cuthbert's MI, Edinburgh]

LAWRIE, ROBERT, son of Robert Lawrie, a gentleman from Edinburgh, settled in St George, St Vincent, died 1770, test., 1782, C.E. [NRS.CC8.8.125]

LAURIE, THOMAS, a mason burgess of Edinburgh, 1779. [EBR]

LAURIE, WILLIAM, son of William Smith in Portsburgh, appr. to Thomas Blair a cutler burgess of Edinburgh, 1737. [ERA]

LAW, GEORGE, son of George Law in Edinburgh, appr. to John Morison a barber wigmaker burgess of Edinburgh, 1728. [ERA]

LAW, THOMAS, a burgess and guilds-brother of Edinburgh, 1765, son of David Law a merchant burgess and guilds-brother. [EBR]

LAWSON, JAMES, a porter burgess of Edinburgh, 1776, husband of Elizabeth dau. of Robert Dickson a weaver burgess. [EBR]

LAWSON, THOMAS, a skipper in Leith, husband of Sarah Innes, 1760. [NRS.S/H]

The People of Edinburgh, 1725-1775

LEARMONT, ALEXANDER, son of John Learmont a schoolmaster, appr. to Thomas Herron a wright burgess of Edinburgh, 1727. [ERA]

LEARMONTH, CHRISTIAN, a milliner in Edinburgh, aunt of John Learmonth in Pennsylvania, a decreet, 1766. [NRS.CS16.1.125]

LEARMONTH, JOHN, son of Alexander Learmonth in Edinburgh, a pilot in Philadelphia, Pennsylvania, before 1781. [New York Gazette and Weekly Mercury, 8 January 1781]

LEE, ARTHUR, a burgess and guilds-brother of Edinburgh, 1761. [EBR]

LEE, CHARLES, son of Umphray Lee an Excise officer, appr. to Samuel Graham a bookbinder burgess of Edinburgh, 1739. [ERA]

LEES, JOHN, a mason in Canongate, released from Edinburgh Tolbooth for transportation to America in 1773. [NRS.HH.11.28]

LEGERTWOOD, WILLIAM, a mariner in Leith, test., 1753, C.E. [NRS]

LEGGAT, FRANCIS, a bookbinder burgess of Edinburgh, 1768, son of William Leggat a surgeon burgess. [EBR]

LEGGAT, JAMES, a vintner burgess of Edinburgh, 1777, son of James Leggat a burgess. [EBR]

LEIGHTON, S., born 1747, a clerk from Edinburgh, to Georgia in July 1775. [TNA.T47.9/11]

LEITCH, PATRICK, son of Patrick Leitch a wright in Pleasance, Edinburgh, appr. to Robert Robertson a wright burgess of Edinburgh, 1747. [ERA]

LENNOX, JAMES, son of Collin Lennox a vintner in Leith, appr. to Edward Caithness a merchant burgess and guildsbrother of Edinburgh, 1745. [ERA]

LESLIE, GEORGE, a merchant burgess and guilds-brother of Edinburgh, 1771, former appr. of George Chalmers a burgess and guilds-brother. [EBR]

LESLIE, WALTER, appr. to John Dale a barber burgess of Edinburgh, 1747. [ERA]

LESLIE, WILLIAM, an ale-seller burgess of Canongate, 1725. [CBR]

LESTER, FRANCIS, born 1756, a hair-dresser from Edinburgh, to Maryland in September 1774. [TNA.T47.9/11]

LETHEM, ARCHIBALD, clerk to Daniel Seton, a merchant burgess of Edinburgh, 1775, son of Robert Letham an upholsterer burgess. [EBR]

LETHAM, ROBERT, a smith burgess of Edinburgh, 1767, former appr. to Thomas Letham deacon and a smith burgess. [EBR]

LETHAM, WALTER, son of Archibald Letham a smith at the Water of Leith, appr. to Edward Letham a tailor burgess of Edinburgh, 1732. [ERA]

LEWIS, JOHN, from Edinburgh, in Boston, New England, 1762, [SCS]

LEYS, WILLIAM, a chairmaster burgess of Edinburgh, 1770. [EBR]

LIDDELL, ANN, wife of Gilbert Mason a merchant in Edinburgh, heir to her uncle Thomas Rendall of Breck, Orkney, who died in January 1755, 1771. [NRS.S/H]

The People of Edinburgh, 1725-1775

LIDDELL, WILLIAM, a weaver in Leith, heir to David Thomson, son of David Thomson a distiller there, 1774. [NRS.S/H]

LIGHTBODY, AGNES, dau. of James Lightbody a wigmaker in Edinburgh, a decreet, 1782. [NRS.CS17.1.1]

LIGHTON, JOHN, a merchant burgess and guilds-brother of Edinburgh, 1778, former appr. of Robert Scott a merchant burgess and guilds-brother. [EBR]

LILLIE, JOHN, son of George Lillie an upholsterer, appr. to James Heriot a cordiner burgess of Edinburgh, 1730. [ERA]

LIND, GEORGE, a merchant burgess and guilds-brother of Edinburgh, 1770, former appr. to Young and Trotter upholsterers in Edinburgh. [EBR]

LIND, Dr JAMES, of Gorgie, a burgess and guilds-brother of Edinburgh, 1771. [EBR]

LIND, JAMES, a cordiner in Leith, son of David Lind a cordiner in Leith, married Isobel Sangster on 4 October 1735, a process of aliment, 1736. [NRS.CC8.6.272]

LIND, JAMES, in Edinburgh, appr. to Simon Fraser a white iron smith burgess of Edinburgh, 1747. [ERA]

LINDSAY, ALEXANDER, eldest son of George Lindsay minister at North Leith, appr. to Alexander Kincaid a bookseller in Edinburgh, 1743. [ERA]

LINDSAY, DAVID, son of Robert Lindsay a spinet maker in Canongate, appr. to Nicol Somervail a painter burgess of Edinburgh, 1745. [ERA]

LINDSAY, DAVID, a skinner burgess of Edinburgh, 1763, former appr. to John Lindsay a skinner burgess. [EBR]

LINDSAY, ELIZA, dau. of William Lindsay, from Edinburgh, settled in Charleston, South Carolina, before 1771. [NRS.RD4.213.1490]

LINDSAY, GEORGE, from North Leith, in Boston, New England, 1762. [SCS]

LINDSAY, JOHN, son of David Lindsay, appr. to James Blair a skinner in Edinburgh, 1747. [ERA]

LINDSAY, MARTIN, a writer in Edinburgh, heir to his cousin Margaret Martin or Melville at Cults, 1777. [NRS.S/H]

LINDSAY, THEODORE, son of James Lindsay a writer, appr. to John Orr a wigmaker burgess of Edinburgh, 1750. [ERA]

LINDSAY, WILLIAM, a plumber burgess of Canongate, 1725. [CBR]

LINDSAY, Captain ...., born in Edinburgh, settled in New York city 1758. [New York Gazette and Weekly Mercury, 18 March 1782]

LITCH, DUNCAN, an ale-seller burgess of Canongate, 1725. [CBR]

LITHGOW, ROBERT, a merchant in Edinburgh, 1739. [NRS.AC11.120]

LITHGOW, ROBERT, born in Leith 1758, settled in Glynn County, Georgia, 1775, died on Colonel's Island, Georgia, 11 October 1802. [E.A. #4077/03; Colonial Museum and Savannah Advertiser, 22.10.1802]

The People of Edinburgh, 1725-1775

LITTLE, JOHN, a wright burgess of Edinburgh, 1772, former appr. to James Brounhill a wright burgess. [EBR]

LITTLEJOHN, ALEXANDER, son of David Littlejohn a skipper in Leith, appr. to James Scott a merchant in Edinburgh, 1754. [ERA]

LITTLEJOHN, DAVID, from Edinburgh, in Boston, New England, 1748. [SCS]

LIVINGSTON, CHARLES, a writer in Edinburgh, heir to his uncle Hugh Inglis, son of Thomas Inglis a writer there, 1774. [NRS.S/H]

LIVINGSTON, JOHN, a printer burgess and guilds-brother of Edinburgh, 1767, son of Alexander Livingston a baxter burgess and guilds-brother. [EBR]

LIVINGSTON, JOHN, son of George Livingston a vintner, appr. to John Murdoch, a clock and watch-maker in Edinburgh, 1769-1776. [ERA]

LIVINGSTON, JOHN, son of William Livingston a carter, appr. to John Brown, a pewterer in Edinburgh, 1770-1776. [ERA]; a burgess of Edinburgh, 1778. [EBR]

LIZARS, ELIZABETH, dau. of William Lizars a baker in Edinburgh, heir to her sister Margaret Lizars, 1770; and to her sister Marion Lizars, 1770. [NRS.S/H]

LIZARS, JANE, dau. of William Lizars a baker in Edinburgh, heir to her sister Margaret Lizars, 1770; and to her sister Marion Lizars, 1770. [NRS.S/H]

LOCH, DAVID, a merchant in Leith, trading with Charleston, South Carolina, Madeira, and the West Indies, 1755-1767. [NRS.E504.22; AC7.51/52]

LOCH, WILLIAM, son of William Loch, from Edinburgh, settled in Savanna-la-Mar, Jamaica, before 1766. [NRS.RD4.227.1187]

LOCKHART, ALEXANDER, son of Samuel Lockhart a minister, appr. to George Cowan a wright burgess of Edinburgh, 1729. [ERA]

LOCKHART, ALEXANDER, an advocate burgess and guilds-brother of Edinburgh, 1761. [EBR]

LOCKHART, JANET, born 1759, a servant from Edinburgh, to Philadelphia, Pennsylvania, in May 1775. [TNA.T47.12]

LOCKHART, THOMAS, a Commissioner of Excise, a burgess and guilds-brother of Edinburgh, 1765. [EBR]

LOCKHART, WILLIAM, a shoemaker burgess of Edinburgh, 1775. [EBR]

LOGAN, ROBERT, a burgess of Canongate, 1725. [CBR]

LOGAN, ROBERT, son of Patrick Logan an Excise officer, appr. to Patrick Graham a goldsmith burgess of Edinburgh, 1730. [ERA]

LOTHIAN, ANDREW, from Edinburgh, in Jamaica, a decreet, 1778. [NRS.CS16.1.173]

LOTHIAN, JOHN, from Edinburgh, a surgeon in the Royal Navy, 1738. [NRS.S/H]

LOTHIAN, JOHN, son of John Low a writer, appr. to James Troop a weaver burgess of Edinburgh, 1740. [ERA]

LOTHIAN, WALTER, a merchant burgess and guilds-brother of Edinburgh, 1779, son of James Lothian a skinner burgess and guilds-brother. [EBR]

The People of Edinburgh, 1725-1775

LOTHIAN, WILLIAM, born 5 November 1740, son of George Lothian a surgeon in Edinburgh, minister at Canongate from 1764 until his death on 17 December 1783, husband of Elizabeth, dau. of Edward Lothian a jeweller in Edinburgh, parents of Edward, William, George, Helen, John, and Thomas. [F.I.25]

LOUDEN, ELIZABETH, spouse of John Boag a mariner in Leith, test., 1748, C.E. [NRS]

LOW, JAMES, son of George Low a staymaker in Canongate, appr. to Robert Clydesdale a watch and clock-maker in Edinburgh, 1755. [ERA]

LOW, JOHN, son of Robert Low a writer, appr. to Robert Low a goldsmith in Edinburgh, 1742. [ERA]

LUGTON, SIMON, a tailor from Edinburgh, transported to the colonies in November 1748. [P.2.354]

LUNDIE, ARCHIBALD, born 1750, a merchant from Edinburgh, to New York in July 1775, settled in Savannah, Georgia, moved to St Augustine, East Florida, in 1776, later a Loyalist refugee in the West Indies. [TNA.T47.9/11; AO13.33.45] [NRS.NRAS.0159.C4; CS16.1.185]

LUNDIE, HENRY, a burgess and guilds-brother of Edinburgh, 1765. [EBR]

LYLE, DAVID, born 1746, a laborer from Edinburgh, to New York in April 1775. [TNA.T47.9/11]

LYON, JOHN, a vintner in Leith, 1737. [NRS.AC10.247]

LYON, JOHN, son of David Lyon a wright, appr. to John Kelly, a white ironsmith, 1775-1782. [ERA]

LYON, WILLIAM, son of John Lyon a vintner in Leith, appr. to Alexander Cairns a wright burgess of Edinburgh, 1728, [ERA]; a wright in Leith, 1738. [NRS.AC11.110]

LYON, WILLIAM, a merchant burgess of Edinburgh, 1775. [EBR]

MCALESTER, JOHN, born 1745, a copper-smith from Edinburgh, to New York or Georgia in May 1775. [TNA.T47.12]

MCALISTER, MATHEW, a merchant in Edinburgh, deeds, 1752. [NRS.RD2,171/2.154/158]

MCALISTER, WALTER, son of John Smith a porter, appr. to Duncan McQueen, a white ironsmith in Edinburgh, 1771-1778. [ERA]

MCALPINE, JOHN, son of Duncan McAlpine in Edinburgh, an appr. to William Weir, a shoemaker in Edinburgh, 1759-1765. [ERA]

MCARBER, JAMES, son of John McArber a farmer, appr. to Patrick Thomson a weaver burgess of Edinburgh, 1733. [ERA]

MCARTHUR, JOHN, a writer in Edinburgh, deeds, 1752. [NRS.RD4.178/2.206,284]; a burgess and guilds-brother of Edinburgh, 1765. [EBR]

The People of Edinburgh, 1725-1775

MCAULAY, ARCHIBALD, Lord Provost of Edinburgh, deeds, 1750. [NRS.RD4.178/1.57, 67]

MCBAIN, LAUCHLAN, a merchant burgess and guilds-brother of Edinburgh, 1766, husband of John Clearichew a vintner burgess and guilds-brother.[EBR]

MCBEATH, JAMES, son of James McBeath a vintner, appr. to James McEwing a barber burgess of Edinburgh, 1731. [ERA]

MCBETH, JAMES, born 1716, from Edinburgh, to Antigua in October 1731. [CLRO/AIA]

MCCALL, WILLIAM, son of Robert McCall a day-laborer, appr. to William McLean, a barber in Edinburgh, 1765-1771. [ERA]

MCCALLUM, ANDREW, son of John McCallum a minister, appr. to William Tod a merchant burgess of Edinburgh, 1730. [ERA]

MCCALLUM, ARCHIBALD, son of John McCallum a minister, appr. to James Herriott a wright burgess of Edinburgh, 1736. [ERA]

MCCANDLISH, ALEXANDER, a surgeon in Leith, heir to his great-grandfather Adam Coutart a merchant burgess of Ayr, 1772. [NRS.S/H]

MCCLEESH, JAMES, a bookseller burgess of Edinburgh, 1778. [EBR]

MACCLELLAN, ROBERT, a merchant in Leith, a decreet, 1754. [NRS.AC7.46.130]

MCCLELLAN, WILLIAM, a merchant from Edinburgh, to Virginia 1759, later in Tarborough, North Carolina, from 1766 until 1777, a Loyalist who moved to London. [TNA.AO12.35.118]

MCCONACHIE, ALEXANDER, a merchant in Leith, 1737. [NRS.AC10.262]

MCCOUL, JAMES, appr. to William Gardiner a candlemaker burgess of Edinburgh, 1747. [ERA]; a burgess and guilds-brother of Edinburgh, 1761.[EBR]

MCCOULL, JOHN, a candlemaker burgess and guilds-brother of Edinburgh, 1778, son of James McCoull a candlemaker burgess and guilds-brother. [EBR]

MCCRUMMON, PETER, son of Donald McCrummon a servant to Norman McLeod, appr. to Robert Morrison, a barber and wig-maker in Edinburgh, 1763-1769. [ERA]

MCCULLOCH, EBENEZER, a merchant in Edinburgh, master of the Leith Linen Manufactury, 1743; trading with Virginia and Carolina, a decreet, 1771. [NRS.AC10.300; CS16.1.143]

MCCULLOCH, GEORGE, a skipper in Lees Quarter, Leith, 1773. [WED.51]

MCCULLOCH, JAMES, son of David McCulloch, appr. to Robert Brown a tailor burgess of Edinburgh, 1738. [ERA]

MCDERMOD, PETER, born 14 January 1768 in Edinburgh, son of Hugh McDermod, a drummer in New York, and his wife Grizel Colvill in New Greyfriars parish, Edinburgh. [Edinburgh Old Parish Register]

MCDIARMID, DONALD, a merchant burgess of Edinburgh, 1762. [EBR]

The People of Edinburgh, 1725-1775

MCDIARMID, JOHN, son of Patrick McDiarmid, from Edinburgh, transported to the colonies in August 1764. [NRS.HCR.I.96]

MCDERMITT, MALCOLM, a poultryman burgess of Edinburgh, 1774. [EBR]

MCDONALD, ARCHIBALD, a merchant burgess of Edinburgh, 1779. [EBR]

MCDONALD, DONALD, a merchant from Edinburgh, died at Cross Creek, North Carolina, 1773. [SM.35.223; EA#972]

MCDONALD, DUNCAN, a writer in Edinburgh, a decreet, 1778. [NRS.CS16.1.174]

MCDONALD, JOHN, a merchant burgess and guilds-brother, 1766. [EBR]

MCDONALD, RONALD, son of James McDonald, appr. to John Edmonston, a goldsmith in Edinburgh, 1757-1764. [ERA]

MCDONALD, UDNEY, son of Simon McDonald in Edinburgh, appr. to James Sutherland, a founder in Edinburgh, 1764-1771. [ERA]

MCDONALD, THOMAS, son of Angus McDonald, appr. to John Cheyne, a surgeon apothecary in Edinburgh, 1769-1774. [ERA]; a burgess and guilds-brother, 1769. [EBR]

MCDONALD, WILLIAM, a writer in Edinburgh, a deed, 1752. [NRS.RD2.172/2.430]

MCDONNELL, ANGUS, a merchant burgess and guilds-brother, 1777. [EBR]

MCDOUGALL, ALEXANDER, an auditor's clerk from the Exchequer in Edinburgh, bound from Leith aboard the <u>Margaret and Peggy of Leith</u> for Charleston, South Carolina, 1757. [NRS.AC9.1591.7]

MCDOUGAL, JAMES, son of Alexander McDougal a writer, appr. to John Callendar a skinner in Edinburgh, 1742. [ERA]

MCDOUGAL, Colonel WILLIAM, of St Kitt's, a burgess and guilds-brother of Edinburgh, 1724. [EBR]

MCDOUGALL, WILLIAM, a merchant in Edinburgh, a deed, 1752. [NRS.RD3.211/2.236]

MCDOWALL, ARCHIBALD, a merchant burgess and guilds-brother of Edinburgh, 1771, son of James McDowall a merchant burgess and guilds-brother. [EBR]

MCDOWALL, JAMES, junior, a merchant in Edinburgh, a deed, 1752. [NRS.RD3.211/2.522]

MCDUFF, JOHN, son of Robert McDuff an officer of the Incorporation of Goldsmiths, appr. to John Clark, a goldsmith in Edinburgh, 1767-1774. [ERA]

MCEWAN, ANDREW, son of James McEwan a dyer in Canongate, appr. to James Gillieland, a goldsmith in Edinburgh, 1762-1769. [ERA]

MCEWAN, ARCHIBALD, keeper of Parliament House and an inn-keeper in Leith, process of scandal, 1737. [NRS.CC8.6.275]

The People of Edinburgh, 1725-1775

MCEWAN, JAMES, a merchant burgess of Edinburgh, 1772, husband of Charlotte dau. of William Stewart a burgess. [EBR]

MCEWAN, JAMES, a clubmaker on Bruntsfield Links, a burgess of Edinburgh, 1775, husband of Janet dau. of John Young a merchant burgess and guilds-brother. [EBR]

MCEWAN, PETER, son of Alexander McEwan a workman, appr. to Patrick Bowie, an orris and livery lace worker in Edinburgh, 1763-1770. [ERA]

MCEWAN, WILLIAM, son of James McEwan a thread dyer, appr. to William Herriot, a gun-smith in Edinburgh, 1772-1779. [ERA]

MCFARLANE, DUNCAN, of Urins, born 1746, died 1774. [Greyfriars MI]

MCFARLANE, DUNCAN, a merchant burgess and guilds-brother of Edinburgh, 1770, former appr. to Thomas Hepburn a merchant burgess and guilds-brother. [EBR]

MCFARLANE, JOHN, from Leith, in Boston, New England, 1758. [SCS]

MCFARLANE, ROBERT, son of Patrick McFarlane in Edinburgh, appr. to James Clark, a weaver in Edinburgh, 1761-1768. [ERA]

MCFARLANE, Dr WILLIAM, a physician in Edinburgh, a deed, 1752. [NRS.RD2.172.423]

MCFARLANE, WILLIAM, from the West Kirk of Edinburgh Charity Workhouse, appr. to William Thomson, a weaver in Edinburgh, 1771-1778. [ERA]

MCFARQUHAR, GEORGE, son of John McFarquhar a writer, appr. to David Cleland a painter burgess of Edinburgh, 1745. [ERA]; a burgess of Edinburgh, 1763. [EBR]

MCFARQUHAR, GEORGE, appr. to David Cleland, a painter in Edinburgh, 1763-1771. [ERA]

MCFARQUHAR, JOHN, son of Andrew McFarquhar an Excise officer in Edinburgh, appr. to George Murray a cordiner in Edinburgh, 1750. [ERA]

MCGACHEN, ROBERT, a merchant burgess and guilds-brother of Edinburgh, 1778, husband of Elizabeth dau. of Archibald Mercer a merchant burgess and guilds-brother. [EBR]

MCGALL, WILLIAM, son of William McGall a weaver in Canongate, appr. to Arthur Miller, a merchant in Edinburgh, 1756-1761. [ERA]; a merchant in Leith, a burgess and guilds-brother of Edinburgh, 1775. [EBR]

MCGHIE, WILLIAM, a writer in Edinburgh, 1748. [NRS.AC11.232]

MCGIBBON, JAMES, a brewer in Edinburgh, 1765. [NRS.AC7.51]

MCGILL, ALEXANDER, son of Alexander McGill in the Pleasance, Edinburgh, appr. to Simon Fraser a white iron smith burgess of Edinburgh, 1741. [ERA]

MCGLASHAN, JAMES, a merchant in Edinburgh, a deed, 1751. [NRS.RD4.178/1.106]

MCGOWAN, JOHN, appr. to Adam Shaw a skinner in Edinburgh, 1726. [ERA]

The People of Edinburgh, 1725-1775

MCGOUAN, JOHN, a writer in Edinburgh, a deed, 1744. [NRS.RD4.178/1.446]
MCGREGOR, JAMES, son of Alexander McGregor professor of the art of defence, appr. to Hendry Walbers in Edinburgh, 1733. [ERA]
MCGROUGAR, THOMAS, a merchant in Edinburgh, 1747. [NRS.AC11.178]
MCGRUTHER, WILLIAM, son of Alexander McGruther, appr. to George Manson a barber burgess of Edinburgh, 1727. [ERA]
MCHARDIE, JOHN, a merchant in Edinburgh, a deed, 1752. [NRS.RD2.171/2.144]
MCHATTIE, ALEXANDER, a ships carpenter aboard HMS Peggie, husband of Janet Maitland in Edinburgh, 1759. [SL.87]
MCHATTIE, ALEXANDER, a merchant burgess of Edinburgh, 1770. [EBR]
MCINTOSH, DUNCAN, a merchant from Edinburgh, died in Jamaica, test., 1744, C.E. [NRS.CC8.8.108]
MCINTOSH, JOHN, son of James McIntosh in Edinburgh, appr. to Alexander Dickson a glazier in Edinburgh, 1755. [ERA]
MCINTYRE, ARCHIBALD, in Edinburgh, a deed, 1752. [NRS.RD2.171/2.295]
MCINTYRE, JOHN, son of Alexander McIntyre a tailor at Multrees Hill, Edinburgh, appr. to Edward Caithness, a merchant in Edinburgh, 1764-1769. [ERA]
MCIVOR, EDWARD, from Edinburgh, in Boston, New England, 1734. [SCS]
MCKAIL, HUGH, a writer in Edinburgh, 1742. [NRS.AC11.144]
MCKAY, ALEXANDER, son of Alexander McKay a journeyman baker, appr. to John Lauder, a coppersmith in Edinburgh, 1761-1767. [ERA]
MCKAY, ANDREW, son of Robert McKay a porter, appr. to James Ferguson, a coppersmith in Edinburgh, 1764-1771. [ERA]
MCKAY, JOHN, a vintner burgess of Canongate, 1733. [CBR]
MCKEAN, JOHN, son of Daniel McKean a sailor, appr. to John Thomas a cordiner burgess of Edinburgh, 1741. [ERA]
MCKENNA, JOHN, a merchant in Edinburgh, 1757; supercargo aboard the Margaret and Peggy of Leith, bound from Leith to Charleston, South Carolina, 1757. [NRS.AC7.49.1293; AC9.1591.7]
MACKENZIE, ANDREW, from Leith, a clerk, later a merchant in Charleston, South Carolina, a Loyalist in 1776. [NA.AO12.51.273]
MCKENZIE, DUNCAN, a shoemaker burgess of Edinburgh, 1770, husband of Magdalen dau. of William Coke a shoemaker burgess. [EBR]
MCKENZIE, FRANCIS, son of Robert McKenzie a skipper in Leith, appr. to John Dalgleish a watch and clock-maker burgess of Edinburgh, 1752. [ERA]
MCKENZIE, GEORGE, a writer in Edinburgh, a bond, 1741. [NRS.RD4.178/1.258]
MCKENZIE, JAMES, a goldsmith burgess of Edinburgh, 1778, former appr. of James McKenzie a goldsmith burgess. [EBR]

The People of Edinburgh, 1725-1775

MCKENZIE, KENNETH, an advocate and professor of Civil Law at Edinburgh University, 1751. [NRS.RD4.178/1.437]

MCKENZIE, KENNETH, a cordiner burgess of Edinburgh, 1764. [EBR]

MCKENZIE, NORMAN, son of Francis McKenzie a servant to Norman McLeod, appr. to John Clark, a goldsmith in Edinburgh, 1759-1766. [ERA]

MCKENZIE, ROBERT, son of George McKenzie a tailor, appr. to Henry Anderson, a shoemaker in Edinburgh, 1766-1772. [ERA]

MCKENZIE, ROBERT, a merchant in Charleston, South Carolina, before 1776, a Loyalist, settled in Leith. [TNA.AO12.51.273][NRS.CS16.17.1/61.123]

MCKERRAS, ANDREW, son of James McKerras a Supervisor of Excise, appr. to John Moubray a wright burgess of Edinburgh, 1742. [ERA]

MCKERTER, JAMES, son of William McKerter a Customs officer in Edinburgh, appr. to James Sommervell a goldsmith in Edinburgh, 1755. [ERA]

MCKEWEN, WILLIAM, a merchant in Edinburgh, a deed, 1752. [NRS.RD2.171/1.32]

MACKIE, DAVID, son of David Mackie a merchant, appr. to John Mein a slater burgess of Edinburgh, 1736. [ERA]

MACKIE, GEORGE, a merchant in Edinburgh, a deed, 1750. [NRS.RD2.171/2.51]

MACKIE, MARION, widow of William Mein senior, a merchant in Edinburgh, a decreet, 1782. [NRS.CS17.1.1]

MCKINLAY, JOHN, son of William McKinlay in Edinburgh, appr. to Thomas Reikie, a glazier in Edinburgh, 1772-1778. [ERA]

MCKINLAY, PHOEBE, sister of Dr Alexander McKinlay, in Jamaica later in Leith, a decreet, 1776. [NRS.CS16.1.170]

MCKINNA, JOHN, a merchant from Edinburgh, later in Jamaica, test., 1766, C.E. [NRS]

MCKINNON, MARTIN, son of Lieutenant John McKinnon, appr. to James Welsh, a jeweller in Edinburgh, 1764-1771. [ERA]

MCKOWN, WILLIAM, a vintner in Edinburgh, a deed, 1752. [NRS.RD4.178/2.505]

MCLACHLAN, HUGH, senior, a merchant from Leith, later in Kingston, Jamaica, 1755. [NRS.AC7.47.598]

MCLAGGAN, CHARLES, son of Daniel McLaggan in Edinburgh, appr. to Patrick Bowie, a weaver in Edinburgh, 1762-1770. [ERA]; a weaver burgess of Edinburgh, 1771. [EBR]

MCLARDIE, ALEXANDER, a merchant burgess of Edinburgh, 1768, son of Archibald McLardie a burgess and guilds-brother. [EBR]

MCLARDIE, JOHN, a vintner burgess of Edinburgh, 1766. [EBR]

MCLAREN, DAVID, a merchant burgess and guilds-brother of Edinburgh, 1777. [EBR]

The People of Edinburgh, 1725-1775

MCLAREN, THOMAS, a merchant burgess and guilds-brother of Edinburgh, 1777. [EBR]

MCLAURIN, DONALD, a surgeon in Canongate, a deed, 1752. [NRS.RD4.178/2.581]

MCLAURIN, DOUGAL, son of Donald McLaurin a surgeon, appr. to James Allan, a painter in Edinburgh, 1759-1767. [ERA]

MCLAURIN, JOHN, of Drygrange, Professor of Mathematics at Edinburgh University, a tack, 1750. [NRS.RD3.211/2.218]

MCLEAN, DANIEL, a chairman in Edinburgh, a deed, 1752. [NRS.RD2.171/1.31]

MCLEAN, GEORGE, a merchant in Edinburgh, a deed, 1752. [NRS.RD2.172.400]

MCLEAN, JAMES, a merchant burgess of Edinburgh, 1776. [EBR]

MCLEAN, JOHN, a merchant in Leith, a burgess and guilds-brother of Edinburgh, 1777. [EBR]

MCLEAN, LAUCHLAN, a merchant burgess of Edinburgh, 1770. [EBR]

MCLEAN, MURDOCH, a merchant from Edinburgh, in America, a decreet, 1776. [NRS.CS16.1.170]

MCLEAN, WILLIAM, son of William McLean in Edinburgh, appr. to John Shaw and Company, upholsterers and merchants in Edinburgh, 1759-1766. [ERA]

MCLEAN, WILLIAM, a barber burgess of Edinburgh, 1763, husband of Christian dau. of James Graham a barber burgess. [EBR]

MCLEAN, WILLIAM, a merchant burgess and guilds-brother of Edinburgh, 1774, former appr. to John McLean a burgess and guilds-brother. [EBR]

MCLELLAN, ALEXANDER, a smith burgess of Edinburgh, 1779, husband of Elizabeth dau. of William Herriot a smith burgess. [EBR]

MCLELLAN, ROBERT, a merchant in Leith, 1750. [NRS.AC11.190]

MCLELLAN, WILLIAM, a merchant from Edinburgh, settled in Virginia 1759 to 1766, moved to Tarborough, North Carolina, 1767, Loyalist later in London, 1777. [TNA.AO12.35.118]

MCLENNAN, COLIN, a printer from Edinburgh, in America, a decreet, 1779. [NRS.CS16.1.177]

MCLEOD, JOHN, a merchant in Edinburgh, trading with Carolina, 1737, and Maryland, 1741. [NRS.GD170.3339; RH9.17.308]

MCLERAN, THOMAS, son of Thomas McLeran a wright, appr. to James Shearer a barber burgess of Edinburgh, 1730. [ERA]

MCLURE, HAMILTON, son of John McClure a writing master, appr. to John Balfour, a surgeon in Edinburgh, 1765-1770. [ERA]; a burgess and guilds-brother of Edinburgh, 1773. [EBR]

MCLURE, JOHN, a writing-master and accountant burgess and guilds-brother of Edinburgh, 1764. [EBR]

The People of Edinburgh, 1725-1775

MCMILLAN, ANDREW, a flesher burgess of Edinburgh, 1776, son of William McMillan a flesher in Dalkeith. [EBR]

MCMILLAN, EUPHAN, relict of Thomas Cochran a flesher and baillie of Edinburgh, 1752. [NRS.RD2.171/2.336]

MCMILLAN, GILBERT, a poulterer burgess of Edinburgh, 1765, husband of Ann dau. of ....Black a burgess. [EBR]

MCMILLAN, JAMES, son of Daniel McMillan a stabler, appr. to Thomas Richardson a locksmith burgess of Edinburgh, 1730. [ERA]

MCMILLAN, JOHN, son of William McMillan in Edinburgh, appr. to William Murray and James Clark shoemakers in Edinburgh, 1765-1770. [ERA]

MCMILLAN, ROBERT, son of Daniel McMillan a stabler, appr. to Robert Arnot a lorimer burgess of Edinburgh, 1728. [ERA]

MCMILLAN, ROBERT, son of James McMillan a sergeant, appr. to John Baxter a barber burgess of Edinburgh, 1734. [ERA]

MCMUCHAN, JOHN, a merchant in Leith, 1749. [NRS.AC11.184]

MCNABB, ALEXANDER, son of John McNabb a glazier in Canongate, appr. to Alexander Cunningham, a white iron smith in Edinburgh, 1762-1768. [ERA]

MCNAB, CHARLES, son of Duncan McNab, appr. to George Campbell a wright burgess of Edinburgh, 1739. [ERA]

MCNAB, CHARLES, a merchant burgess of Edinburgh, 1777. [EBR]

MCNAB, JOHN, a merchant in Edinburgh, a deed, 1752. [NRS.RD2.171/2.376]

MCNAUGHTON, JAMES, son of Archibald McNaughton a shoemaker in Nicholson Street, Edinburgh, appr. to William Gibb, book-seller in Edinburgh, 1772-1778. [ERA]

MCNAUGHTON, JAMES, a merchant burgess and guilds-brother of Edinburgh, 1777, former appr. to John McLean a merchant burgess and guilds-brother. [EBR]

MCNAUGHTON, MALCOLM, a merchant burgess of Edinburgh, 1773. [EBR]

MCNAUGHTON, PETER, a merchant burgess and guilds-brother of Edinburgh, 1774/1777. [EBR]

MCNEIL, ANDREW, son of Archibald McNeil a town officer, appr. to Archibald Howie deacon of the weavers of Edinburgh, 1735. [ERA]

MCNICOL, ALEXANDER, a writer in Edinburgh, a deed, 1751. [NRS.RD2.171/1.37]

MCNIGHT, ROBERT, son of Robert McNight a tailor burgess, appr. to Thomas McNight a merchant burgess of Edinburgh, 1725. [ERA]

MCPHAIL, DAVID, a merchant in Edinburgh, a deed, 1752. [NRS.RD2.171/2.377];

MCPHERSON, ANGUS, a tailor burgess and guilds-brother of Edinburgh, 1763, son of William McPherson a writer burgess and guilds-brother. [EBR]

The People of Edinburgh, 1725-1775

MCPHERSON, DAVID, a merchant burgess and guilds-brother of Edinburgh, 1770, son of William McPherson a writer burgess and guilds-brother. [EBR]

MCPHERSON, DAVID, a merchant burgess and guilds-brother of Edinburgh, 1771, son of Angus McPherson a merchant tailor burgess and guilds-brother. [EBR]

MCPHERSON, JAMES, a master mason in St Cuthbert's parish, Edinburgh, a deed, 1752. [NRS.RD3.211/2.196]

MCPHERSON, JAMES, a merchant in Edinburgh, later a Lieutenant of Montgomery's Highlanders in America by 1759. [NRS.CS16.1.105/78]

MCPHERSON, JOHN, a musician in Edinburgh, a bond, 1744. [NRS.RD2.172.559]

MCPHERSON, JOHN, born in Edinburgh 1726, son of William McPherson, a writer burgess, and his wife Jean Adamson, settled in Philadelphia, Pennsylvania, as a shipmaster and privateer before 1751, died there on 6 September 1792. [AP#259]; late commander of HMS Britannia in the West Indies, a burgess of Edinburgh, 1764. [EBR]

MCPHERSON, NORMAND, a watchmaker burgess and guilds-brother of Edinburgh, 1763, son of William McPherson a writer burgess and guilds-brother. [EBR]

MCPHERSON, ROBERT, a clerk in the Fisheries office, a burgess and guilds-brother of Edinburgh, 1764. [EBR]

MCQUEEN, DUNCAN, son of Anne Logan in Edinburgh, appr. to James Auchenleck a white iron-smith burgess of Edinburgh, 1750. [ERA]

MCRABIE, WILLIAM, son of James McRabie, appr. to William Armstrong, a coppersmith in Edinburgh, 1771-1777. [ERA]

MCROBIE, JAMES, a gardener burgess of Canongate, 1733. [CBR]

MCSYMMOND, JAMES, son of Thomas McSymmond a shoemaker in Canongate, appr. to Alexander Gardiner, a goldsmith in Edinburgh, 1762-1769. [ERA]

MCTAGGART, WALTER, a rope-maker in Leith, a decreet, 1779. [NRS.CS16.1.175]

MCVICAR, NEIL, born 1672, minister in Edinburgh, died 29 January 1747, his wife Lilias Dunbar, born 1685, died 12 December 1732. [St Cuthbert's MI]

MCVICAR, NEIL, a merchant burgess and guilds-brother of Edinburgh, 1775, son of Neil McVicar a merchant burgess and guilds-brother. [EBR]

MABON, WILLIAM, a cutler burgess of Edinburgh, 1777, husband of Jean dau. of John Bell a baxter burgess. [EBR]

MACK, JOHN, a mason in Edinburgh, husband of Sarah Swinton, a sasine, 1756. [NRS.SC27.146.421]

MAIN, GEORGE, a jeweller burgess of Edinburgh, test., 1739, C.E. [NRS]

The People of Edinburgh, 1725-1775

MAITLAND, ALEXANDER, a merchant burgess of Edinburgh, 1777, son of O'Brian Malcolm a shoemaker burgess. [EBR]

MALCOLM, DOUGAL, a burgess and guilds-brother of Edinburgh, 1761. [EBR]

MALCOLM, JOHN, a barber and wigmaker burgess of Edinburgh, 1763, husband of Maria dau. of Charles Ramsay a barber and wigmaker burgess. [EBR]

MALCOLM, JOHN, son of William Malcolm a staymaker in Canongate, appr. to William Deas, a painter in Edinburgh, 1776-1782. [ERA]

MALCOLM, ROBERT, a merchant in Edinburgh, 1739. [NRS.AC11.122]

MALCOLM, ROBERT, son of William Malcolm a staymaker in Canongate, appr. to Daniel Ker, a goldsmith in Edinburgh, 1766-1773. [ERA]

MALCOLM, THOMAS, a shoemaker burgess of Edinburgh, 1774, son of William Henry Malcolm a shoemaker burgess. [EBR]

MALCOLM, WILLIAM HENRY, a shoemaker burgess of Edinburgh, 1768, husband of Lillias dau. of William Michelson a wright burgess. [EBR]

MALICE, DONALD, a flesher burgess of Canongate, 1729. [CBR]

MALLOCH, ANDREW, an ale-seller burgess of Canongate, 1726. [CBR]

MALTMAN, JAMES, a druggist burgess and guilds-brother of Edinburgh, 1778. [EBR]

MANDERSON, GEORGE, a wright in Edinburgh, 1733. [NRS.AC10.199]

MANN, THOMAS, a skipper in Leith, son of John Mann a ship's carpenter, test., 1777, C.E. [NRS]

MANN, WILLIAM, a merchant in Edinburgh, 1748. [NRS.AC11.183]

MANN, WILLIAM, son of James Mann a vintner, appr. to William Phin, a silk weaver and member of the Incorporation of Waulkers in Edinburgh, 1775-1781. [ERA]

MANSFIELD, JAMES, a merchant in Edinburgh, 1742/1756. [NRS.AC11.225; AC7.48.970]

MANSON, JOHN, son of John Manson a smith, appr. to James Auchinleck a white iron-smith burgess of Edinburgh, 1726. [ERA]

MANSON, JOHN, a wright burgess of Canongate, 1729. [CBR]

MANSON, WILLIAM, of Rotterdam, a burgess and guilds-brother of Edinburgh, 1761. [EBR]

MANUEL, CHARLES, son of John Manuel a merchant, appr. to George Farquhar, a painter in Edinburgh, 1767-1773. [ERA]

MANUEL, JOHN, son of John Manuel a keeper of Parliament House, appr. to James Mansfield a merchant burgess of Edinburgh, 1731. [ERA]

MANUEL, THOMAS, son of John Manuel a merchant, appr. to Patrick Robertson, a goldsmith in Edinburgh, 1765-1772. [ERA]

MARJORYBANKS, JAMES, a merchant in Edinburgh, 1729. [NRS.AC10.146]

The People of Edinburgh, 1725-1775

MARJORYBANKS, JOHN, a barber and wigmaker burgess of Edinburgh, 1777. [EBR]

MARSHALL, DAVID, son of William Marshall a shipmaster in Leith, appr. to James Campbell a goldsmith in Edinburgh, 1757-1764. [ERA]

MARSHALL, FRANCIS, son of David Marshall a tailor, appr. to James Miller a merchant in Edinburgh, 1736. [ERA]

MARSHALL, JAMES, son of James Marshall in Edinburgh, appr. to Laurence Brown a barber and wigmaker in Edinburgh, 1750. [ERA]

MARSHALL, JANET, from Cowgate, Edinburgh, transported to the colonies in January 1767. [NRS.JC27][SM.29.221]

MARSHALL, JOHN, a cooper from Leith, to Brunswick, North Carolina, in June 1775. [TNA.T47.12]

MARSHALL, WILLIAM, a goldsmith and jeweller burgess of Edinburgh, son of Robert Marshall of Riddoch and his wife Helen Dundas, test., 1738, C.E. [NRS]

MARSHALL, WILLIAM, a skipper in Weighhouse Wynd, Leith, 1773, [WED.51]; husband of Marion Falconer, 1776. [NRS.S/H]

MARSHALL, ZORABEL, former gaoler in Edinburgh, released from Edinburgh Tolbooth on condition of leaving Scotland, 1742. [NRS.HH11.21]

MARTIN, ALEXANDER, son of William Mason a tailor in Canongate, appr. to James Hill, a goldsmith in Edinburgh, 1763-1770. [ERA]

MARTIN, CHARLES, son of Robert Martin a barber and wigmaker, appr. to Andrew Bell, a barber and wigmaker in Edinburgh, 1768-1774. [ERA]; a burgess of Edinburgh, 1774. [EBR]

MARTIN, ELLIS, a merchant in Leith, a burgess and guilds-brother of Edinburgh, 1775. [EBR]

MARTIN, HENRY, a turner burgess of Edinburgh, 1762, son of William Martin a wheelwright burgess. [EBR]

MARTIN, JAMES, a writer burgess of Edinburgh, 1762, husband of Rachel dau. of Charles Blair a goldsmith burgess. [EBR]

MARTIN, JOHN, a mariner in Leith, test., 1756, C.E. [NRS]

MARTIN, JOHN, son of John Martin a whipmaker, appr. to John Orrock, a cutler in Edinburgh, 1771-1777. [ERA]

MARTIN, MARY, born 1759, a servant from Edinburgh, to Philadelphia, Pennsylvania, in May 1775. [TNA.T47.12]

MARTIN, SAMUEL, a burgess and guilds-brother of Edinburgh, 1763. [EBR]

MARTINE, THOMAS, a founder burgess of Edinburgh, 1767, former appr. to John Miln a founder burgess. [EBR]

MASON, GILBERT, a merchant in Edinburgh, a decreet, 1779. [NRS.CS16.1.177]

MASON, JAMES, a baker burgess and guilds-brother of Edinburgh, 1772, son of John Mason a baker burgess and guilds-brother. [EBR]

The People of Edinburgh, 1725-1775

MASON, JOHN, a mason in Leith, a burgess of Edinburgh, 1769, husband of Jean dau. of James Square a flesher burgess. [EBR]

MASON, JOHN, a baker burgess of Edinburgh, 1772, son of John Mason a baker burgess. [EBR]

MASON, WILLIAM, in Canongate, appr. to William Hill, a weaver in Edinburgh, 1762-1768. [ERA]

MASSON, JOHN, a journeyman wright burgess of Edinburgh, 1774. [EBR]

MASTERMAN, THOMAS, a skipper in Leith, test., 1758, C.E. [NRS]

MATHER, JOHN, a skipper in North Leith, test., 1743, C.E. [NRS]

MATHIE, GEORGE, gardener to the Surgeons of Edinburgh, a burgess of Canongate, 1731. [CBR]

MATHIE, GEORGE, son of George Mathie in Edinburgh, appr. to Andrew Cockburn a white iron smith in Edinburgh, 1741. [ERA]

MATHIE, PETER, son of Peter Mathies a baker in Canongate, appr. to William David, a goldsmith in Edinburgh, 1759-1763. [ERA]; a jeweller and goldsmith burgess of Edinburgh, 1776. [EBR]

MATHIE, THOMAS, a merchant burgess and guilds-brother of Edinburgh, 1761/1763, husband of Jean dau. of James Hunter a cordiner burgess. [EBR]

MATHIESON, ALEXANDER, a master of Edinburgh High School, a burgess and guilds-brother of Edinburgh, 1762. [EBR]

MATHIESON, DOUGAL, a sailor in Leith, test., 1760, C.E. [NRS]

MATHIESON, E., born 1758, from Edinburgh, to New York in April 1775. [TNA.T47.12]

MAULE, JOHN, son of Henry Maule a Writer to the Signet, appr. to Patrick Gibb a cordiner burgess of Edinburgh, 1732, [ERA]; a cordiner in Canongate, 1737. [NRS.AC10.249]

MAVOR, PATRICK, a baxter burgess and guilds-brother of Edinburgh, 1767, husband of Ann dau. of George Begbie a baxter burgess and guilds-brother. [EBR]

MAXTON, JAMES, a clerk from Edinburgh, transported to the colonies in January 1767. [NRS.HCR.I.99]

MAXWELL, DANIEL, brother of Archibald Maxwell a writer in Edinburgh, settled in Beaufort County, North Carolina, as a merchant, a Loyalist, killed in 1775. [TNA.AO13.95.397]

MAXWELL, JOHN, son of Robert Maxwell in Edinburgh, appr. to John Allen a freeman weaver burgess of Edinburgh, 1729. [ERA]; a burgess of Edinburgh, 1778. [EBR]

MAXWELL, ROBERT, son of John Maxwell a brewer's servant, appr. to William Robison, a white iron smith in Edinburgh, 1764-1770. [ERA]

The People of Edinburgh, 1725-1775

MAXWELL, WILLIAM, son of Robert Maxwell a calsey-layer, appr. to Alexander Fairbairn a locksmith burgess of Edinburgh, 1729. [ERA]

MAXWELL, WILLIAM, son of Robert Maxwell a writer, appr. to John Dalgleish a watchmaker in Edinburgh, 1748. [ERA]

MAY, ROBERT, a sailor aboard the Seahorse, husband of Christian McFarlane in Canongate, 1757. [SL.82]

MEAD, WILLIAM, son of Joseph Mead a sergeant, appr. to James Shearer a barber burgess of Edinburgh, 1734. [ERA]

MEEK, ROBERT, a merchant burgess and guilds-brother of Edinburgh, 1764, husband of Charlotte dau. of John Coupar a merchant burgess and guilds-brother. [EBR]

MEGGAT, JOHN, a burgess and guilds-brother of Edinburgh, 1776, son of John Meggat a merchant burgess and guilds-brother. [EBR]

MEIKLE, GEORGE, a brewer in Leith, a burgess of Edinburgh, 1761, husband of Jean dau. of William Wightman, a skipper in Leith and a burgess and guilds-brother of Edinburgh. [EBR]

MEIN, ANDREW, a merchant burgess and guilds-brother of Edinburgh, 1778, son of William Mellis a merchant burgess and guilds-brother. [EBR]

MEIN, DAVID, a coach-maker burgess of Canongate, 1731. [CBR]

MEIN, JOHN, son of John Mein, a book-seller from Edinburgh, settled in Boston, New England, 1765. [SCS][REB.1765.138]

MELLIS, JOHN, a merchant in Edinburgh, 1749. [NRS.AC11.234]

MELLIS, PETER, son of Donald Mellis a flesher, appr. to Andrew Melliss a flesher in Edinburgh, 1759-1764. [ERA]; a burgess of Edinburgh, 1765. [EBR]

MELLIS, WILLIAM, a flesher burgess of Edinburgh, 1769, son of William Mellis a flesher burgess. [EBR]

MELVIL, ROBERT, a Lieutenant Colonel and Governor in Chief of the conquered islands in the West Indies, a burgess and guilds-brother of Edinburgh, 1763. [EBR]

MELVIL, WILLIAM, a merchant burgess of Edinburgh, 1763. [EBR]

MENZIES, JOHN, a merchant from Edinburgh, died 1768 in Jamaica, test., 1769, C.E. [NRS.CC8.8.121]

MENZIES, WILLIAM, former servant to Harbert Wilson a bookseller, appr. to Mathew Dinning a merchant in Edinburgh, 1745. [ERA]

MERRILEES, ANDREW, son of William Merrilees a weaver in Edinburgh, appr. to John Burd a weaver burgess of Edinburgh, 1731. [ERA]

MERRILEES, PATRICK, an ale-seller burgess of Canongate, 1727. [CBR]

METHVEN, JAMES, a painter burgess of Edinburgh, 1767, husband of Janet dau. of George Hardie a baxter burgess. [EBR]

The People of Edinburgh, 1725-1775

MICHIE, THOMAS, son of Finlay Michie in Edinburgh, appr. to John Shaw upholsterer in Edinburgh, 1764-1771. [ERA]; a merchant burgess and guilds-brother of Edinburgh, 1767. [EBR]

MIDCUFF, JOHN, son of William Midcuff a silk manufacturer in Leith, appr. to Thomas Laing, an edge-tool maker in Edinburgh, 1777-1784. [ERA]

MIDDLEMIST, ROBERT, a baxter burgess of Edinburgh, 1766, son of John Middlemist a baxter burgess. [EBR]

MIDDLEMIST, THOMAS, a merchant burgess and guilds-brother of Edinburgh, 1773. [EBR]

MIDDLETON, JOHN, born 1760, from Edinburgh, to Philadelphia, Pennsylvania, in May 1775. [TNA.T47.12]

MIDDLETON, ROBERT, a skipper in Leith, test., 1732, C.E. [NRS]

MILLER, ALEXANDER, son of Robert Miller a wright, appr. to John Veitch, an ironmonger in Edinburgh, 1762-1767. [ERA]

MILLER, ALEXANDER, a merchant burgess and guilds-brother of Edinburgh, 1768, former appr. to James Cargill a merchant burgess and guilds-brother. [EBR]

MILLER, CHARLES, son of Joseph Miller tenant in Pleasance, Edinburgh, appr. to Charles Butter a wright burgess of Edinburgh, 1744. [ERA]

MILLER, CHARLES, son of Andrew Miller a wheelwright in the Fishmarket, appr. to Gilbert Auchenleck, a cutler in Edinburgh, 1761-1767. [ERA]

MILLER, DAVID, a surgeon in Westmoreland, Jamaica, heir to his uncle William Hill a writer in Edinburgh, 1770. [NRS.S/H]

MILLER, GEORGE, a pensioner on the New Greyfriars Kirk Session, appr. to David Brown a weaver burgess of Edinburgh, 1732. [ERA]

MILLER, GEORGE, a merchant burgess and guilds-brother of Edinburgh, 1764, son of William Miller a merchant burgess and guilds-brother. [EBR]

MILLER, GEORGE, a merchant burgess and guilds-brother of Edinburgh, 1771, former appr. of William and Thomas Tod merchant burgesses and guilds-brothers. [EBR]

MILLER, JAMES, son of James Miller in Edinburgh, appr. to James Mansfield a merchant burgess of Edinburgh, 1728, [ERA]; a merchant in Edinburgh, 1746. [NRS.AC11.170]

MILLER, JAMES, son of Malcolm Miller a gardener, appr. to James Norrie a painter burgess of Edinburgh, 1733. [ERA]

MILLER, JAMES, appr. to Nathan Porteous a skinner burgess of Edinburgh, 1751. [ERA]; a burgess of Edinburgh, 1762. [EBR]

MILLER, JOHN, born 1710, from Edinburgh, to New York or Pennsylvania in July 1728. [CLRO/AIA]

The People of Edinburgh, 1725-1775

MILLER, JOHN, son of Malcolm Miller a gardener, appr. to George Buchanan a bookbinder burgess of Edinburgh, 1729. [ERA]

MILLER, JOHN, son of George Miller a merchant burgess, appr. to William Aiton a goldsmith jeweller burgess of Edinburgh, 1732. [ERA]

MILLER, JOHN, son of John Miller, appr. to Alexander Kincaid a bookseller burgess of Edinburgh, 1735. [ERA]

MILLER, JOHN, eldest son of James Miller a baxter in Canongate, appr. to James Baillie and James Seton merchants in Edinburgh, 1751. [ERA]

MILLER, JOHN, son of John Miller a merchant in Canongate, appr. to John Scott, a gunsmith in Edinburgh, 1764-1770. [ERA]; a burgess in 1775. [EBR]

MILLER, ROBERT, son of Robert Miller a coach-maker in Canongate, appr. to Alexander Brown, a saddler in Edinburgh, 1773-1779. [ERA]

MILLER, ROBERT, a boy from George Watson's Hospital, appr. to Alexander Thomson, a grocer in Edinburgh, 1775-1780. [ERA]

MILLER, THOMAS, a waulker burgess of Edinburgh, 1762, husband of Alison dau. of Duncan Robertson a waulker burgess. [EBR]

MILLER, THOMAS, a glazier burgess of Edinburgh, 1768, son of Alexander Miller a glazier burgess. [EBR]

MILLER, WILLIAM, a painter burgess of Edinburgh, 1768, son of Alexander Miller a painter burgess. [EBR]

MILLER, WILLIAM, son of John Miller a vintner in Canongate, appr. to Gilbert Auchenleck, a cutler in Edinburgh, 1764-1771. [ERA]

MILLER, WILLIAM, a merchant burgess and guilds-brother of Edinburgh, 1774. [EBR]

MILNE, DAVID, son of David Milne in Canongate, appr. to Robert Paterson a merchant burgess of Edinburgh, 1747. [ERA]

MILNE, DAVID, son of David Milne a tailor in Canongate, appr. to John Hope, a merchant in Edinburgh, 1760-1765. [ERA]; a merchant burgess and guilds-brother of Edinburgh, 1764. [EBR]

MILNE, JAMES, a tailor in Leith, pressed into the Royal Navy, 1755. [ECL.36]

MILNE, JAMES, a tobacconist burgess of Edinburgh, 1765. [EBR]

MILNE, JAMES, a tanner burgess of Edinburgh, 1772, son of John Milne a founder burgess. [EBR]

MILNE, JOHN, son of John Milne a weaver, appr. to John Williamson a poultryman burgess of Edinburgh, 1730. [ERA]

MILNE, JOHN, jr., a founder burgess of Edinburgh, 1772, son of John Milne sr., a founder burgess. [EBR]

MILNE, JOHN, son of William Milne an advocate's servant, appr. to James Russell, an upholsterer in Edinburgh, 1772-1778. [ERA]

The People of Edinburgh, 1725-1775

MILNE, THOMAS, son of Henry Milne a blacksmith in Canongate, appr. to Andrew Douglas a merchant in Edinburgh, 1752. [ERA]

MILNE, WILLIAM, a skipper in Leith, test., 1732, C.E. [NRS]

MIRRYLEES, ALEXANDER, a brewer from Leith, later in South Carolina, 1779. [NRS.CS16.1.175]

MITCHELL, ADAM, a wright burgess of Edinburgh, 1762, son of William Mitchell a wright burgess. [EBR]

MITCHELL, ANDREW, brewer in the Yardheads of Leith, process of scandal, 1726. [NRS.CC8.6.218]

MITCHELL, CATHCART, son of George Mitchell a miller at the Water of Leith, appr. to John Kinloch, a white iron-smith in Edinburgh, 1771-1777. [ERA]

MITCHELL, COLIN, a goldsmith in Canongate, test., 1753, C.E. [NRS]

MITCHELL, JAMES, son of Walter Mitchell a coppersmith, appr. to George Forrester a white iron smith in Edinburgh, 1748. [ERA]

MITCHELL, JAMES, a jeweeler in Edinburgh, test., 1767, C.E. [NRS]

MITCHELL, JAMES, son of William Mitchell a former Excise officer, appr. to James Yorstoun, a cutler in Edinburgh, 1765-1772. [ERA]

MITCHELL, JEAN, relict of Nicol Mason a skipper in Leith, test., 1743, C.E. [NRS]

MITCHELL, JOHN, a merchant in North Leith, process of scandal, 1738. [NRS.CC8.6.278]

MITCHELL, JOHN, a merchant burgess of Edinburgh, 1772. [EBR]

MITCHELL, ROBERT, born 1704, a school-master from Edinburgh, to Maryland in November 1723. [CLRO/AIA]

MITCHELL, ROBERT, a merchant burgess of Edinburgh, 1764. [EBR]

MITCHELL, THOMAS, a goldsmith burgess of Edinburgh, test., 1769, C.E. [NRS]

MITCHELL, THOMAS, born 1750, a blacksmith from Edinburgh, to Dominica in December 1773. [TNA.T47.9/11]

MITCHELL, WILLIAM, a merchant in Leith, a burgess and guilds-brother of Edinburgh, 1770, son of William Mitchell a burgess and guilds-brother. [EBR]

MITCHELSON, JAMES, a goldsmith and jeweller in Edinburgh, test., 1758, C.E. [NRS]

MOFFAT, CUMBERLAND, a druggist burgess and guilds-brother of Edinburgh, 1777, son of William Moffat a glass-grinder burgess and guilds-brother. [EBR]

MOFFAT, GEORGE, son of George Moffat a weaver in Portsburgh, Edinburgh, appr. to Robert Raeburn, a weaver in Edinburgh, 1756-1762. [ERA]

MOFFAT, GEORGE, son of George Moffat the elder, a weaver in Portsburgh, Edinburgh, appr. to John Malcolm, a barber in Edinburgh, 1772-1777. [ERA]

MOIR, DAVID, son of John Moir a flax-dresser, appr. to Patrick Moir, a shoemaker in Edinburgh, 1771-1777. [ERA]

The People of Edinburgh, 1725-1775

MOIR, JAMES, steward to the Marquis of Lothian, a burgess of Canongate, 1731. [CBR]

MOLLISON, JOHN, a writer burgess and guilds-brother of Edinburgh, 1761, husband of May dau. of Charles Sawers a merchant burgess and guilds-brother. [EBR]

MONCRIEFF, GEORGE, late in Antigua, a merchant burgess and guilds-brother of Edinburgh, 1757. [EBR]

MONCUR, ROBERT, a shoemaker burgess of Edinburgh, 1775, husband of Alison dau. of Aeneas Bailie a shoemaker burgess. [EBR]

MONEYEY, WILLIAM, born 1752 in Edinburgh, a merchant in Charleston, South Carolina, died in Savannah, Georgia, on 30 September 1819. [Savannah Republican: 30.9.1819]

MONRO, ANDREW, a merchant in Edinburgh, factor for the Swedish East India Company, 1741. [NRS.AC10.290]

MONRO, JANET, from Edinburgh, transported to the colonies in May 1770. [SM.32.337]

MONRO, JOHN, a merchant burgess and guilds-brother, 1761. [EBR]

MONRO, PHILIP, a wig-maker burgess of Canongate, 1725. [CBR]

MONTEITH, ALEXANDER, a burgess of Canongate, 1729. [CBR]

MONTEITH, JAMES, a peuterer burgess of Edinburgh, 1767, former appr. to Archibald Inglis a peuterer burgess. [EBR]

MONTEITH, LOUIS, son of William Monteith a writer, appr. to James Herriot a cordiner in Edinburgh, 1727. [ERA]

MONTGOMERY, FRANCIS, a barber and wigmaker burgess of Canongate, 1733. [CBR]

MONTGOMERY, JAMES, one of HM solicitors, a burgess and guilds-brother of Edinburgh, 1761. [EBR]

MONTGOMERY, WILLIAM, a merchant in Leith, married Elizabeth, dau. of Sir Edward Eizatt MD, in 1723, process of divorce, 1738. [NRS.CC8.6.279]

MONTGOMERY, WILLIAM, a wigmaker burgess of Edinburgh, 1761, son of Francis Montgomery a wigmaker burgess. [EBR]

MOODIE, ROBERT, a sailor in Leith, son and heir of John Moodie a ships carpenter in Leith, 1753. [NRS.S/H]

MOODIE, ROBERT, a merchant in Savannah-la-Mar, Jamaica, later in Leith, test., 1776. [NRS.CC8.8.123]

MOOR, BENJAMIN, a carpenter in Canongate, 1762, son of William Moor a joiner in Pisealoqua, Rariton River, Middlesex County, New Jersey. [NRS.RS27.160.215]

MORE, CHARLES, son of John More a book-binder, appr. to James Scott, a merchant in Edinburgh, 1766-1771. [ERA]

The People of Edinburgh, 1725-1775

MORE, JACOB, son of William More a merchant, appr. to Robert Norrie, a painter in Edinburgh, 1764-1770. [ERA]

MORE, JOHN, a painter burgess of Edinburgh, 1770, son of John More a bookbinder burgess. [EBR]

MORE, JOHN, a gunsmith burgess of Edinburgh, 1772, former appr. to Andrew Wilson a smith burgess. [EBR]

MOREM, ROBERT, son of Robert Morem a flesher, appr. to George Mellis, a flesher in Edinburgh, 1772-1777. [ERA]

MORGAN, Dr JOHN, a burgess and guilds-brother of Edinburgh, 1763. [EBR]

MORGAN, THOMAS, a watchmaker burgess of Edinburgh, 1777, former appr. to William Nicol a clock and watchmaker. [EBR]

MORISON, CHARLES, son of Alexander Morison a merchant in Canongate, appr. to James Hill, a goldsmith in Edinburgh, 1760-1767. [ERA]

MORRISON, HENRIETTA, in Canongate, a deed, 1775. [NRS.RD2.218/18]

MORRISON, JAMES, a writer burgess and guilds-brother of Edinburgh, 1768, son of John Morrison a merchant burgess and guilds-brother. [EBR]

MORISON, ROBERT, born 1724, a baker on Crosscauseway, Edinburgh, died 1764. [St Cuthbert's MI, Edinburgh]

MORISON, THOMAS, son of James Morison an advocate, appr. to William Gib a surgeon apothecary burgess of Edinburgh, 1726. [ERA]

MOSSMAN, HUGH, in Edinburgh, a deed, 1769. [NRS.RD2.218/205]

MOWAT, JOHN, a merchant burgess of Edinburgh, 1774, son of John Mowat a burgess and guilds-brother, and as former appr. to John Mosman a merchant burgess and guilds-brother. [EBR]

MOWBRAY, ALEXANDER, son of William Mowbray a wright in Leith, appr. to William Falconer a wigmaker in Edinburgh, 1736. [ERA]; a merchant guilds-brother of Edinburgh, 1766. [EBR]

MOWBRAY, MARTIN, a merchant burgess and guilds-brother of Edinburgh, 1773, husband of Jean dau. of William Johnston a brewer burgess and guilds-brother. [EBR]

MOWBRAY, ROBERT, son of John Mowbray a barber, appr. to John Paterson a merchant burgess of Edinburgh, 1748. [ERA]

MOWBRAY, WILLIAM, a baxter, appr. to John Adamson, a burgess of Canongate, 1727. [CBR]

MOYES, ROBERT, a flesher burgess of Edinburgh, 1763, husband of Margaret dau. of James Square a flesher burgess. [EBR]

MOYES, SHADRACH, a Customs House clerk, a burgess and guilds-brother of Edinburgh, 1762. [EBR]

The People of Edinburgh, 1725-1775

MUDIE, ROBERT, master of the <u>Lyon</u>, arrived in the Rappahannock River, Virginia, in July 1767 from Leith, [VaGaz#845]; a skipper in Tolbooth Wynd, Leith, 1773. [WED.51]

MUIR, ADAM, a merchant, possibly from Edinburgh, settled in Maryland around 1746 and in Virginia by 1756. [NRS.CS16.1.99][MAGU#35]

MUIR, JANET, born 1746, a servant from Edinburgh, to Philadelphia, Pennsylvania, in May 1775. [TNA.T47.12]

MUIR, THOMAS, a vintner in Edinburgh, a decreet, 1756. [NRS.CS16.1.99]

MUIR, THOMAS, a wright from Edinburgh, transported to the colonies in 1773. [NRS.HH11.29]

MUIR, WILLIAM, a stabler burgess of Edinburgh, 1764. [EBR]

MUIRHEAD, ALEXANDER, a waulker burgess of Edinburgh, 1776, son of Edward Muirhead a waulker burgess. [EBR]

MUIRHEAD, GEORGE, son of Alexander Muirhead a causey layer, appr. to James Auchenleck a white iron smith burgess of Edinburgh, 1729. [ERA]

MUIRHEAD, GEORGE, a writer in Edinburgh, papers, 1723-1752. [NRS.B30.21.102]

MUIRHEAD, ROBERT, son of Robert Muirhead a writer, appr. to John More a bookbinder in Edinburgh, 1749. [ERA]

MUIRHEAD, ROBERT, son of Robert Muirhead a weaver at the Water of Leith, appr. to Robert Brown, a founder in Edinburgh, 1770-1777. [ERA]

MUNDELL, ROBERT, a printer burgess of Edinburgh, 1762, son of James Mundell a schoolmaster burgess. [EBR]

MUNN, JOHN, son of John Munn a journeyman cordiner, appr. to William Cock a cordiner burgess of Edinburgh, 1743. [ERA]

MUNRO, Reverend HARRY, DD, born 1730, rector of St Peter's, Albany, New York, died in Edinburgh 30 May 1801. [St Cuthbert's MI, Edinburgh]

MUNRO, WILLIAM, a merchant burgess and guilds-brother of Edinburgh, 1761. [EBR]

MURDIESON, ANDREW, son of John Murdieson a tenant, appr. to Andrew Tweedie a merchant in Edinburgh, 1738. [ERA]

MURDOCH, ARCHIBALD, a merchant burgess and guilds-brother of Edinburgh, 1770, son of Archibald Murray a merchant burgess. [EBR]

MURDOCH, JOHN, a watchmaker burgess, 1766, son of Robert Murdoch a threadmaker burgess. [EBR]

MURE, STEPHEN, in Quebec, a merchant burgess and guilds-brother of Edinburgh, 1763. [EBR]

MURRAY, ALEXANDER, a skipper in Leith, husband of Grizel Sutherland, 1754. [NRS.S/H]

The People of Edinburgh, 1725-1775

MURRAY, ANDREW, a merchant burgess of Edinburgh, 1770, husband of Margaret dau. of Thomas Tully a merchant burgess. [EBR]

MURRAY, ARCHIBALD, son of Robert Murray, appr. to William Newton a weaver burgess of Edinburgh, 1729. [ERA]

MURRAY, DANIEL, born 1744, late merchant in Edinburgh, died 29 March 1780. [St Cuthbert's MI, Edinburgh]

MURRAY, DAVID, a merchant burgess of Edinburgh, 1765. [EBR]

MURRAY, DAVID, son of William Murray in Edinburgh, appr. to James Cowan, a clock and watch-maker in Edinburgh, 1769-1776. [ERA]; a burgess of Edinburgh, 1779. [EBR]

MURRAY, FRANCIS, son of Christian Grant in Edinburgh, appr. to John Scott, a gunsmith in Edinburgh, 1775-1781. [ERA]

MURRAY, JAMES, a merchant from Leith, in Virginia, a decreet, 1744. [NRS.CS16.1.73]

MURRAY, JAMES, appr. to Thomas Giffard a smith in Edinburgh, 1747. [ERA]

MURRAY, JAMES, a merchant in Edinburgh, 1750. [NRS.AC10.351]

MURRAY, JAMES, a writer from Edinburgh, in Jamaica, 1764. [NRS.CS16.1.117]

MURRAY, JAMES, son of George Murray, a druggist from Edinburgh, died in New York during September 1767. [SM.29.557]

MURRAY, JEAN, dau. of William Murray and his wife Janet Shaw, from Edinburgh, wife of Daniel Stewart, to Dominica before 1778. [NRS.RD4.223.624]

MURRAY, JOHN, Captain Lieutenant of the 55th Regiment of Foot, died in North America, brother of Duncan and Evan Murray in Edinburgh, probate, May 1759, PCC.

MURRAY, JOHN, a druggist in Edinburgh, a decreet, 1761. [NRS.CS16.1.107]

MURRAY, JOHN, a skipper in Leith, test., 1770, C.E. [NAS]

MURRAY, JOHN, a baker burgess of Edinburgh, 1771, former appr. to John Symington a baker burgess. [EBR]

MURRAY, ROBERT, son of Robert Murray a tailor in Leith, appr. to James Murray, a merchant in Edinburgh, 1768-1773. [ERA]

MURRAY, WILLIAM, a shoemaker burgess of Edinburgh, 1764. [EBR]

MURRAY, WILLIAM, a merchant in Edinburgh, trading with Charleston, South Carolina, 1767. [NRS.AC7.52]

MURRAY, WILLIAM, son of William Murray a brewer in Pleasance, appr. to George Blair, a baker in Edinburgh, 1767-1773. [ERA]; a baker burgess of Edinburgh, 1775, husband of Margaret dau. of George Home a baker burgess and guilds-brother. [EBR]

MURRAY, ZACHARIAS, son of David Murray a stabler, appr. to William Laurie, a cutler in Edinburgh, 1771-1777. [ERA]

The People of Edinburgh, 1725-1775

NAIRN, JOHN, a burgess of Canongate, 1729. [CBR]

NAIRN, JOHN, son of John Nairn a tailor, appr. to James Ronaldson a cordiner burgess of Edinburgh, 1738. [ERA]

NAIRN, JOHN, a merchant burgess and guilds-brother of Edinburgh. 1776. [EBR]

NAIRNE, WILLIAM, an advocate in Edinburgh, a letter, 1773. [NRS.B26.1.78]

NAISMITH, JAMES, of Earlshaugh, a writer in Edinburgh, a deed, 1742. [NRS.RD4.178/1.242]

NAPIER, JAMES, a writer in Edinburgh, a deed, 1752. [NRS.RD3.211/2.433]

NAPIER, JAMES, son of James Napier a writer, appr. to Adam Burnet, a wright in Edinburgh, 1758-1764. [ERA]

NAPIER, JAMES, a merchant burgess and guilds-brother of Edinburgh, 1769, husband of Rachel dau. of George Manderston a wright burgess and guilds-brother. [EBR]

NASMITH, JOHN, son of James Nasmith of Earlshaugh, a merchant from Edinburgh, died in Virginia, 1747, test., 1752, C.E. [NRS.CC8.8.114]

NASMITH, MICHAEL, son of Michael Nasmith a wright, appr. to Thomas Herriot, a wright in Edinburgh, 1770-1776. [ERA]

NAVIE, ROBERT, son of David Navie a brewer, appr. to Thomas Hutton a freeman burgess of Edinburgh, 1740. [ERA]

NEAL, JOHN, a merchant burgess and guilds-brother of Edinburgh, 1761. [EBR]

NEIL, JAMES, appr. to Turnbull and Aitchison, clock and watch-makers in Edinburgh, 1775-1782. [ERA]

NEIL, JOHN, a sailor in Leith, test., 1757, C.E. [NRS]

NEIL, JOHN, a coppersmith burgess of Edinburgh, 1767, former appr. to William Armstrong a coppersmith burgess. [EBR]

NEILL, PATRICK, son of Thomas Neill in Edinburgh, appr. to James Cochrane a printer burgess of Edinburgh, 1739. [ERA]

NEILSON, GILBERT, a merchant burgess of Edinburgh, 1767, husband of Catharine dau. of James Aikenhead a merchant burgess and guilds-brother. [EBR]

NEILSON, JAMES, in Edinburgh, a deed, 1752. [NRS.RD3.211/2.556]

NEILSON, JAMES, son of James Neilson a wright in Leith, appr. to Alexander Weir, a painter in Edinburgh, 1768-1774. [ERA]

NEILSON, Dr JOHN, heir to his brother William Neilson a merchant in Edinburgh, 1776. [NRS.S/H]

NEILSON, RICHARD, a linen manufacturer in Canongate, a deed, 1752. [NRS.RD3.211/2.465]

NEILSON, SAMUEL, a mason in Edinburgh, a deed, 1750. [NRS.RD4.178/2.461]

NEILSON, THOMAS, appr. to David Loch a weaver in Edinburgh, 1725. [ERA]

The People of Edinburgh, 1725-1775

NEILSON, WALTER, a merchant in Canongate, a deed, 1752. [NRS.RD2.171/2.42]

NEILSON, WILLIAM, a wright in Leith, a bond, 1747. [NRS.RD3.211/2.271]

NEVAY, JEAN, wife of James Oliphant a goldsmith from Edinburgh, in America, 1780. [NRS.CS16.1.179]

NEVAY, MARGARET, in Edinburgh, a decreet, 1780. [NRS.CS16.1.179]

NEWART, ARCHIBALD, a merchant in Edinburgh, a bond, 1724. [NRS.RD3.211/2.383]

NEWBIGGING, JOHN, a hatter burgess of Edinburgh, 1761, son of John Newbigging a hatter burgess. [EBR]

NEWBIGGING, PETER, a hatter burgess of Edinburgh, 1763, son of John Newbigging a hatter burgess. [EBR]

NEWLANDS, ALEXANDER, a merchant burgess of Edinburgh, 1765, son of Alexander Newlands a merchant burgess. [EBR]

NEWLANDS, JAMES, to Virginia in 1731, brother of Alexander Newlands a skinner in Edinburgh. [NRS.RH15.5412]

NEWLANDS, JOHN, son of Alexander Newlands a skinner, appr. to his father, 1769-1774. [ERA]

NEWTON, MATHEW, a merchant burgess of Edinburgh, 1779, son of Hugh Newton a weaver burgess. [EBR]

NICHOL, WILLIAM, a merchant in Edinburgh, 1738, 1743. [NRS.AC11.108/226]

NICHOLSON, JAMES, a wright on Multray's Hill, Edinburgh, 1743. [NRS.AC10.301]

NICOLL, GEORGE, in Edinburgh, a deed, 1752. [NRS.RD4.178/1.203]

NICOLL, JAMES, a watchmaker burgess of Canongate, 1729; a deed, 1752. [CBR][NRS.RD3.211/2.607]

NICOLL, JAMES, a wright and trunk-maker in Edinburgh, husband of Isobel Watson, a deed, 1752. [NRS.RD2.171/2.108]

NICOLL, JOHN, in Canongate, a deed, 1752. [NRS.RD4.178/1.245]

NICOLL, LEWIS, born 1710, from Edinburgh, to Jamaica in August 1730. [CLRO/AIA]

NICOLL, ROBERT, a mason burgess of Canongate, 1733. [CBR]

NICOLL, WILLIAM, a merchant in Edinburgh, a deed, 1752. [NRS.RD2.171/1.69]; a burgess and guilds-brother of Edinburgh, 1767, son of George Nicoll a merchant burgess and guilds-brother. [EBR]

NICOLSON, WILLIAM, son of John Nicolson a bottlemaker in the South Leith bottle works, appr. to Alexander Nicolson a plumber in Edinburgh, 1749. [ERA]

NIELSON, DAVID, of the Leith Soap Works, a decreet, 1765. [NRS.AC8/1183]

NIMMO, GEORGE, in Leith, a deed, 1775. [NRS.RD2.218/932]

NIMMO, JOHN, a burgess of Canongate, 1728. [CBR]

The People of Edinburgh, 1725-1775

NIMMO, WILLIAM, a weaver burgess of Edinburgh, 1773, son of William Fraser a weaver burgess. [EBR]

NISBET, ALEXANDER, a merchant from Edinburgh, settled in Charleston, South Carolina, by 1715, died there 1753, probate, 1753, South Carolina. [NRS.GD237.10.1.42; GD237.1.153.9; RD4.116.1084; AC9.455]

NISBET, ALEXANDER, a student of law a burgess and guildsbrother of Edinburgh, 1761, son of Alexander Nisbet of Northfield convenor of the Trades. [EBR]

NISBET, ALEXANDER, a merchant burgess and guilds-brother of Edinburgh, 1765/1767. [EBR]

NISBET, ALEXANDER, a weaver burgess of Edinburgh, 1773, son of William Nisbet a weaver burgess. [EBR]

NISBET, DAVID, of Glasgow, a merchant burgess and guilds-brother of Edinburgh, 1766, son of James Nisbet a minister in Edinburgh. [EBR]

NISBET, JAMES, born 1677, a minister in Edinburgh, died 1756, his wife Mary Pitcairn, born 1685, died 1757. [Greyfriars MI, Edinburgh]

NISBET, JOHN, a merchant and confectioner burgess and guilds-brother of Edinburgh, 1763, husband of Elizabeth dau. of James Jardine a merchant burgess and guildsbrother. [EBR]

NISBET, JOHN SCOTT, of Craigentinny, born 1729, died 1764. [Greyfriars MI]

NOBLE, MARK, son of Mark Noble late of H.M. Lifeguards, appr. to Alexander Drysdale, a coppersmith in Edinburgh, 1769-1775. [ERA]

NORRIE, GEORGE, heir to his father George Norrie a painter in Edinburgh, 1776. [NRS.S/H]

NORRIE, ..., a painter, son of James Norrie a painter, a burgess of Canongate, 1732. [CBR]

NUGENT, THOMAS, son of Augustine Nugent a skipper in Leith, appr. to George Laing, a barber in Edinburgh, 1776-1782. [ERA]

OATTS, CHARLES, a shoemaker burgess of Edinburgh, 1778. [EBR]

OCHILTRIE, ARCHIBALD, a goldsmith burgess of Edinburgh, 1776, son of George Ochiltrie a weaver. [EBR]

OGILVIE, ALEXANDER, of the Edinburgh Ropery Company, 1762. [NRS.AC8.1067]

OGILVIE, ALEXANDER, a merchant in Leith, trading with America, decreets, 1779, 1780, 1783. [NRS.CS16.1.181; AC7.57/59]

OGILVIE, DAVID, a skipper in Precious Wynd, Leith, 1773. [WED.51]; a burgess and guilds-brother of Edinburgh, 1777, son of James Ogilvy a skipper in Leith, a burgess and guilds-brother. [EBR]

OGILVIE, JAMES, a skipper in Precious Wynd, Leith, 1773. [WED.51]

OGILVIE, JAMES, from Leith, died in Georgia 1790. [GaGaz, 19.8.1790]

The People of Edinburgh, 1725-1775

OGILVIE, MALCOLM, appr. to John Ogilvie deacon of the skinners in Edinburgh, 1730. [ERA]

OGILVIE, MALCOLM, a merchant in Edinburgh, husband of Jean Walker, a sasine, 1753. [NRS.RS27.142.426]

OGSTON, CHARLES, a writer in Edinburgh, 1734. [NRS.AC11.79]

OGSTON, JAMES, a writer in Edinburgh, 1734. [NRS.AC11.79]

OLIPHANT, CHARLES, son of Charles Oliphant a writer, appr. to George Winter a barber and wigmaker burgess of Edinburgh, 1747. [ERA]; a perfumer burgess of Edinburgh, 1773. [EBR]

OLIPHANT, GEORGE, son of William Oliphant a minister, appr. to David Knox a surgeon apothecary burgess of Edinburgh, 1727. [ERA]

OLIPHANT, JAMES, a goldsmith burgess of Edinburgh, 1763, former appr. to Robert Low a goldsmith burgess. [EBR]

OMAN, DANIEL, born 1760, a servant from Leith, to Philadelphia, Pennsylvania, in May 1775. [TNA.T47.12]

OMAN, MARY, born 1754, a milliner from Edinburgh, to Philadelphia, Pennsylvania, in May 1775. [TNA.T47.12]

ORD, GEORGE, a merchant in Edinburgh, 1742/1743. [NRS.AC10.305; AC11.226]

ORMISTON, THOMAS, a merchant from Edinburgh, to Savannah, Georgia, 1736. [SPC.143.148][TNA.CO5.668; 670.293/308]

ORR, JOHN, a journeyman baker, appr. to Henry Allan, a baker in Edinburgh, 1775-1780. [ERA]

ORR, WILLIAM, son of William Orr a porter, appr. to William Herriot, a gunsmith in Edinburgh, 1774-1780. [ERA]

ORROCK, ALEXANDER, a cutler burgess of Canongate, 1733. [CBR]

ORROCK, JOHN, son of Andrew Orrock a cutler in Canongate, appr. to Robert Boog, a cutler in Edinburgh, 1758-1764. [ERA]

ORROCK, ROBERT, a barber burgess of Edinburgh, 1743. [NRS.AC11.157]

ORROCK, WALTER, son of Alexander Orrock, appr. to John Brown a cordiner burgess of Edinburgh, 1728, [ERA]; a cordiner in Edinburgh, bound for Virginia, 1748. [NRS.AC10.338]

ORROCK, WILLIAM, a saddler burgess of Edinburgh, 1775, former appr. to George Boswell a saddler burgess. [EBR]

OSWALD, WILLIAM, son of John Oswald a coffee house keeper, appr. to Walter and Thomas Rudiman printers in Edinburgh, 1747. [ERA]

OWENS, THOMAS, a sailor from Leith, master of the Sea Flower of Leith, died in Jamaica, 1740, test., 1777, C.E. [NRS. CC8.8.124/1]

OWENS, THOMAS, a mariner from Leith, in Jamaica, a decreet, 1774. [NRS.CS16.1.164]

The People of Edinburgh, 1725-1775

PARIS, ROBERT, a tailor burgess of Canongate, 1727. [CBR]
PARK, JAMES, a druggist burgess and guilds-brother of Edinburgh, 1761. [EBR]
PARK, JOHN, a shoemaker burgess of Canongate, 1727. [CBR]
PARKHILL, JOHN, a merchant in Edinburgh, 1740s. [NRS.CS181.Misc.27/1]
PATERSON, ALEXANDER, a skipper in Leith, 1735. [NRS.AC11.88]
PATERSON, ALEXANDER, son of Hugh Paterson a tailor, appr. to George Forbes a goldsmith burgess of Edinburgh, 1740. [ERA]
PATERSON, BERNARD, a glover burgess of Edinburgh, 1761, son of William Paterson a skinner burgess. [EBR]
PATERSON, EUPHAME, a merchant in Edinburgh, 1734. [NRS.AC11.79]
PATERSON, HUGH, son of Hugh Paterson a writer, appr. to Neill McKinnon a wigmaker burgess of Edinburgh, 1743. [ERA]
PATERSON, JAMES, son of Thomas Paterson a pewterer, appr. to George Paterson a glazier burgess of Edinburgh, 1728. [ERA]
PATERSON, JAMES, of Woodside, tide surveyor in Leith, process of scandal, 1739; 1741. [NRS.CC8.6.286; AC11.139]
PATERSON, JAMES, a merchant in Leith, a burgess and guilds-brother of Edinburgh, 1762. [EBR]
PATERSON, JAMES, a skipper in Leith, test., 1774, C.E. [NRS]
PATERSON, JOHN, son of James Paterson a freeman tailor in Canongate, appr. to Francis Davidson, a tailor in Edinburgh, 1757-1762. [ERA]; a burgess of Edinburgh, 1762. [EBR]
PATERSON, JOHN, a skipper in Leith, test., 1774, C.E. [NRS]
PATERSON, MOSES, son of James Paterson in Edinburgh, appr. to Alexander Easton a cordiner burgess of Edinburgh, 1747. [ERA]
PATERSON, ROBERT, a writer in Edinburgh, 1730. [NRS.AC10.156]
PATERSON, THOMAS, appr. to John Lang a wigmaker in Edinburgh, 1726. [ERA]
PATERSON, THOMAS, a rope-maker from Leith, later in Maryland and Virginia, great-grandson of Gilbert Story a maltster in Leith, decreets, 1771, 1777, 1779, 1780. [NRS.CS16.1.146/171/175/179; S/H.24.2.1780]
PATERSON, WILLIAM, son of James Paterson a journeyman mason, appr. to James Duff, a clock and watch-maker in Edinburgh, 1771-1778. [ERA]
PATISON, JOHN, town clerk of Leith, a burgess and guilds-brother of Edinburgh, 1776, husband of Christian dau. of John Watson a writer burgess and guilds-brother. [EBR]
PATON, ALEXANDER, son of Thomas Paterson a merchant, appr. to Alexander Edmonston a goldsmith in Edinburgh, 1751. [ERA]
PATON, ANDREW, son of William Paton a brewer in Leith, appr. to George Boyd, a merchant in Edinburgh, 1770-1775. [ERA]

The People of Edinburgh, 1725-1775

PATON, CHARLES, son of Thomas Paton a merchant, appr. to Andrew Currie late deacon of the weavers in Edinburgh, 1743. [ERA]

PATON, JAMES, a merchant in Edinburgh, 1735. [NRS.AC11.87]

PATON, JAMES, a merchant burgess and guilds-brother of Edinburgh, 1774, son of Robert Paton minister at Lasswade a burgess and guilds-brother. [EBR]

PATON, JAMES, a wright in Leith, a decreet, 1776. [NRS.CS16.1.170]

PATON, NEIL, son of George Paton a barber and wigmaker, appr. to James Gulland, a goldsmith in Edinburgh, 1757-1765. [ERA]

PATON, PHILIP, appr. to William Hog a merchant in Edinburgh, 1725. [ERA]

PATON, WILLIAM, son of James Paton in Potterrow, Edinburgh, appr. to Thomas Aird a cooper burgess of Edinburgh, 1742. [ERA]

PATON, WILLIAM, a skipper, Sheriffbrae, Leith, 1773. [WED.60]

PATON, WILLIAM, jr., a skipper on New Quay, Leith, 1773. [WED.60]

PEARSON, JOHN, a dyer burgess of Canongate, 1728. [CBR]

PEAT, JOHN, a merchant burgess and guilds-brother of Edinburgh, 1767, husband of ..... dau. of Simon Mathieson a merchant burgess and guilds-brother. [EBR]

PEDDIE, ANDREW, a peuterer burgess of Edinburgh, 1767, husband of Margaret dau. of Robert Brown a peuterer burgess. [EBR]

PEEBLES, JOHN, son of James Peebles porter at the Edinburgh Weigh-house, appr. to Andrew Cockburn a white iron smith burgess of Edinburgh, 1755. [ERA]

PENDRIGH, WILLIAM, son of William Pendrigh, appr. to David Alison a cordiner burgess of Edinburgh, 1728. [ERA]

PENMAN, ARCHIBALD, a merchant from Edinburgh, settled in Florida before 1785. [NES.CS17.1.4/193]

PENMAN, EDWARD, a goldsmith in Edinburgh, husband of Margaret Durie, test., 1733, C.E. [NRS]

PENMAN, EDWARD, son of George Penman, a merchant from Edinburgh, settled in Charleston, South Carolina, before 1784. [NRS.RD3.245.725]

PENMAN, HUGH, a goldsmith and jeweller in Edinburgh, a sasine, 1755. [NRS.RS27.144.405]; test., 1785, C.E. [ERA]

PENMAN, HUGH, a merchant in Charleston, South Carolina, 1783. [NRS.CS17.1.2/343]

PENMAN, JAMES, born 1649, goldsmith and assay master of HM Mint, died 21 February 1733. [Greyfriars MI, Edinburgh]

PENMAN, JAMES, a merchant from Edinburgh, settled in St Augustine, Florida, and in Charleston, South Carolina, before 1772, probate 1789 South Carolina. [NRS.AC7.59.1788; NRAS.771.bundle 29/491; NRAS.0181]

PENNANT, THOMAS, a burgess and guilds-brother of Edinburgh, 1772. [EBR]

The People of Edinburgh, 1725-1775

PERKLE, JAMES, born 1752, a printer from Edinburgh, to Maryland in September 1774. [TNA.T47.9/11]

PETER, WILLIAM, a tailor burgess of Edinburgh, 1766, former appr. to Robert Brown a tailor burgess. [EBR]

PETRIE, ALEXANDER, son of John Petrie a journeyman baker, appr. to deacon William Thomson a weaver in Edinburgh, 1771-1776. [ERA]; a burgess of Edinburgh, 1775. [EBR]

PETRIE, JOHN, a merchant in Edinburgh, 1744. [NRS.AC11.159]

PEW, JOHN, a burgess of Canongate, 1726. [CBR]

PHARLEN, JAMES, a merchant burgess and guilds-brother of Edinburgh, 1767, husband of Catherine dau. of Christopher Alexander a merchant burgess and guilds-brother. [EBR]

PHILIP, JAMES, a merchant in North Leith, a burgess of Canongate, 1727. [CBR]

PHILIP, JAMES, a burgess and guilds-brother of Edinburgh, 1763. [EBR]

PHILIP, JOHN, a gardener burgess of Canongate, 1726. [CBR]

PHILIP, MARGARET, born 1757, a servant from Edinburgh, to Philadelphia, Pennsylvania, in May 1775. [TNA.T47.12]

PHILIP, RICHARD, a burgess and guilds-brother of Edinburgh, 1763. [EBR]

PHILP, ALEXANDER, a merchant in Leith, later purser of HMS Thetis, husband of Isobel Bell, test., 1757, C.E. [NRS]

PHILP, JAMES, a merchant in Leith, 1728. [NRS.AC11.38]

PHILP, JOHN, a merchant burgess of Edinburgh, 1765, husband of Jean dau. of Thomas Dick a cordiner burgess. [EBR]

PHINN, THOMAS, an engraver in Edinburgh, husband of Agnes McBrair, a sasine, 1760. [NRS.RS27.156.226]; an engraver burgess of Edinburgh, 1768, son of John Phinn a wigmaker burgess. [EBR]

PHIN, WILLIAM, a waulker burgess of Edinburgh, 1762, son of John Phin a waulker burgess. [EBR]

PHIN, WILLIAM, a cooper burgess of Edinburgh, 1777, son of William Phin a waulker burgess. [EBR]

PILLANS, JAMES, son of John Pillans a brewer, appr. to Alexander Stevenson a merchant burgess of Edinburgh, 1750. [ERA]

PILLANS, JAMES, appr. to Thomas Rannie a merchant burgess and guilds-brother of Edinburgh, 1767. [EBR]

PILLANS, JOHN, a merchant burgess and guilds-brother of Edinburgh, 1769, son of John Pillans a brewer burgess and guilds-brother. [EBR]

PILLANS, THOMAS, a merchant in Leith, 1739. [NRS.AC11.121]

PILLANS, THOMAS, a skipper in Leith, 1752. [SL.71]; test., 1771, C.E. [NRS]

PILLANS, WILLIAM, a sailor in Leith, husband of Isabel Leswair, 1743, [SL.51]; master of the James of Leith wrecked 17 December 1750, [AJ.159]; a burgess and guilds-brother of Edinburgh, 1761, husband of Beatrix dau. of William Wightman a skipper in Leith, [EBR]; a skipper on New Quay, Leith, 1773. [WED.60]

PIRRIE, GEORGE, a merchant burgess of Edinburgh, 1769, husband of James McAlpine a tailor burgess. [EBR]

PIRRIE, WILLIAM, a merchant burgess and guilds-brother of Edinburgh, 1765, husband of Margaret dau. of Alexander Ritchie a merchant burgess and guilds-brother. [EBR]

PITCAIRN, JAMES, son of Thomas Pitcairn minister at the West Kirk of Edinburgh, appr. to James Hunter a wright burgess of Edinburgh, 1742. [ERA]

PITCUR, JAMES, son of Walter Pitcur in Edinburgh, appr. to William Cumming a burgess of Edinburgh, 1731. [ERA]

PLENDERLEITH, DAVID, a burgess and guilds-brother of Edinburgh, 1765. [EBR]

POLLOCK, DANIEL, a skipper in Leith, 1759. [SL.85]

POLLOCK, DUNCAN, a skipper in Leith, died in September 1761. [South Leith Kirk Session Records, 7.9.1761]

POLLOCK, JAMES, a smith and farrier burgess of Edinburgh, 1778, husband of Alison dau. of William Waddell a smith burgess. [EBR]

POLSON, WILLIAM, a flax manufacturer and merchant in Edinburgh, a sasine, 1758. [NRS.RS27.152.357]

PORTEOUS, DAVID, a painter burgess of Edinburgh, 1768, son of Adam Porteous a painter burgess. [EBR]

PORTEOUS, JOHN, son of George Porteous in Edinburgh, appr. to Robert Dalgleish a smith burgess of Edinburgh, 1740. [ERA]

PORTEOUS, ROBERT, a servant from Craigentinny, Edinburgh, transported to the colonies in August 1768. [NRS.JC27.D35]

PORTEOUS, WILLIAM, son of George Porteous an Excise officer, appr. to James Thomson a barber burgess of Edinburgh, 1742. [ERA]

PORTERFIELD, Dr WILLIAM, in Edinburgh, a deed, 1766. [NRS.RD4.218/907]

POTTS, HENRY, secretary to the general postmasters, a burgess and guilds-brother of Edinburgh, 1767. [EBR]

POUSTIE, JOHN, a tailor from Edinburgh, husband of Elizabeth Yeaman, transported to the colonies in November 1748. [P.3.256]

POWELL, SAMUEL, a burgess and guilds-brother of Edinburgh, 1763. [EBR]

PRESTON, WILLIAM, born in Edinburgh during 1718, son of George Preston, educated at Balliol College in Oxford, 1735-1739, an Episcopalian minister in New Jersey from 1767 to 1777, died in Shreswbury, N.J., 7 March 1781. [CCMC]

PRIDIE, HAMDEN, a hatter burgess of Edinburgh, 1768, former appr. of David Anderson a hatter burgess. [EBR]

PRIDIE, ROBERT, a skipper in Leith, test., 1749, C.E. [NRS]

The People of Edinburgh, 1725-1775

PRINGLE, ANDREW, from Edinburgh, in Boston, New England,1734. [SCS]
PRINGLE, DUNBAR, a merchant burgess and guilds-brother of Edinburgh, 1772, son of Robert Pringle a merchant burgess and guilds-brother. [EBR]
PRINGLE, GEORGE, son of William Pringle, appr. to Michael Anderson a merchant burgess of Edinburgh, 1731. [ERA]
PRINGLE, JAMES, a merchant burgess and guilds-brother of Edinburgh, 1771. [EBR]
PRINGLE, JOHN, an advocate burgess and guilds-brother of Edinburgh, professor of history, 1765. [EBR]
PRINGLE, PATRICK, son of John Pringle a skinner burgess, appr. to Patrick Campbell a plumber burgess of Edinburgh, 1739. [ERA]
PRINGLE, WILLIAM, appr. to William Nimmo a weaver burgess of Edinburgh, 1731. [ERA]
PROCTOR, ROBERT, servant to Robert Gordon a minister in Edinburgh, appr. to Robert Morison a barber and wigmaker burgess of Edinburgh, 1754. [ERA]
PROUDFOOT, JOHN, born 1752, a hair-dresser from Edinburgh, to Virginia in November 1774. [TNA.T47.9/11]
PULLAR, JOHN, a merchant in Canongate, husband of Elizabeth Wilson, a sasine, 1759. [NRS.RS27.154.345]
PURDIE, JAMES, appr. to William McVey a wright burgess of Edinburgh, 1747. [ERA]
PURSELL, WILLIAM, a merchant burgess and guilds-brother of Edinburgh, 1772, husband of Janet dau. of Alexander Dallas a silk dyer and deacon of the dyers. [EBR]
PYM, JOSEPH, a merchant burgess and guilds-brother of Edinburgh, 1771. [EBR]
PYOT, JOHN, a printer burgess of Edinburgh, 1761, husband of Margaret dau. of James Leggat a burgess. [EBR]
RAE, GEORGE, son of Robert Rae a silk weaver, appr. to Noel le Conte a merchant and upholsterer in Edinburgh, 1749. [ERA]
RAE, JOHN, a merchant burgess and guilds-brother of Edinburgh, 1777. [EBR]
RAE, WILLIAM, a surgeon burgess of Edinburgh, 1777, son of James Rae a surgeon burgess and guilds-brother. [ERA]
RAEBURN, ANDREW, son of Andrew Raeburn a gardener, appr. to James Beatson a wright burgess of Edinburgh, 1732. [ERA]
RAEBURN, ROBERT, a weaver in Edinburgh, a sasine, 1758. [NRS.RS27.151.459]
RAEBURN, WILLIAM, son of Robert Raeburn a weaver, appr. to Neill McVicar a merchant in Edinburgh, 1755. [ERA]
RAEBURN, WILLIAM, a perfumer and hairdresser burgess of Edinburgh, 1778. [EBR]

The People of Edinburgh, 1725-1775

RAINIE, THOMAS, in Edinburgh, a deed, 1774. [NRS.RD2.217/1.586]

RAIT, JAMES, a burgess of Canongate, 1732. [CBR]

RAIT, THOMAS, son of Lieutenant Rait, appr. to David Brown a merchant burgess of Edinburgh, 1738. [ERA]

RAMAGE, JOHN, son of James Ramage a mealmaker, appr. to William Scoullar a tanner and currier burgess of Edinburgh, 1748. [ERA]

RAMIDGE, JAMES, a merchant burgess and guilds-brother of Edinburgh, 1772, husband of Margaret dau. of William Inglis a brewer burgess and guilds-brother. [EBR]

RAMSAY, ALEXANDER, a skipper in Leith, 1738. [NRS.AC11.112]

RAMSAY, ALEXANDER, a slater in Canongate, a burgess there in 1728, husband of Jean Walker, sasine, 1753. [NRS.RS27.142.341][CBR]

RAMSAY, ALEXANDER, son of Alexander Ramsay a mason, appr. to Thomas Mylne a mason burgess of Edinburgh, 1740. [ERA]

RAMSAY, ALEXANDER, a slater guilds-brother of Edinburgh, 1761. [EBR]

RAMSAY, ANDREW, a merchant in Canongate, trading with Pennsylvania, decreets, 1773, 1780. [NRS.CS16.1.157/179]

RAMSAY, CHARLES, appr. to George Balderston a surgeon apothecary in Edinburgh, 1728. [ERA]

RAMSAY, DAVID, a shipmaster in Leith, 1737; a sasine, 1756. [NRS.AC10.262; RS27.146.452]

RAMSAY, ELIZABETH, wife of William Adams master of HMS Druid, test., 1766, C.E. [NRS]

RAMSAY, FANNY, born 1752, from Edinburgh, to New York in April 1775. [TNA.T47.12]

RAMSAY, GEORGE, a stabler in Edinburgh, a sasine, 1751. [NRS.RS27.139.40]

RAMSAY, JAMES, son of Alexander Ramsay a slater, appr. to Simon Andrew a slater in Edinburgh, 1747. [ERA]

RAMSAY, KATHERINE and ANN, milliners in Edinburgh, a decreet, 1769. [NRS.CS16.1.138]

RAMSAY, KATHERINE, wife of William Davidson a writer in Edinburgh, a decreet, 1779. [NRS.CS16.1.174]

RAMSAY, MARTIN, in Canongate, a deed, 1775. [NRS.RD4.207/751]

RAMSAY, PETER, a merchant burgess and guilds-brother of Edinburgh, 1763. [EBR]

RAMSAY, ROBERT, a merchant in Edinburgh, 1743. [NRS.AC11.158]

RAMSAY, Dr ROBERT, a physician burgess and guilds-brother of Edinburgh, Regius Professor of Natural History, 1770. [EBR]

RAMSAY, THOMAS, born 1756, a gentleman-planter from Edinburgh, to Jamaica in December 1773. [TNA.T47.9/11]

The People of Edinburgh, 1725-1775

RAMSAY, WALTER, late brewer at Hamilton's Folly, now an Excise officer burgess and guilds-brother of Edinburgh, 1775, former appr. to Thomas Trotter of Mortonhall, a brewer burgess and guilds-brother. [EBR]

RAMSAY, WILLIAM, a merchant burgess and guilds-brother of Edinburgh, 1761, former appr. to James Ramsay a merchant. [EBR]

RANDAL, ROBERT, born 1753, a printer and book-binder from Edinburgh, to Maryland in July 1774. [TNA.T47.9/11]

RANKEN, CHARLES, a miller at the Water of Leith, heir to his uncle Alexander Moffat a mason in Burghmuirhead, 1770. [NRS.S/H]

RANKINE, JAMES, a lapidary burgess of Edinburgh, 1772, husband of Janet dau. of Robert Proctor a burgess and guilds-brother. [EBR]

RANKIN, WILLIAM, born 1736, a turner from Edinburgh, to Jamaica in February 1754. [CLRO/AIA]

RANNIE, DAVID, heir to his father Thomas Rannie a merchant in Edinburgh, 1775. [NRS.S/H]

RANNIE, DAVID, heir to his brother Alexander Rannie, son of Mungo Rannie a brewer in Portsburgh, Edinburgh, 1778. [NRS.S/H]

RANNIE, THOMAS, jr., a merchant burgess and guilds-brother of Edinburgh, 1762, son of David Rannie a merchant burgess and guilds-brother. [EBR]

RATTRAY, ALEXANDER, appr. to Patrick Henderson a merchant burgess of Edinburgh, 1747. [ERA]

RATTRAY, JAMES, heir to his mother Christian Main, wife of John Rattray a surgeon in Edinburgh, 1776. [NRS.S/H]

RATTRAY, JANET, heir to her mother Christian Main, wife of John Rattray a surgeon in Edinburgh, 1776. [NRS.S/H]

RATTRAY, JOHN, a merchant in Edinburgh, a burgess of Canongate, 1725. [CBR]

RATTRAY, JOHN, son of Dr Thomas Rattray, appr. to John Semple a surgeon apothecary burgess of Edinburgh, 1728. [ERA[

RATTRAY, JOHN, heir to his mother Christian Main, wife of John Rattray a surgeon in Edinburgh, 1776. [NRS.S/H]

RATTRAY, MARGARET, heir to her mother Christian Main, wife of John Rattray a surgeon in Edinburgh, 1776. [NRS.S/H]

REDLAY, JAMES, a merchant in Leith, heir to his father James Redlay a skipper there, 1776. [NRS.S/H]

REID, ALEXANDER, son of Charles Reid a wigmaker in Leith, appr. to Edward Lothian a goldsmith in Edinburgh, 1750. [ERA]

REID, ALEXANDER, a sailor, heir to his cousin Janet Bruce, dau. of Alexander Bruce a merchant in Edinburgh, 1770. [NRS.S/H]

The People of Edinburgh, 1725-1775

REID, ALEXANDER, a merchant burgess and guildsbrother of Edinburgh, 1765/1776. [EBR]

REID, ALEXANDER, a mason burgess of Edinburgh, 1772, husband of May dau. of William Cochran a glazier burgess and guilds-brother. [EBR]

REID, ANDREW, a surgeon, heir to his cousin Janet Bruce, dau. of Alexander Bruce a merchant in Edinburgh, 1770. [NRS.S/H]

REID, ANDREW, a wright burgess of Edinburgh, 1770. [EBR]

REID, ANDREW, in Canongate, a bond, 1771. [NRS.RD4.218/1036]

REID, CHARLES, son of James Reid, appr. to Thomas Gifford a blacksmith burgess of Edinburgh, 1729. [ERA]

REID, CHARLES, a burgess of Edinburgh, 1777, husband of Janet dau. of William Richardson a baker burgess. [EBR]

REID, CHRISTIAN, a jeweller in Edinburgh, heir to his cousin Janet Bruce, dau. of Alexander Bruce a merchant in Edinburgh, 1770. [NRS.S/H]

REID, FRANCIS, a tailor burgess and guilds-brother of Edinburgh, 1763, husband of Catharine dau. of John Hamilton a merchant burgess and guilds-brother. [EBR]

REID, HUGH, son of Thomas Reid a carter, appr. to Andrew Currier a weaver burgess of Edinburgh, 1729. [ERA]

REID, JAMES, master of the <u>Charles of Charleston</u>, a burgess and guilds-brother of Edinburgh, 1737. [EBR]

REID, JAMES, son of Charles Reid a smith, appr. to William Davie a goldsmith in Edinburgh, 1749. [ERA]

REID, JAMES, a coach-maker in Canongate, a sasine, 1756. [NRS.RS27.147.377]

REID, JOHN, an ale-seller burgess of Canongate, 1731. [CBR]

REID, JOHN, a printer burgess and guilds-brother of Edinburgh, 1761, former appr. to Alexander Murray a printer burgess. [EBR]

REID, KEITH, a mariner in Leith, test., 1777, C.E. [NRS]

REID, MARION, dau. of Andrew Reid a brewer in Canongate, heir to his cousin Janet, dau. of Alexander Bruce a merchant in Edinburgh, 1770. [NRS.S/H]

REID, MARY, born 1758, a servant from Edinburgh, to Philadelphia, Pennsylvania, in May 1775. [TNA.T47.12]

REID, ROBERT, a brewer and late bailie of Canongate, husband of Elizabeth Gifford, a sasine, 1755. [NRS.RS27.145.32]

REID, WILLIAM, a merchant in Edinburgh, 1750; a sasine, 1755. [NRS.AC10.352; RS27.146.314]

REID, WILLIAM, in Leith, a sailor aboard <u>HMS Buckingham</u>, husband of Jean Morrison, 1760. [SL.91]

REIKIE, JAMES, a glazier burgess of Edinburgh, 1766, son of Thomas Reikie a glazier. [EBR]

The People of Edinburgh, 1725-1775

REIKIE, THOMAS, son of James Reikie a wright, appr. to James Crawford a glazier burgess of Edinburgh, 1734. [ERA]

RENNIE, JAMES, a cooper in Leith, 1737.[NRS.AC11.100]

RHIND, WILLIAM, son of James Rhind a stabler, appr. to James Ferguson, a coppersmith in Edinburgh, 1759-1765. [ERA]; a burgess of Edinburgh, 1776. [EBR]

RICHARDSON, GEORGE, a writer in Edinburgh, a letter, 1740. [NRS.B59.24.10.20]

RICHARDSON, JAMES, a tailor burgess of Edinburgh, 1775, husband of Eupham dau. of Alexander Coutts a tailor burgess. [EBR]

RICHARDSON, JOHN, a merchant burgess of Edinburgh, 1761. [EBR]

RICHARDSON, JOHN, a printer burgess and guilds-brother of Edinburgh, 1766, former appr. to Thomas and Walter Ruddiman printer burgesses and guildsbrothers of Edinburgh. [EBR]

RICHARDSON, RICHARD, a merchant burgess and guilds-brother of Edinburgh, 1769, husband of Anne dau. of Robert Watson a merchant burgess and guilds-brother. [EBR]

RICHARDSON, WILLIAM, a writer burgess and guilds-brother of Edinburgh, 1762, son of John Richardson a merchant burgess and guilds-brother. [EBR]

RICHARDSON, WILLIAM, jr., a smith burgess of Edinburgh, 1772, son of William Richardson sr. a smith burgess. [EBR]

RICHARDSON, WILLIAM, born 1752, a printer from Edinburgh, to Maryland in July 1774. [TNA.T47.9/11]

RICHMOND, JAMES, a merchant burgess and guilds-brother of Edinburgh, 1774. [EBR]

RIDDELL, JOHN, a sailor in Leith, husband of Marion Cornwall, 1728. [SL.24]

RIDDELL, ROBERT, a skipper in Leith, a burgess of Edinburgh, 1775, son of Charles Riddell a merchant in Leith. [EBR]

RIDLEY, JOHN, a sailor in Leith, husband of Margaret Campbell, 1779. [SL.114]

RITCHIE, ALEXANDER, a skinner burgess of Edinburgh, 1765, former appr. to William Mitchell a skinner burgess. [EBR]

RITCHIE, ALEXANDER, a skipper in Broad Wynd, Leith, 1773. [WED.64]

RITCHIE, ALEXANDER, jr., a skipper on The Shore, Leith, 1773. [WED, appx.1]

RITCHIE, GEORGE, a vintner in Leith, 1746; 1748. [NRS.AC11.171; AC10.332]

RITCHIE, GEORGE, a skipper in Broad Wynd, Leith, 1773. [WED.64]

RITCHIE, JAMES, a burgess of Canongate, 1732. [CBR]

RITCHIE, JOHN, a sailor in Leith, 1764. [ECL.41]

RITCHIE, JOSEPH, son of Alexander Ritchie in Canongate, appr. to Patrick Robertson, a goldsmith in Edinburgh, 1761-1768. [ERA]; a goldsmith and

The People of Edinburgh, 1725-1775

jeweller burgess of Edinburgh, 1778, husband of Katherine dau. of William Syme. [EBR]

RITCHIE, ROBERT, a cordiner in Leith, a sasine, 1751. [NRS.RS27.138.297]

RITCHIE, WILLIAM, a mariner in Leith, husband of Isobel Duncan, 1756. [SL.93]

RITCHIE, WILLIAM, a merchant burgess of Edinburgh, 1762. [EBR]

RITCHIE, WILLIAM, a skinner burgess of Edinburgh, 1773, former appr. to Alexander Farquhar a skinner burgess. [EBR]

ROB, WILLIAM, a merchant burgess and guilds-brother of Edinburgh, 1764, husband of Katherine dau. of James Brownlie a merchant burgess. [EBR]

ROBERTS, MERCER, son of Edward Roberts a saddler in Williamsburg, Virginia, appr. to Baillie Blinshall, a saddler in Edinburgh, 1778-1785. [ERA]

ROBERTSON, ALEXANDER, a tailor, husband of Jean Buchan, a burgess of Canongate, 1732. [CBR]

ROBERTSON, ALEXANDER, son of Charles Robertson a flesher, appr. to Robert Clark, a goldsmith in Edinburgh, 1763-1770. [ERA]

ROBERTSON, ALEXANDER, a merchant burgess and guilds-brother of Edinburgh, 1777, husband of Christian dau. of George Howison a skipper in Leith and a burgess and guilds-brother. [EBR]

ROBERTSON, ANDREW, a sailor in Leith, husband of Elizabeth Campbell, 1759. [SL.86]

ROBERTSON, ARCHIBALD, a merchant from Edinburgh, emigrated to America by 1743, settled in Petersburg, Virginia. [VMHB.34.77][NRS.SC36.63.2][WMQ.5.185/237]

ROBERTSON, ARTHUR, a boy from George Watson's Hospital, appr. to James Farquhar, a merchant in Edinburgh, 1768-1773. [ERA]

ROBERTSON, CRAIGIE, son of John Robertson in Edinburgh, appr. to George Winter, a barber in Edinburgh, 1770-1776. [ERA]

ROBERTSON, DAVID, a block-maker in Leith, 1734. [NRS.AC11.76]

ROBERTSON, DAVID, a glover burgess of Edinburgh, 1769, husband of Janet dau. of Walter Brown a skinner burgess. [EBR]

ROBERTSON, DAVID, a merchant burgess and guilds-brother of Edinburgh, 1776, former appr. to Samuel Paterson a merchant burgess and guilds-brother. [EBR]

ROBERTSON, DONALD, a manufacturer burgess of Edinburgh, 1777, former appr. to William Allan a manufacturer burgess. [EBR]

ROBERTSON, GEORGE, a sailor in Leith, husband of Marjory Hamilton, 1729. [SL.26]

ROBERTSON, GEORGE, a skipper on The Shore, Leith, 1773. [WED.65]

ROBERTSON, HUGH, a writer in Edinburgh, 1749. [NRS.AC10.344]

The People of Edinburgh, 1725-1775

ROBERTSON, JAMES, son of George Robertson a writer in Edinburgh, an appr. weaver who absconded in 1743. [NRS.AC10.300]

ROBERTSON, JAMES, a packman, married Margaret Scott, a servant, in Edinburgh, 1754. [DUAS.BrMs3.Dc/12]

ROBERTSON, JAMES, son of Hugh Robertson in Edinburgh, appr. to Samuel Brown, a clock and watch-maker in Edinburgh, 1758-1764. [ERA]

ROBERTSON, JAMES, son of Alexander Robertson a wine-cooper in Leith, appr. to James Murray, a merchant in Edinburgh, 1766-1772. [ERA]

ROBERTSON, JAMES, a brewer burgess of Canongate, 1725. [CBR]

ROBERTSON, JAMES, a mason in Edinburgh, a sasine, 1753. [NRS.RS27.141.323]

ROBERTSON, JAMES, son of William Robertson a porter, appr. to Robert Armstrong, a founder in Edinburgh, 1767-1773. [ERA]

ROBERTSON, JAMES, a boy from George Watson's Hospital, appr. to Dewar and McFarlane, merchants in Edinburgh, 1771-1776. [ERA]

ROBERTSON, JAMES, a printer and book-seller in Edinburgh, later a newspaper publisher in Charleston, South Carolina, then a printer in Boston, New York, and Norwich, Connecticut, a Loyalist in 1776, settled in Nova Scotia, 1783. [NRS.CS236.R12/3][TNA.AO12.19.289, etc]

ROBERTSON, or BYERS, JEAN, from Edinburgh, transported to the colonies in January 1767. [NRS.JC27][SM.29.221]

ROBERTSON, JOHN, son of William Robertson, a cooper burgess of Canongate, 1725. [CBR]

ROBERTSON, JOHN, born 1652, brewer and portioner of the Water of Leith, died 11 November 1748, his wife Helen Pirrie, born 1653, died 1716, their son James Robertson a brewer, born 1686 died 1766. [St Cuthbert's MI, Edinburgh]

ROBERTSON, JOHN, a merchant in Edinburgh, 1735. [NRS.AC11.86]

ROBERTSON, JOHN, a burgess of Edinburgh, 1761, son of John Robertson a printer and former appr. to Thomas Lumsden a printer burgess. [EBR]

ROBERTSON, JOHN, son of John Robertson, servant to William Alston a writer, appr. to James Cadell, an upholsterer in Edinburgh, 1761-1767. [ERA]

ROBERTSON, JOHN, a merchant burgess of Edinburgh, 1762. [EBR]

ROBERTSON, JOHN, a burgess of Edinburgh, 1762, appr. to James Williamson a flesher burgess. [EBR]

ROBERTSON, JOHN, a goldsmith burgess of Edinburgh, 1763, son of William Robertson a beltmaker burgess. [EBR]

ROBERTSON, JOHN, a barber and wigmaker burgess of Edinburgh, 1766. [EBR]

ROBERTSON, JOHN, a chairmaster burgess of Edinburgh, 1770. [EBR]

ROBERTSON, JOHN, a flesher burgess of Edinburgh, 1771. [EBR]

ROBERTSON, JOHN, a jeweller in Edinburgh, a decreet, 1779. [NRS.CS16.1.175]

The People of Edinburgh, 1725-1775

ROBERTSON, JOSEPH, a surgeon apothecary burgess and guilds-brother of Edinburgh, 1768. [EBR]

ROBERTSON, KATHERINE, relict of Robert Moncur a skipper in Leith, test., 1767, C.E. [NRS]

ROBERTSON, PATRICK, a shipbuilder in Leith, 1734. [NRS.AC11.74/75]

ROBERTSON, PATRICK, a merchant from Edinburgh, in New London, New England, son of William Robertson a merchant in Edinburgh and his wife Agnes Fleming, decreets, 1742, 1744, a deed, 1772. [NRS.CS16.1.70/75; RD4.211.547]

ROBERTSON, PAUL, a chairmaster burgess of Edinburgh, 1767. [EBR]

ROBERTSON, PETER, a merchant burgess and guilds-brother of Edinburgh, 1765/1766. [EBR]

ROBERTSON, PETER, a clerk to James Alexander a merchant in Edinburgh, in America, a decreet, 1776. [NRS.CS16.1.170]

ROBERTSON, ROBERT, born 6 April 1740 in Edinburgh, a freeman and merchant of New York 1769, died 6 November 1805, buried in Trinity Churchyard. [ANY.I.218]

ROBERTSON, ROBERT, a candlemaker burgess of Edinburgh, 1762, son of John Robertson a merchant burgess. [EBR]

ROBERTSON, ROBERT, a burgess of Edinburgh, 1763, husband of Ann dau. of John Robertson a chairmaster burgess. [EBR]

ROBERTSON, ROBERT, a journeyman wright from Edinburgh, transported to the colonies in December 1774. [NRS.HCR.I.112]

ROBERTSON, THOMAS, a cordiner in Calton, a burgess of Canongate, 1725. [CBR]

ROBERTSON, THOMAS, a barber and wigmaker burgess of Edinburgh, 1764, son of Thomas Robertson a barber wigmaker burgess. [EBR]

ROBERTSON, WILLIAM, a sailor in Leith, husband of Margaret Thom, 1738. [ECL.48]

ROBERTSON, WILLIAM, from Edinburgh, to New York before 1750. [NRS.RD4.176.448]

ROBERTSON, Dr WILLIAM, a minister in Edinburgh, a burgess and guilds-brother of Edinburgh, 1761, [EBR]; a deed, 1766. [NRS.RD2.217/2/712]

ROBERTSON, WILLIAM, a sailor in Leith, husband of Jean Kennedy, 1767. [SL.102]

ROBERTSON, WILLIAM, a merchant burgess and guilds-brother of Edinburgh, 1774, son of William Robertson a tobacconist burgess and guilds-brother. [EBR]

ROBERTSON, WILLIAM, a boy from George Watson's Hospital, appr. to Robert Brown, a founder in Edinburgh, 1771-1777. [ERA]

ROBERTSON, WILLIAM, a skipper in Leith, husband of Isabel Steven, 1774. [NRS.S/H]; test., 1783, C.E. [NRS]

The People of Edinburgh, 1725-1775

ROBINSON, CHRISTOPHER, a burgess and guilds-brother of Edinburgh, 1767. [EBR]

ROBINSON, ROBERT, an architect burgess and guilds-brother of Edinburgh, 1773. [EBR]

ROBISON, JOHN, Professor of Natural Philosophy, a burgess and guilds-brother of Edinburgh, 1774. [EBR]

ROBISON, WILLIAM, a white-iron smith burgess, 1761, former appr. to Andrew Cockburn a white iron smith burgess. [EBR]

ROCHEAD, JAMES, from Edinburgh, a merchant in New York, probate 26 January 1740, Monmouth, New Jersey. [Monmouth Wills lib.C fo.378]

ROCHEAD, JAMES, a merchant in Edinburgh, a sasine, 1758. [NRS.RS27.150.406]

RODGER, ROBERT, a merchant in Coalhill, North Leith, a burgess of Canongate, 1732. [ERA]

ROEBUCK, JOHN, MD, a burgess and guilds-brother of Edinburgh, 1763. [EBR]

ROGERS, THOMAS, a merchant burgess of Edinburgh, 1771. [EBR]

ROLLANDS, WILLIAM, a skipper in Leith, test., 1753, C.E. [NRS]

ROLLO, ARCHIBALD, a poulterer burgess of Edinburgh, 1761. [EBR]

ROLLO, JOHN, appr. to Henry Bethune a goldsmith in Edinburgh, 1724. [ERA]; a goldsmith in Edinburgh, 1731-1735. [NRS.GD56.X.164/1]

ROLLO, ROBERT, a merchant burgess of Edinburgh, 1776, husband of Helen dau. of William Anderson a burgess and guilds-brother. [EBR]

ROLLO, WILLIAM, from Edinburgh, in Boston, New England,1766. [SCS]

RONALDSON, ANDREW, son of James Ronaldson a glazier, appr. to William Good, a wright in Edinburgh, 1764-1770. [ERA]

RONALDSON, JAMES, born 1768 in Gorgie, Edinburgh, son of William Ronaldson and his wife Marion Cleghorn, a printer who settled in Philadelphia, Pennsylvania, 1794, died 29 March 1841. [AP#305]

RONALDSON, WILLIAM, a shoemaker burgess of Edinburgh, 1764, son of James Ronaldson a cordiner burgess. [EBR]

RONALDSON, WILLIAM, a baker burgess and guilds-brother of Edinburgh, 1763/1774, former appr. of Andrew Hardie a baxter burgess. [EBR]

ROSS, ALEXANDER, from Edinburgh, settled in Savannah, Georgia, on 28 December 1734. [ESG#94]

ROSS, ALEXANDER, a sailor in Leith, husband of Henrietta Charles, 1756. [SL.80]

ROSS, ALEXANDER, son of Alexander Ross a shoemaker in Crosscauseway, Edinburgh, appr. to James Methven, a painter in Edinburgh, 1769-1775. [ERA]

ROSS, ANDREW, a clothier in Edinburgh, a decreet, 1739. [NRS.CS16.1.69]

ROSS, ARTHUR, a bookbinder burgess of Edinburgh, 1762, former appr. of George Stewart a bookseller burgess. [EBR]

ROSS, DAVID, a skipper in Tolbooth Wynd, Leith, 1773. [WED.65]

ROSS, DAVID, an accountant in Edinburgh, a decreet, 1775. [NRS.CS16.1.165]

ROSS, GEORGE, a skipper in Leith, 1770. [NRS.RS38.XII.451]

ROSS, JAMES, a burgess of Canongate, 1732. [CBR]

ROSS, JAMES, born 1727, a carpenter from Edinburgh, transported to the Leeward Islands 5 May 1747, landed on Martinique. [P.3.288][TNA.SP36.102]

ROSS, JAMES, a writer in Edinburgh, a decreet, 1764. [NRS.CS16.1.117]

ROSS, JOHN, a burgess and guilds-brother of Edinburgh, 1764. [EBR]

ROSS, JOHN, son of Hugh Ross in Edinburgh, appr. to James Cumming, a painter in Edinburgh, 1776-1782. [ERA]

ROSS, THOMAS, son of Robert Ross in Edinburgh, appr. to William Gray, a bookbinder in Edinburgh, 1761-1770. [ERA]

ROSS, THOMAS, a mariner in South Leith, test., 1782, C.E. [NRS]

ROSS, WILLIAM, born 1734, a painter from Edinburgh, to Philadelphia, Pennsylvania, in May 1774. [TNA.T47.9/11]

ROW, WILLIAM, a merchant in Edinburgh, deceased, his widow Janet Constable, and children Samuel and Margaret, a sasine, 1754. [NRS.RS27.143.388]

ROY, JAMES, son of James Roy, appr. to John Aitken, a watchmaker in Edinburgh, 1762-1768. [ERA]

RUDDIMAN, JOHN, son of John Ruddiman a tailor, appr. to John Edmonston, a goldsmith in Edinburgh, 1766-1773. [ERA]

RUDDIMAN, THOMAS, keeper of the Advocates' Library in Edinburgh, deceased, and his widow Ann Smith, sasines, 1756-1758. [NRS.RS27.147.60/213; 152/54]; born 1674, died 1757, born 1694, died 1769. [Greyfriars MI, Edinburgh]

RUDDIMAN, WALTER, a printer in Edinburgh, sasines, 1758. [NRS.RS27.151.263/267]

RUNCIMAN, ALEXANDER, a painter burgess of Edinburgh, 1762, former appr. of Robert Norrie a painter burgess. [EBR]

RUSH, BENJAMIN, of Philadelphia, Pennsylvania, a burgess and guilds-brother of Edinburgh, 1767. [EBR]

RUSSELL, CLAUD, in Edinburgh, a deed, 1775. [NRS.RD4.218/15]

RUSSELL, DAVID, in Edinburgh, a deed, 1775.]NRS.RD3.234/356]

RUSSELL, FRANCIS, a surgeon apothecary in Edinburgh, 1730. [NRS.AC10.155]

RUSSELL, FRANCIS, a merchant in Leith, trading with South Carolina and New Providence, ledger, 1752-1760. [NRS.CS96.1583; CS228.MISC,27/2]

The People of Edinburgh, 1725-1775

RUSSELL, JAMES, son of Thomas Russell a brewer, appr. to David Alison a cordiner, 1725. [ERA]

RUSSELL, JAMES, from Edinburgh, in Boston, New England,1745. [SCS]

RUSSELL, JAMES, appr. to John Shaw, a merchant and upholsterer in Edinburgh, 1760-1767. [ERA]; a burgess and guilds-brother of Edinburgh, 1767. [EBR]

RUSSELL, JAMES, a surgeon burgess and guilds-brother of Edinburgh, 1777, son of James Russell a surgeon burgess and guilds-brother. [EBR]

RUSSELL, WALTER, a merchant burgess and guilds-brother of Edinburgh, 1776, son of Robert Russell a merchant burgess and guilds-brother. [EBR]

RUTHERFORD, JAMES, from Edinburgh, a gold and silver-smith in Charleston, South Carolina, 1751. [South Carolina Gazette #914]

RUTHERFORD, JAMES, son of James Rutherford a carter in West Kirk parish, Edinburgh, appr. to John Kinloch, a white iron smith in Edinburgh, 1766-1772. [ERA]

RUTHERFORD, JOHN, eldest son of Thomas Rutherford a merchant in Edinburgh, a decreet, 1744. [NRS.CS16.1.73]

RUTHERFORD, JOHN, a surgeon in Antigua, second son of Thomas Rutherford a merchant in Edinburgh, a decreet, 1744. [NRS.CS16.1.73]

RUTHERFORD, Dr JOHN, a physician burgess and guilds-brother of Edinburgh, 1766. [EBR]

RUTHERFORD, ROBERT, a sailor in Leith, husband of Grizel Provan, 1754. [NRS.S/H]

RUTHVEN, WILLIAM, junior, a writer in Edinburgh, a sasine, 1751. [NRS.RS27.138.376]

SALTER, ISAAC, a brewer burgess and guilds-brother of Edinburgh, 1779, husband of Margaret dau. of Robert Ponton in Damhead a burgess and guilds-brother. [EBR]

SALTON, ALEXANDER, a glazier burgess of Edinburgh, 1773, former appr. to Robert Salton a glazier burgess.]EBR]

SALTON, ROBERT, a glazier burgess of Edinburgh, 1764, former appr. to James Veitch a glazier burgess. [EBR]

SAMUEL, GEORGE, born 1729, a book-binder from Edinburgh, transported to the Leeward Islands 5 May 1747, landed on Martinique. [P.3.298][TNA.SP36.102]

SAMUEL, JAMES, son of Robert Samuel servant to John Clarkson a baker, appr. to said John Clarkson, 1772-1777. [ERA]

SAMUEL, JOHN, a burgess of Canongate, 1728. [CBR]

SAMUEL, JOHN, a baker in Edinburgh, 1742. [NRS.AC11.143]

The People of Edinburgh, 1725-1775

SANDERS, ARCHIBALD, son of William Sanders a Post Office clerk, appr. to William Dempster a goldsmith in Edinburgh, 1751. [ERA]

SANDILANDS, JOHN, son of John Sandilands a tailor on Crosscauseway, Edinburgh, appr. to William Bruce, an upholsterer in Edinburgh, 1772-1778. [ERA]

SANDS, ALEXANDER, born 1758, a chapman from Edinburgh, to Philadelphia, Pennsylvania, in May 1775. [TNA.T47.12]

SAVAGE, JOHN, in Canongate, a deed, 1752. [NRS.RD2.172.217]

SAVAGE, ROBERT, a wig-maker and hair merchant in Potter-row, Edinburgh, a sasine, 1757, a decreet, 1779. [NRS.RS27.149.369; CS16.1.177]

SAUNIE, WILLIAM, an upholsterer burgess of Edinburgh, 1764. [EBR]

SAWERS, ARCHIBALD, a baker burgess of Edinburgh, 1771, son of Charles Sawers a burgess. [EBR]

SAWERS, JOHN, a farmer at Bell's Milns, a burgess and guilds-brother of Edinburgh, 1775, son of Charles Sawers a merchant burgess and guilds-brother. [EBR]

SAWERS, WILLIAM, a merchant burgess and guilds-brother of Edinburgh, 1765. [EBR]

SCEALES, ADOLPHUS, a merchant in Leith, a burgess and guilds-brother of Edinburgh, 1772. [EBR]

SCEALES, ANDREW, a merchant burgess and guilds-brother of Edinburgh, 1773. [EBR]

SCOBIE, WILLIAM, an ale seller, a burgess of Canongate, 1725. [CBR]

SCOTLAND, JOHN, a merchant in Edinburgh, a deed, 1752; to Antigua before 1773. [NRS.RD2.171/2.182; RD3.232.432]

SCOTLAND, WILLIAM, a burgess and guilds-brother of Edinburgh, 1763, son of John Scott a merchant burgess and guilds-brother. [EBR]

SCOTT, ALEXANDER, son of Archibald Scott a brewer in Potterrow, Edinburgh, appr. to Robert Scott the younger, a merchant in Edinburgh, 1768-1773. [ERA]

SCOTT, ALEXANDER, son of Alexander Scott in the Abbey of Holy Rood, Canongate, appr. to James Caddel, an upholsterer in Edinburgh, 1770-1777. [ERA]

SCOTT, ARCHIBALD, a merchant burgess and guilds-brother of Edinburgh, former appr. to Archibald Campbell a brewer burgess and guilds-brother. [EBR]

SCOTT, CHRISTINA, heir to her brothers Andrew and William, sons of William Scott professor of Greek at Edinburgh University, 1771. [NRS.S/H]

SCOTT, DAVID, a glover in Edinburgh, a sasine, 1757. [NRS.RS27.149.212]

SCOTT, DAVID, a weaver burgess of Edinburgh, 1772. [EBR]

SCOTT, DAVID, a merchant from Edinburgh, to Antigua before 1779. [NRS.RD4.226.1004]

The People of Edinburgh, 1725-1775

SCOTT, GEORGE, sometime baxter in Canongate, a burgess there in 1724, afterwards a tax gatherer at the West Port of Edinburgh, sasines 1759. [NRS.RS27.155.116/123][CBR]

SCOTT, JAMES, a writer in Edinburgh, 1741. [NRS.AC10.291]

SCOTT, JAMES, a shipwright, son of James Scott a baker in Leith, test., 1745, C.E. [NRS]

SCOTT, JAMES, of Houden, a writer in Edinburgh, a bond, 1750. [NRS.RD2.171/1.284]

SCOTT, JAMES, a druggist in Edinburgh, a bond, 1750. [NRS.RD2.171/1.34]

SCOTT, JAMES, a tailor in Canongate, a deed, 1752. [NRS.RD3.211/2.437]

SCOTT, JAMES, son of Walter Scott a shoemaker in Potterrow, Edinburgh, appr. to Alexander Storie, a candlemaker in Edinburgh, 1765-1771. [ERA]

SCOTT, JAMES, son of William Scott a brewer in Leith, appr. to Robert Straiton, a wright in Edinburgh, 1760-1766. [ERA]

SCOTT, JAMES, born 1707, a merchant, died 1785. [Greyfriars MI, Edinburgh]

SCOTT, JOHN, son of William Scott a flesher, appr. to William Galloway a wright burgess of Edinburgh, 1725. [ERA]

SCOTT, JOHN, a gunsmith in Canongate, a sasine, 1760. [NRS.RS27.156.202]

SCOTT, JOHN, a flesher burgess of Edinburgh, 1767, son of John Scott a flesher burgess. [EBR]

SCOTT, JOHN, son of James Scott, a druggist in Edinburgh, a decreet, 1782. [NRS.CS17.1.1]

SCOTT, KATHERINE, a vintner in Leith, spouse of John Snelling a skipper in Leith, test., 1782, C.E. [NRS]

SCOTT, MUNGO, a glazier in Edinburgh, a sasine, 1754. [NRS.RS27.144.231]

SCOTT, PATRICK, a tailor, former appr. to William Henderson, a burgess of Canongate, 1725. [CBR]

SCOTT, PHILIP, son of Walter Scott a surgeon, appr. to John Anderson a cordiner burgess of Edinburgh, 1738. [ERA]

SCOTT, ROBERT, son of Robert Scott a tailor in Potterrow, Edinburgh, appr. to John Grieve, a merchant in Edinburgh, 1766-1771. [ERA]

SCOTT, ROBERT, a journeyman wright in Edinburgh, a decreet, 1771. [NRS.CS161.1.146]

SCOTT, ROBERT, a merchant in Leith, 1741; a deed, 1752. [NRS.AC10.291; RD2.172.399]

SCOTT, ROBERT, a baker burgess of Edinburgh, 1773, former appr. to Thomas Murray a baker burgess. [EBR]

SCOTT, WALTER, son of Walter Scott in Fisher Row, appr. to Patrick Gibb late deacon of the cordiners in Edinburgh, 1735. [ERA]

SCOTT, WALTER, a merchant in Edinburgh, a deed, 1752. [NRS.RD4.178/2.469]

The People of Edinburgh, 1725-1775

SCOTT, WILLIAM, a burgess of Canongate, 1731. [CBR]

SCOTT, WILLIAM, a wright in Canongate, a deed, 1752. [NRS.RD4.178/2.321]

SCOTT, WILLIAM, a brewer in Leith, a sasine, 1757. [NRS.RS27.149.272]

SCOTT, WILLIAM, a plumber burgess of Edinburgh, 1768, son of John Scott a plumber burgess. [EBR]

SCOTT, WILLIAM, a merchant burgess and guilds-brother of Edinburgh, 1774, former appr. to Samuel Foggo a merchant burgess and guilds-brother. [EBR]

SCOTT, WILLIAM, a peuterer burgess of Edinburgh, 1779, son of William Scott a peuterer burgess. [EBR]

SCOTT, WILLIAM HENRY, son of Alexander Scott a merchant in Edinburgh, a merchant in St Eustatia, died 1789 in Antigua. [GM.XII.01/212]

SCOTT-MONCREIFF, ROBERT, a merchant burgess and guilds-brother of Edinburgh, 1762, former appr. of William Hog a merchant burgess and guilds-brother. [EBR]

SCOUGALL, JOHN, a skipper at Coalhill, Leith, 1773. [WED.71]; a burgess and guilds-brother of Edinburgh, 1773, husband of Jean youngest dau. of John Tod a shipbuilder in Leith, a burgess and guilds-brother. [EBR]

SCOUGALL, RICHARD, a shipmaster in Leith, husband of Margaret Shepherd, a sasine, 1756. [NRS.RS27.147.402]; master of the Margaret of Leith, 1751. [AJ.158]; at Tolbooth Wynd, Leith, 1773. [WED.71][NRS.B3.7.4]

SCOULLER, ALEXANDER, a tanner in Edinburgh, a tack, 1750. [NRS.RD2.172.141]

SCRIMGEOUR, HENRY, Writer to the Signet, a deed, 1751. [NRS.RD3.211/2.69]

SCRIMGEOUR, JOHN, a weaver from North Leith, transported to the colonies in August 1753. [SM.15.420][NRS.JC3.29.274]

SCYTH, ROBERT, an upholsterer burgess and guilds-brother of Edinburgh, 1777, former appr. to James Caddell a burgess and guilds-brother. [EBR]

SEAMAN, GEORGE, son of Alexander Seaman a baxter in Leith, appr. to Charles Crockett a merchant burgess of Edinburgh, 1721. [ERA]; a merchant burgess and guilds-brother of Edinburgh, 1730. [EBR]

SEAMAN, GEORGE, born 1735, son of Alexander Seaman, a merchant from Leith, settled in South Carolina by 1755, died 1769 in Charleston, probate 1769. PCC, probate South Carolina, 1769. [NRS.RD3.210.491; CS16.1.120/170; AC7.49.14; AC9.1960]

SEAMAN, JAMES, a skipper in Leith, 1755. [ECL.52]

SEATON, JAMES, jr., a merchant in Edinburgh, 1745. [NRS.AC10.317]

SELBY, ROBERT, a plumber in Canongate, a burgess and guilds-brother of Edinburgh, 1761, husband of Elizabeth dau. of Thomas Miln a mason burgess and guilds-brother. [EBR]

SELKIRK, ANDREW, a cordiner burgess of Canongate, 1729. [CBR]

The People of Edinburgh, 1725-1775

SELLERS, WILLIAM, a writer in Edinburgh, a burgess of Canongate, 1731. [CBR]
SEMPLE, HUGH, in Edinburgh, appr. to George Gray a barber burgess of Edinburgh, 1731. [ERA]
SETON, GILBERT, a merchant burgess and guilds-brother of Edinburgh, 1773, son of Daniel Seton a merchant burgess and guilds-brother. [EBR]
SETON, JAMES, a merchant in Edinburgh, a deed, 1752. [NRS.RD4.178/2.2]
SETON, WALTER, a merchant burgess and guilds-brother of Edinburgh, 1777, son of David Seton a merchant burgess and guilds-brother. [EBR]
SETTERS, WILLIAM, a sailor at Coalhill, Leith, 1766. [SL.105]
SHACHAN, ADAM, son of John Shachan a baxter, appr. to William Glen a weaver burgess of Edinburgh, 1732. [ERA]
SHAND, ALEXANDER, a merchant in Edinburgh, 1737; deeds, 1752; a sasine, 1754. [NRS.RD2.172.553; RD4.178/2.308; RS27.143.416]
SHAND, FRANCIS, a merchant burgess and guilds-brother of Edinburgh, 1777. [EBR]
SHAND, JOHN, a merchant burgess and guilds-brother of Edinburgh, 1764, husband of Jean dau. of Duncan Finlayson a merchant burgess. [EBR]
SHARP, ALEXANDER, a merchant in Edinburgh, 1737. [NRS.AC11.96]
SHARP, GILES, son of Henry Sharp in St Kitts, West Indies, appr. to Charles Congalton, an apothecary in Edinburgh, 1764-1769. [ERA]
SHARP, JAMES, a sailor in Leith, husband of Margaret Miller, 1764. [SL.98]
SHARP, THOMAS, in Edinburgh, a deed, 1775. [NRS.RD4.218/469]
SHAW, ALEXANDER, a writer from Edinburgh, in America, a decreet, 1780. [NRS.CS16.1.181]
SHAW, DAVID, born 1708, a joiner and carpenter from Edinburgh, to Jamaica in May 1731. [CLRO/AIA]
SHAW, DAVID, appr. to Adam Burnet a wright in Edinburgh, 1724. [ERA]
SHAW, JAMES, of Jamaica, a burgess and guilds-brother of Edinburgh, 1763. [EBR]
SHAW, JAMES, a burgess and guilds-brother of Edinburgh, 1764. [EBR]
SHAW, JAMES, a grocer burgess of Edinburgh, 1771, son of William Shaw a chairmaster burgess. [EBR]
SHAW, JAMES, a skipper in Leith, test., 1771, C.E. [NRS]
SHAW, JOHN, a writer in Edinburgh, a sasine, 1753. [NRS.RS27.142.185]
SHAW, JOHN, an upholsterer in Edinburgh, a sasine, 1758. [NRS.RS27.151.333]
SHAW, JOHN, a merchant in Edinburgh, register of bonds, 1757-1770. [NRS.CS228.MISC.24/5]
SHAW, SAMUEL, a brewer burgess of Canongate, 1728. [CBR]
SHEARER, ARCHIBALD, a journeyman wright in Edinburgh, a sasine, 1759. [NRS.RS27.155.67]

The People of Edinburgh, 1725-1775

SHEARER, RACHEL, in Edinburgh, a deed, 1775. [NRS.RD4.218/108]
SHEDDEN, PATRICK, a tailor in St Mary's Wynd, Canongate, a deed, 1751. [NRS.RD2.171/2.136]
SHEILLS, DANIEL, a carter in Leith, sasines, 1752. [NRS.RS27.140.273/275]
SHEILLS, EDWARD, son of James Sheills a brewer in Portsburgh, appr. to Thomas Murray late deacon of the baxters of Edinburgh, 1742. [ERA]
SHEILLS, FRANCIS, a baker burgess of Edinburgh, 1771, former appr. of Walter Colvil a baker burgess. [EBR]
SHEILLS, HENRY, in North Leith, a burgess of Canongate, 1726. [CBR]
SHEILS, JOHN, a druggist burgess of Edinburgh, 1772. [EBR]
SHEPHERD, DAVID, a merchant burgess of Edinburgh, 1762. [EBR]
SHERIDAN, THOMAS, a burgess and guilds-brother of Edinburgh, 1761. [EBR]
SHERIFF, CHARLES, a merchant in Leith, 1748; a bond, 1751. [NRS.AC10.332; RD3.211/2.545]
SHERIFF, DAVID, son of William Sheriff a tobacconist, appr. to Alexander Dickson a smith burgess of Edinburgh, 1749. [ERA]
SHERIFF, GILBERT, a skipper at Leith Bridge, 1773; husband of Ann Drysdale, 1769. [SL.106][NRS.S/H][WED.71]
SHERIFF, WILLIAM, son of Alexander Sheriff a janitor, appr. to Hugh Barclay a clockmaker burgess of Edinburgh, 1727. [ERA]
SHERIFF and GUTHRIE, trading between Leith and South Carolina, 1765. [NRS.E504.22]
SHIPLEY, WILLIAM, a sailor in Leith, husband of Catherine ...., 1759. [SL.85]
SHIRREFF, JOHN, a slater in Leith, a deed, 1752. [NRS.RD2.172.237]
SHORT, JAMES, Fellow of the Royal Society, a burgess and guilds-brother of Edinburgh, 1766. [EBR]
SHORT, JAMES, a cooper burgess of Edinburgh, 1779, husband of Johan dau. of Robert Kennedy a cooper burgess. [EBR]
SHORT, THOMAS, an optician in Leith, a sasine, 1760. [NRS.RS27.156.382]
SHORT, THOMAS, in Edinburgh, a decreet, 1783. [NRS.CS17.1.2]
SIBBALD, DAVID, a smith burgess of Canongate, 1725. [CBR]
SIBBALD, JOHN, a smith burgess of Edinburgh, 1763, son of Patrick Sibbald a burgess. [EBR]
SIBBALD, JOHN, a smith burgess of Edinburgh, 1779, son of Thomas Sibbald a smith burgess. [EBR]
SIBBALD, PATRICK, son of John Sibbald a writer, appr. to James Angus a wright burgess of Edinburgh, 1738. [ERA]
SIBBALD, WILLIAM, a merchant burgess and guilds-brother of Edinburgh, 1770, former appr. to Robert and John Jamieson merchant burgesses and guild-brothers. [EBR]

The People of Edinburgh, 1725-1775

SIBLEY, JOHN, a sailor in Leith, husband of Anne Douglas, 1746. [SL.55]
SIEVEWRIGHT, JAMES, a combmaker burgess of Edinburgh, 1761. [EBR]
SILVER, WILLIAM, a tailor burgess of Canongate, 1732. [CBR]
SIME, JOHN, a carpenter in Leith, a deed, 1752. [NRS.RD4.178/2.505]
SIME, JOHN, a shipbuilder in North Leith, 1746; a deed, 1752. [NRS.AC10.316; RD4.178/1.426]; a burgess and guilds-brother of Edinburgh, 1772, husband of Janet dau. of Alexander Lawson a merchant burgess and guilds-brother. [EBR]
SIME, JOHN, jr., a ship carpenter in Leith, a burgess and guilds-brother of Edinburgh, 1772, son of John Sime a ship carpenter burgess and guilds-brother. [EBR]
SIMPSON, ADAM, son of Mathew Simpson a minister, appr. to James Steel a saddler burgess of Edinburgh, 1730. [ERA]
SIMPSON, ALEXANDER, a merchant tailor in Edinburgh, a decreet, 1779. [NRS.AC7.58]
SIMPSON, ANDREW, son of James Simpson a writer, appr. to Charles Butter a wright burgess of Edinburgh, 1731. [ERA]
SIMPSON, ANDREW, a tobacconist in Leith, 1742. [NRS.AC10.299; AC11.225]
SIMPSON, DAVID, son of William Simpson a schoolmaster, appr. to Robert Hamilton a merchant burgess of Edinburgh, 1731. [ERA]
SIMPSON, GEORGE, a merchant tailor in Leith, 1741. [NRS.AC10.291]
SIMPSON, GEORGE, born 1732, a book-keeper from Edinburgh, to Jamaica in August 1749. [CLRO/AIA]
SIMPSON, JAMES, son of John Simpson, a jeweller at the Water of Leith, appr. to John Fairholm, deacon of the skinners of Edinburgh, 1763-1769. [ERA]; a burgess of Edinburgh, 1763. [EBR]
SIMPSON, JAMES, a baker burgess of Edinburgh, 1769, former appr. of David Simpson a baker burgess. [EBR]
SIMPSON, JAMES, son of James Simpson a schoolmaster, appr. to James Scott, a merchant in Edinburgh, 1765-1770. [ERA]
SIMPSON, JOHN, a merchant in Leith, husband of Ann Mosman, a sasine, 1754. [NRS.RS27.143.90]
SIMPSON, RICHARD, a merchant burgess and guilds-brother of Edinburgh, 1771. [EBR]
SIMPSON, ROBERT, son of James Simpson, appr. to John Livingston a candlemaker burgess of Edinburgh, 1728. [ERA]
SIMPSON, ROBERT, son of Alexander Simpson a workman, appr. to Claud Inglis a merchant burgess of Edinburgh, 1751. [ERA]
SIMPSON, WILLIAM, a slater in Leith, 1748; a sasine, 1755. [NRS.AC11.181; RS27.145.206]

The People of Edinburgh, 1725-1775

SIMPSON, WILLIAM, from Edinburgh, Chief Justice of Georgia in 1763, probate 1768 Georgia. [NRS.NRAS#0771]

SIMPSON, WILLIAM, son of Charles Simpson in Edinburgh, appr. to Nicol Somerville, a painter in Edinburgh, 1770-1778. [ERA]

SINCLAIR, ALEXANDER, son of John Sinclair a barber in Canongate, appr. to Norman McPherson, a watchmaker in Edinburgh, 1767-1773. [ERA]

SINCLAIR, ANGUS, in Edinburgh, 1744. [NRS.AC11.161]

SINCLAIR, DANIEL, a sailor in Leith, husband of Catherine McGhie, 1759. [SL.85]

SINCLAIR, GUSTAVUS, a merchant in Edinburgh, trading with Boston, New England,1736; 1738. [NRS.AC13.1; AC10.246; AC7.43.493]

SINCLAIR, JOHN, a writer in Edinburgh, a sasine, 1759. [NRS.RS27.153.325]

SINCLAIR, NEIL, a merchant burgess of Edinburgh, 1772, son of Malcolm Sinclair a tailor burgess. [EBR]

SINCLAIR, WILLIAM, son of Angus Sinclair in Edinburgh, appr. to Hugh Gordon a jeweller in Edinburgh, 1740. [ERA]

SKAE, DAVID, a merchant burgess of Edinburgh, 1767, husband of Ann dau. of David Sloan a guilds-brother. [EBR]

SKELTON, GEORGE, son of John Skelton a writer, appr. to William Downie, a clock and watchmaker in Edinburgh, 1773-1780. [ERA]

SKENE, JOHN, in Edinburgh, a bond, 1773. [NRS.RD4.217/887]

SKIPPEN, WILLIAM, a burgess and guilds-brother of Edinburgh, 1761. [EBR]

SKIRVING, JOHN, a clock and watchmaker burgess of Edinburgh, 1772, husband of Janet dau. of John Paterson a merchant burgess and guilds-brother. [EBR]

SLATER, MARGARET, relict of James Jervy a skipper in Leith, test., 1738, C.E. [NRS]

SLEATH, JOSEPH, a sailor in Leith, husband of Janet Walker, 1759. [SL.87]

SLOAS, DAVID, son of John Sloas a gauger, appr. to Gavin Hamilton, John Balfour, and Patrick Neill, printers in Edinburgh, 1751. [ERA]

SLOZER, CHARLES, from Edinburgh, in Boston, New England, 1762. [SCS]

SMALL, CHARLES, son of Thomas Small a journeyman tailor, appr. to William Innes, a barber and wigmaker in Edinburgh, 1763-1769. [ERA]; a burgess of Edinburgh, 1770. [EBR]

SMALL, JOHN, a sailor in Leith, 1757. [ECL.38]

SMART, ARCHIBALD, a candle-maker in Canongate, a burgess there in 1726, husband of Ann Morton, a sasine, 1754. [NRS.RS27.143.106][CBR]

SMART, THOMAS, a sailor in Leith, husband of Janet Law, 1728. [SL.24]

SMITH, ADAM, a flesher in Leith, 1735. [NRS.AC11.89]

SMITH, DAVID, a vintner burgess of Canongate, 1728. [CBR]

The People of Edinburgh, 1725-1775

SMITH, DONALD, in Edinburgh, a bond, 1775. [NRS.RD4.218/67]

SMITH, DUNCAN, son of Archibald Smith a workman in Canongate, appr. to John McCoul, a shoemaker in Edinburgh, 1763-1769. [ERA]

SMITH, GEORGE, son of John Smith in Edinburgh, appr. to James Beatson a baxter burgess of Edinburgh, 1736. [ERA]

SMITH, GEORGE, a skipper in North Leith, test., 1743, C.E. [NRS]

SMITH, GILBERT, a merchant in Edinburgh, 1750. [NRS.AC10.355]

SMITH, JAMES, son of Alexander Smith a farmer, appr. to Thomas Dunlop a wright burgess of Edinburgh, 1730. [ERA]

SMITH, JAMES, jr., a writer in Edinburgh, married Katherine Ferguson, in South Leith on 14 November 1747. [LER]

SMITH, JANET, wife of Alexander Hay a wright in Edinburgh, heir toher brother John, son of William Smith tenant in Nethershiels, 1778. [NRS.S/H]

SMITH, JOHN, born 1708, a husbandman from Edinburgh, to Jamaica in May 1731. [CLRO/AIA]

SMITH, JOHN, a tailor burgess of Canongate, 1726. [CBR]

SMITH, JOHN, son of Thomas Smith a brewer in the Abbey of Holyroodhouse, appr. to Arthur Miller a merchant, 1755. [ERA]

SMITH, JOHN, of Christiansands, Norway, a burgess and guilds-brother of Edinburgh, 1761. [EBR]

SMITH, JOHN, a smith burgess of Edinburgh, 1767, husband of Grizel dau. of William Graham a saddler burgess. [EBR]

SMITH, JOHN, a skipper on Dub Row, Leith, 1773. [WED.71]; a burgess and guilds-brother of Edinburgh, 1778, husband of Rachael, dau. of John Cleland a merchant burgess and guilds-brother. [EBR]

SMITH, MARGARET, wife of James Shaw a writer in Leith, heir to her father John Smith a baker in Haddington, 1773. [NRS.S/H]

SMITH, MARY, born 1750, from Edinburgh, to New York in April 1775. [TNA.T47.12]

SMITH, PETER, a shoemaker burgess of Edinburgh, 1762, son of James Smith a shoemaker burgess. [EBR]

SMITH, ROBERT, a burgess and guilds-brother of Edinburgh, 1764. [EBR]

SMITH, ROBERT, son of William Smith a journeyman smith, appr. to David Robertson, a locksmith in Edinburgh, 1771-1777. [ERA]

SMITH, ROBERT, a wright burgess of Edinburgh, 1777, son of James Smith in Edinburgh. [EBR]

SMITH, THOMAS, son of Thomas Smith in Edinburgh, appr. to David Baird and David Inglis merchant burgesses of Edinburgh, 1739. [ERA]

SMITH, THOMAS, a skipper on The Shore, Leith, 1773. [WED.71]

The People of Edinburgh, 1725-1775

SMITH, THOMAS, a merchant burgess and guilds-brother of Edinburgh, 1776, former appr. of James Inglis a merchant burgess and guilds-brother.[EBR]

SMITH, THOMAS LOUGHTON, from South Carolina, a burgess and guilds-brother of Edinburgh, 1769. [EBR]

SMITH, WALTER, son of William Smith clerk to the Chancery, appr. to George Stevenson, a wright in Edinburgh, 1756-1762. [ERA]; a wright burgess and guilds-brother of Edinburgh, 1769, son of William Smith a writer burgess and guilds-brother. [EBR]

SMITH, WILLIAM, son of Walter Smith a minister, appr. to Robert Antonius a wright burgess of Edinburgh, 1725. [ERA]

SMITH, WILLIAM, son of Walter Smith a lecturer, appr. to Adam Lindsay a surgeon apothecary burgess of Edinburgh, 1727. [ERA]

SMITH, WILLIAM, a gardener burgess of Canongate, 1728. [CBR]

SMITH, WILLIAM, son of James Smith a dyster, appr. to John Christie a baxter burgess of Edinburgh, 1730. [ERA]

SMITH, WILLIAM, a merchant burgess and guilds-brother of Edinburgh, 1763, [EBR], trading with New York, 1766. [NRS.CS16.1.126]

SMITH, WILLIAM, a skipper in Leith, 1762; on The Shore, Leith, 1773. [South Leith Kirk Session Records, 15.7.1762][WED.71]

SMITH, WILLIAM, a grocer burgess of Edinburgh, 1772. [EBR]

SMITH, WILLIAM, a skipper in North Leith, 1773. [WED.71]

SMITH, WILLIAM, son of Alexander Smith a weaver, appr. to George Winter, a barber and wigmaker in Edinburgh, 1775-1781. [ERA]

SMITON, ALEXANDER, son of George Smith a writer, appr. to Robert Low a goldsmith in Edinburgh, 1754. [ERA]

SMITON, GEORGE, son of George Smiton a writer, appr. to James Baillie and James Seton merchants in Edinburgh, 1749. [ERA]

SMITON, GEORGE, paymaster aboard <u>HMS Guadaloupe</u>, son of George Smiton a writer in Edinburgh and his wife Janet Edmond, 1764. [NRS.S/H]

SMITON, JAMES, son of John Smiton a tailor, appr. to John Gilchrist a barber wigmaker burgess of Edinburgh, 1726. [ERA]

SMITON, JOHN, a sailor in Leith, 1740. [SL.45]

SOMERS, JAMES, a comb-maker in Edinburgh, a sasine, 1753. [NRS.RS27.141.410]

SOMERVAIL, RICHARD, son of James Somervail a mason, appr. to Andrew Miller a mason burgess of Edinburgh, 1731. [ERA]

SOMERVEIL, SAMUEL, a baxter burgess of Edinburgh, 1762, former appr. to Robert Allen a baxter burgess. [EBR]

SOMERVELL, NICOL, a painter in Edinburgh, a sasine, 1757. [NRS.RS27.149.180]

The People of Edinburgh, 1725-1775

SOMERVILLE, JAMES, son of John Somerville a gunsmith in Canongate, appr. to Walter Ruddiman and John Richardson, printers in Edinburgh, 1760-1766. [ERA]

SOMERVILLE, JOHN, a sailor in Leith, husband of Jean Lovette, 1749. [SL.63]

SOMERVILLE, JOSEPH, a sailor in Leith, husband of Helen Callander, 1763; at Coalhill, Leith, 1773. [SL.96][WED.71]

SOMERVILLE, PATRICK, a sailor in Leith, husband of Cockburn Christie, 1774. [SL.111]

SOMERVILLE, PETER, a sailor in Leith, husband of Isobel Drysdale, 1751. [SL.67]

SOMERVILLE, WILLIAM, a sailor in Leith, dead by 1741, husband of Catherine Robertson. [SL.45]

SOMMERS, THOMAS, a merchant burgess and guilds-brother of Edinburgh, 1762, husband of Ann dau. of James Abercrombie a merchant burgess and guilds-brother. [EBR]

SPALDING, ALEXANDER, son of John Spalding a saddler, appr. to Edward Lothian, a goldsmith in Edinburgh, 1759-1766. [ERA]

SPALDING, CHARLES, a merchant burgess and guilds-brother of Edinburgh, 1766. [EBR]

SPALDING, JAMES, son of Thomas Spalding of Leith Milnes, appr. to Edward Caithness a merchant burgess and guilds-brother of Edinburgh, 1751. [ERA]

SPALDING, JAMES, son of James Spalding in Bonnington Mill, a merchant from Edinburgh, to East Florida and Georgia by 1772. [NRS.GD174; RD4.259.758; CS16.1.138; RS27.201.215]

SPALDING, JAMES, a merchant burgess of Edinburgh, 1776. [EBR]

SPANKIE, GEORGE, a tailor in Edinburgh, a sasine, 1758. [NRS.RS27.152.348]

SPANKIE, GEORGE, son of George Spankie a tailor, appr. to William Mercer, a merchant in Edinburgh, 1771-1776. [ERA]; a burgess and guilds-brother of Edinburgh, 1779. [EBR]

SPANKIE, JAMES, in Edinburgh, a deed, 1767. [NRS.RD3.234/176]

SPARK, JOHN, son of Robert Spark a gardener at the Dean, Edinburgh, appr. to Alexander Aberdower, a founder in Edinburgh, 1762-1768. [ERA]

SPEIRS, ALEXANDER, born 1714, a merchant from Edinburgh, settled in Elderslie, Virginia, died in Glasgow 1782. [NRS.B10.15.5943]

SPENCE, DAVID, son of David Spence a Writer to the Signet, appr. to John Campbell a surgeon apothecary burgess and guilds-brother of Edinburgh, 1744. [ERA]

SPENCE, HENRY, a writer in Edinburgh, 1741. [NRS.AC11.141]

SPENCE, JAMES, a hairdresser burgess of Edinburgh, 1772. [EBR]

SPENCE, JOHN, a painter burgess of Edinburgh, 1768, son of William Spence a painter burgess. [EBR]

The People of Edinburgh, 1725-1775

SPENCE, LAWRENCE, a writer in Edinburgh, a decreet, 1783. [NRS.CS17.1.2]

SPENCE, THOMAS, a weaver in Edinburgh, husband of Helen Watt, parents of Ann, a sasine, 1760. [NRS.RS27.156.125]

SPENCE, WALTER, born 1750, a merchant from Edinburgh, to Georgia in July 1775. [TNA.T47.12]

SPENCE, WILLIAM, appr. to James Norrie a painter in Edinburgh, 1727. [ERA]

SPENCE, WILLIAM, a tailor from Edinburgh, to America before 1783. [NRS.CS17.1.2.79]

SPENS, NATHANIEL, a surgeon in Edinburgh, husband of Mary Mulliken, Episcopalians in Edinburgh, 1757. [DUAS.BrMsDC3/12]

SPOTTISWOOD, JOHN, a merchant burgess of Edinburgh, 1775, former appr. to Thomas Rannie a merchant burgess. [EBR]

SPOTTISWOOD, MAURICE, a baker burgess of Edinburgh, 1778, former appr. of George Home a baker burgess. [EBR]

SPROTT, ALEXANDER, a merchant burgess and guilds-brother of Edinburgh, 1769, son of John Sprott a candlemaker burgess and guildsbrother. [EBR]

SPROTT, JOHN, a skinner burgess of Edinburgh, 1770, son of Mark Sprott a skinner burgess. [EBR]

SPROTT, ROBERT, a candlemaker burgess and guilds-brother of Edinburgh, 1764, son of John Sprott a candlemaker burgess and guilds-brother. [EBR]

SPROTT, THOMAS, a candlemaker burgess of Edinburgh, 1761, former appr. to John Sprott a candlemaker burgess. [EBR]

SPROUL, DAVID, appr. to James Cumming a barber in Edinburgh, 1727. [ERA]

SQUAIR, JOHN, son of John Squair, appr. to James Squair a freeman flesher of Edinburgh, 1729. [ERA]

STEADMAN, JOHN, son of James Stedman, appr. to John Moir, a merchant in Edinburgh, 1766-1771. [ERA]

STEADMAN, WILLIAM, a sailor in Leith, husband of Janet Grieve, 1768. [SL.106]

STEEL, ALEXANDER, a chairmaster burgess of Edinburgh, 1778. [EBR]

STEELE, GEORGE, in Edinburgh, a deed, 1775. [NRS.RD3.234/780]

STEEL, HUGH, a skipper on The Shore, Leith, 1773. [WED.71]

STEEL, ROBERT, from Edinburgh, in Boston, New England, 1756. [SCS]

STEEL, ROBERT, a merchant burgess of Edinburgh, 1772. [EBR]

STEILL, ADAM, a silk dyer burgess of Edinburgh, 1769, son of Adam Steill a baker burgess. [EBR]

STEILL, GEORGE, a skipper in Leith, 1750. [NRS.AC10.348]

STEILL, PATRICK, son of James Steill a sclaiter, appr. to Adam Anderson a barber burgess of Edinburgh, 1739. [ERA]

STENHOUSE, JAMES, a horse seller burgess of Edinburgh, 1765, husband of Anne dau. of William Merrylees a weaver burgess. [EBR]

The People of Edinburgh, 1725-1775

STENHOUSE, JOHN, a skipper in South Leith, test., 1729, C.E. [NRS]
STENHOUSE, THOMAS, son of Thomas Stenhouse, a smith burgess of Canongate, 1732. [CBR]
STENNIS, JOHN, a skipper in Leith, burgess of St Andrews, 1727. [NRS.B65.8.7]
STEPHEN, JAMES, a skipper in Leith, husband of Elizabeth Messon, 1748. [SL.60]
STEPHEN, JOHN, a merchant in Leith, 1735. [NRS.AC10.215]
STEPHEN, JOHN, a merchant in Edinburgh, 1742/1743. [NRS.AC10.305; AC11.226]
STEPHENS, THOMAS, a sailor in Leith, 1743. [ECL.28]
STEVEN, JAMES, a sailor in Leith, husband of Christian Baillie, 1726, 1747. [SL.22][ECL.31]
STEVEN, JOHN, in Edinburgh, a deed, 1773. [NRS.RD4.217/224]
STEVENSON, ALEXANDER, son of Alexander Stevenson a merchant, appr. to Patrick Haddoway a baxter in Edinburgh, 1739. [ERA]
STEVENSON, ALEXANDER, son of Alexander Stevenson in Edinburgh, appr. to James Young a bookbinder in Edinburgh, 1747. [ERA]
STEVENSON, ANDREW, son of James Stevenson, appr. to Charles Hoburn a barber wigmaker burgess of Edinburgh, 1725. [ERA]
STEVENSON, ANDREW, a writer burgess and guilds-brother of Edinburgh, 1765, husband of Frances dau. of Reverend James Hart in Edinburgh.[EBR]
STEVENSON, DAVID, in Leith, a deed, 1775. [NRS.RD2.207/1.954]
STEVENSON, JOHN, Professor of Philosophy at Edinburgh University, 1735. [NRS.AC11.88]; account book, from 1740, died 1776. [NRS.CS229.MISC.15/6]
STEVENSON, JOHN, appr. to Alexander Stevenson a stabler's servant, appr. to John Ferguson a coppersmith burgess of Edinburgh, 1741. [ERA]
STEVENSON, JOHN, a skipper in Leith, husband of Margaret Ferguson, 1775. [NRS.S/H]
STEVENSON, JOHN, son of John Stevenson a wright in Potterrow, Edinburgh, appr. to Robert Dewar, a glazier in Edinburgh, 1773-1779. [ERA]
STEVENSON, ROBERT, born 1708, a book-binder from Edinburgh, to Antigua in August 1728. [CLRO/AIA]
STEVENSON, ROBERT, a horse-hirer in Pleasance, a burgess of Canongate, 1733. [CBR]
STEVENSON, ROBERT, a burgess and guilds-brother of Edinburgh, 1763, son of Robert Stevenson a merchant burgess and guilds-brother. [EBR]
STEVENSON, WILLIAM, a teacher of book-keeping burgess and guilds-brother of Edinburgh, 1766. [EBR]
STEWART, ALEXANDER, son of Peter Stewart a writer, appr. to James Gordon a saddler burgess of Edinburgh, 1725. [ERA]

The People of Edinburgh, 1725-1775

STEWART, ALEXANDER, a barber and wigmaker burgess of Edinburgh, 1777, former appr. to John Stewart a barber and wigmaker burgess. [EBR]

STEWART, ANDREW, from Edinburgh, settled at Massacre Rivulet, Dominica, in 1763. [PCCol.4.568]

STEWART, ANTHONY, a merchant from Edinburgh, settled in Annapolis, Maryland, 1753. [NRS.CS17.1.2][TNA.AO12.6.322]

STEWART, ARCHIBALD, a merchant in Edinburgh,1743; member of the Carruber's Close Episcopal congregation, husband of Charlotte Baillie, parents of John baptised 1754. [DUAS.BrMS3.Dc/12][NRS.AC11.226]

STEWART, CHARLES, son of Duncan Stewart a shoemaker, appr. to William Downie, a watchmaker in Edinburgh, 1767-1774. [ERA]

STEWART, DAVID, a skinner burgess of Edinburgh, 1763, husband of Katherine dau. of Archibald Colquhoun a skinner burgess. [EBR]

STEWART, DAVID, a merchant burgess and guilds-brother of Edinburgh, 1777, former appr. of John Coutts a merchant burgess and guilds-brother. [EBR]

STEWART, GABRIEL or GILBERT, a blacksmith from Calton, Edinburgh, transported to the colonies in January 1767. [NRS.HCR.I.99][SM.29.221]

STEWART, GEORGE, son of James Stewart an attorney in the Court of the Exchequer, appr. to William Hogg a merchant in Edinburgh, 1737. [ERA]

STEWART, GEORGE, born 14 May 1765, son of Lewis Stewart and his wife Elizabeth Steel, died 21 February 1771. [St Cuthbert's MI, Edinburgh]

STEWART, GILBERT, in Edinburgh, a letter, 1733. [NRS.GD38.2.4.96]

STEWART, JAMES, son of Patrick Stewart a mason, appr. to James Troup late deacon of the weavers in Edinburgh, 1730. [ERA]

STEWART, JAMES, son of James Stewart a wigmaker, appr. to John Blair a wigmaker and barber burgess of Edinburgh, 1731, [ERA]; a barber and wigmaker in Edinburgh, husband of Margaret Cook, a sasine, 1757. [NRS.RS27.149.307]

STEWART, JAMES, son of James Stewart in Edinburgh, appr. to William Boreland a weaver burgess of Edinburgh, 1736. [ERA]

STEWART, JAMES, son of James Stewart an attorney in the Exchequer, appr. to George Chalmers a merchant in Edinburgh, 1747. [ERA]

STEWART, JAMES, a merchant burgess of Edinburgh, 1762, husband of Katherine dau. of James Aytoun a perfumer burgess. [EBR]

STEWART, JAMES, born 1752, a clerk or book-keeper from Edinburgh, to Philadelphia in October 1774. [TNA.T47.9/11]

STEWART, JAMES, a boy from George Watson's Hospital, appr. to Claud Inglis, a merchant in Edinburgh, 1767-1772. [ERA]

The People of Edinburgh, 1725-1775

STEWART, JAMES, a merchant burgess and guilds-brother of Edinburgh, 1774; son of James Stewart a merchant burgess and former appr. to Claud Inglis a merchant burgess and guilds-brother. [EBR]

STEWART, JOHN, son of James Stewart an attorney in the Exchequer, appr. to Andrew Bonnar a merchant in Edinburgh, 1745. [ERA]; a burgess and guilds-brother of Edinburgh, 1764. [EBR]

STEWART, MANSFIELD, son of David Stewart a merchant, appr. to James Thompson, a skinner in Edinburgh, 1768-1774. [ERA]

STEWART, MARJORY, in Edinburgh, a tack, 1773. [NRS.RD3.134/451]

STEWART, PATRICK, a wigmaker in Edinburgh, 1729. [NRS.AC10.153]

STEWART, PATRICK, son of James Stewart, a merchant and late bailie of Edinburgh, a sasine, 1753. [NRS.RS27.142.8]

STEWART, PETER, a goldsmith in Edinburgh, test., 1741, C.E. [NRS]

STEWART, RICHARD, born 1754, a baker from Edinburgh, to Maryland in May 1774. [TNA.T47.9/11]

STEWART, ROBERT, son of James Stewart in Canongate, appr. to Andrew Stroak a weaver burgess of Edinburgh, 1738. [ERA]

STEWART, THOMAS, son of William Stewart a grocer, appr. to William Fraser, a white iron-smith in Edinburgh, 1772-1779. [ERA]

STEWART, WALTER, an advocate burgess and guilds-brother of Edinburgh, 1761. [EBR]

STEWART, WILLIAM, son of William Stewart a merchant, appr. to William Gilchrist, a goldsmith in Edinburgh, 1772-1779. [ERA]

STEWART, WILLIAM, a merchant burgess and guilds-brother of Edinburgh, husband of Alexandrina dau. of John Gray a barber and wigmaker burgess and guilds-brother, 1775. [EBR]

STILL, ROBERT, a merchant burhess of Edinburgh, 1763, husband of Elizabeth dau. of Adam Anderson a pewterer and grand-dau. of James Raitt a pewterer burgess and guilds-brother. [EBR]

STIRLING, ALEXANDER, a wigmaker in Edinburgh, heir to his grandfather Alexander Gentles or Gentleman a writer in Falkirk, 1773. [NRS.SH]

STIRLING, CHARLES, son of William Stewart a surgeon, appr. to James Troup a weaver burgess of Edinburgh, 1735. [ERA]

STIRLING, GEORGE, son of John Stirling, a soldier from Edinburgh, died in Georgia, probate 1749 PCC

STIRLING, JAMES, a mathematician, born 1692, died 1770. [Greyfriars MI]

STIRLING, JAMES, a merchant in Edinburgh, a sasine, 1751. [NRS.RS27.138.376]

STIRLING, JOHN, son of John Stirling a teacher of English, appr. to James McKenzie a goldsmith burgess of Edinburgh, 1749. [ERA]

The People of Edinburgh, 1725-1775

STOBIE, JAMES, son of James Stobie a merchant in Charleston, appr. to John Young, a locksmith in Edinburgh, 1773-1779. [ERA]

STOBS, JOHN, a sailor in Leith, husband of Elizabeth Sanderson, 1733. [SL.36]

STOCKEL, JOSEPH, a merchant burgess and guilds-brother of Edinburgh, 1772. [EBR]

STOCKTON, ROCHARD, a Councillor at Law in New Jersey, a burgess and guilds-brother of Edinburgh, 1767. [EBR]

STODDART, ADAM, son of James Stoddart, appr. to John Stenhouse a merchant burgess of Edinburgh, 1747. [ERA]

STODDART, JAMES, in Edinburgh, a deed, 1762. [NRS.RD2.218/1229]

STODDART, ROBERT, son of John Stoddart, appr. to Patrick Cargill a cutler burgess of Edinburgh, 1748. [ERA]

STODDART, WILLIAM, a merchant burgess and guilds-brother of Edinburgh, 1767, former appr. of Alexander Johnston a merchant burgess, [EBR]; trading between Leith and South Carolina, 1775. [NRS.E504.22]

STODDART and FAIRBAIRN, merchants in Edinburgh, trading with Jamaica and Antigua, 1767-1787. [NRS.CS96.147, etc]

STORRIE, GEORGE, a baker burgess of Edinburgh, 1775, former appr. of Walter Colvil a baker burgess. [EBR]

STORRY, JOHN, a sailor in Leith, heir to his great grandfather James Littlejohn a groom and burgess of Linlithgow, 1773. [NRS.S/H]

STORY, HELEN, dau. of Gilbert Story a maltster in Leith, a decreet, 1777. [NRS.CS16.1.171]

STOVE, MAGNUS, a sailor in Leith, aboard the <u>Concord</u> bound for the West Indies, 1732. [SL.35]

STRACHAN, DAVID, a merchant in Leith, a sasine, 1751. [NRS.SC27.138.65]

STRACHAN, GEORGE, son of George Strachan a journeyman, appr. to William Thomson in Edinburgh, 1772-1777. [ERA]

STRACHAN, JOHN, a merchant burgess of Edinburgh, 1766, son of David Strachan a merchant in Leith, a burgess and guilds-brother. [EBR]

STRAITON, ARCHIBALD, son of Charles Straiton, appr. to Alexander Brownlie a watchmaker burgess of Edinburgh, 1726. [ERA]

STRATTON, ARTHUR, son of Arthur Stratton, a barber in Edinburgh, a sasine, 1754. [NRS.SC27.144.219]

STRATTON, CHARLES, shipmaster in Leith, deceased, husband of Margaret Garrioch, a sasine, 1753. [NRS.RS27.142.290]

STRONG, JAMES, a skipper at Leith Bridge, 1773. [WED.71]

STRONG, LAWRENCE, a skipper at Leith Bridge, 1773, master of the <u>Shetland Packet</u>. [WED.71]

STRONG, ROBERT, a merchant at Leith Bridge, 1748. [NRS.AC11.180]

The People of Edinburgh, 1725-1775

STUART, CHARLES, a shoemaker burgess of Edinburgh, 1770, husband of Margaret, dau. of Andrew Low a shoemaker burgess. [EBR]

STUART, DONALD, a chair-master burgess of Edinburgh, 1769. [EBR]

STUART, DOUGALD, a professor at Edinburgh University, a burgess and guilds-brother of Edinburgh, 1775. [EBR]

STUART, JAMES, a chairman from Edinburgh, transported to Antigua in December 1752. [AJ#260]

STUART, JAMES, a druggist burgess and guilds-brother of Edinburgh, 1767, husband of Margaret, dau. of Alexander Duncan a druggist burgess and guilds-brother. [EBR]

STUART, JOHN, a burgess and guilds-brother of Edinburgh, 1765. [EBR]

STURROCK, ALEXANDER, a smith burgess of Edinburgh, 1771, former appr. to Thomas Sibbald a smith burgess. [EBR]

SUDDLETON, JOHN, a mariner in Leith, husband of Agnes Bruce, 1764. [SL.99]

SULLIVAN, RICHARD, a sailor in Leith, died in Jamaica, 1744. [ECL.29]

SUMMERS, JAMES, a writer in Edinburgh, a decreet, 1772. [NRS.CS16.1.148]

SUMMERS, THOMAS, a glazier burgess of Edinburgh, 1766, former appr. of David Alston a glazier burgess. [EBR]

SUTHERLAND, ALEXANDER, only son of William Swan, a brewer in Edinburgh, a sasine, 1756. [NRS.SC27.148.42]

SUTHERLAND, ANN, wife of Richard Vernan a shoemaker in Edinburgh, heir of her father James Sutherland a founder there, 1774. [NRS.S/H]

SUTHERLAND, JAMES, a merchant in Leith, 1740. [NRS.AC11.126]

SUTHERLAND, ROBERT, a sailor in Leith, husband of Grizel Provan, 1754. [NRS.S/H]

SUTHERLAND, WILLIAM, a tailor in North Leith, a burgess of Canongate, 1733. [CBR]

SUTHERLAND, WILLIAM, a brewer in Edinburgh, 1749. [NRS.AC11.186]

SUTHERLAND, WILLIAM, son of Alexander Sutherland a breeches maker, appr. to Peter Smith, a shoemaker in Edinburgh, 1765-1771. [ERA]

SUTHERLAND, WILLIAM, a merchant burgess of Edinburgh, 1774, husband of Isobel, dau. of Alexander Noble a burgess. [EBR]

SUTOR, JAMES, a sailor in Leith, husband of Magdalene Robertson, 1761. [SL.91]

SWAN, JAMES, a barber and wig-maker burgess of Edinburgh, 1777, former appr. to James Innes a freeman burgess barber wigmaker and hairdresser. [EBR]

SWAN, ROBERT, eldest son of James Swan, sometime a tailor in Edinburgh, a sasine, 1757. [NRS.RRS27.150.157]

SWINTON, JAMES, son of Andrew Swinton a sergeant, appr. to John Balfour a locksmith burgess of Edinburgh, 1725. [ERA]

SYME, ALEXANDER, a painter in Edinburgh, a sasine, 1755. [NRS.SC27.145.96]

SYME, ANDREW, a cooper in Edinburgh, a sasine, 1756. [NRS.SC27.147.136]

SYME, ANDREW, son of Andrew Syme a merchant, appr. to David Robertson, a skinner in Edinburgh, 1770-1775. [ERA]

SYME, GEORGE, a slater in Edinburgh, a sasine, 1759, [NRS.SC27.154.209]; a burgess and guilds-brother of Edinburgh, 1765. [EBR]

SYME, HENRY, a baker in Portsburgh, a burgess of Edinburgh, 1776, husband of Marion, dau. of William Callander a merchant burgess. [EBR]

SYME, JAMES, a slater in Edinburgh, a sasine, 1757. [NRS.SC27.148.391]

SYME, JAMES, a glover and skinner burgess of Edinburgh, 1763, son of David Syme a glover. [EBR]

SYME, JAMES, a lint-dresser burgess of Edinburgh, 1768. [EBR]

SYMMER, ALEXANDER, a writer in Edinburgh, 1733. [NRS.AC10.203; AC11.69]

SYMMER, ALEXANDER, son of Alexander Symmer a bookseller and his wife Elizabeth Forrest, a merchant from Edinburgh, to Maryland before 1756. [SM.18.524]

SYMMER, ANDREW, son of Alexander Symmer, a merchant from Edinburgh, to Maryland before 1756. [SM.18.524]

SYMMERS, JAMES, a merchant burgess of Edinburgh, 1765. [EBR]

SYMONS, FREDERICK, a skipper in North Leith, 1773. [NRS.S/H]

SYMONS, SARAH, dau. of Frederick Symons a skipper in North Leith, test., 1752, C.E. [NRS]

TAAS, WILLIAM, son of John Taas a sawyer, appr. to William Taylor, a goldsmith in Edinburgh, 1764-1771. [ERA]

TAILFER, PATRICK, a physician from Edinburgh, settled on River Neuse, Georgia, in 1733. [TNA.CO5.70.106]

TAIT, ALEXANDER, a merchant in Edinburgh, 1728. [NRS.AC10.133]

TAIT, BENJAMIN, a goldsmith burgess of Edinburgh, 1763, former appr. of Alexander Aitchison a goldsmith burgess. [EBR]

TAIT, GEORGE, a smith burgess of Edinburgh, 1764, former appr. of George Aikin a smith burgess. [EBR]

TAIT, JAMES, conjunct deputy clerk, a burgess and guilds-brother of Edinburgh, 1763, son of James Tait a jeweller burgess. [EBR]; an indenture, 1766. [NRS.RD4.216/335]

TAIT, JOHN, a skipper in Leith, test., 1734, C.E. [NRS]

TAIT, PATRICK, in Edinburgh, a bond, 1771. [NRS.RD4.216/459]

TAIT, WILLIAM, son of John Tait a servant, appr. to George Aitken a locksmith burgess of Edinburgh, 1736. [ERA]

The People of Edinburgh, 1725-1775

TARBUT, ROBERT, a sailor in Leith, 1730. [SL.29]
TAIT, JAMES, a wright burgess of Edinburgh, 1772, son and former appr. of James Tate senior a wright burgess. [EBR]
TAWSE, JOHN, a writer in Edinburgh, a decreet, 1776. [NRS.CS16.1.168]
TAYLOR, ALEXANDER, late of Charleston, South Carolina, then in Caltonhill, Edinburgh, 1776, 1778. [NRS.RS27.229/231, etc]
TAYLOR, ALEXANDER, a wright burgess of Edinburgh, 1777, husband of Isabella, dau. of Robert Wight a wright burgess. [EBR]
TAYLOR, ARCHIBALD, son of John Taylor a weaver, appr. to Charles McLagan, an orris and livery lace maker in Edinburgh, 1774-1781. [ERA]
TAYLOR, DAVID, son of John Taylor, appr. to James Spittle a cordiner burgess of Edinburgh, 1726. [ERA]
TAYLOR, GEORGE, a sailor in Leith, husband of Penelope Ramsay, 1738. [SL.42]
TAYLOR, JAMES, son of James Taylor a Customs House waiter, appr. to Alexander Scott a merchant burgess and guilds-brother of Edinburgh, 1740. [ERA]
TAYLOR, JAMES, son of Robert Taylor a coachman, appr. to Alexander Fairbairn, a locksmith in Edinburgh, 1758-1764. [ERA]
TAYLOR, JOHN, an ale-seller, a burgess of Canongate, 1725. [CBR]
TAYLOR, JOHN, son of Andrew Taylor a tailor at Canongate Head, appr. to James Scott a barber burgess of Edinburgh, 1734. [ERA]
TAYLOR, JOHN, son of William Taylor in Edinburgh, appr. to David Scott a skinner burgess of Edinburgh, 1744. [ERA]
TAYLOR, JOHN, a mariner in Leith, husband of Margaret Grahame, 1762. [SL.94]
TAYLOR, JOHN, son of Robert Taylor a baker in Canongate, appr. to William Gilchrist, a goldsmith in Edinburgh, 1763-1770. [ERA]; a burgess of Edinburgh, 1763. [EBR]
TAYLOR, JOHN, son of Robert Taylor a bottle blower in Leith, appr. to John Taylor, a goldsmith in Edinburgh, 1764-1771. [ERA]
TAYLOR, ROBERT, from Edinburgh, in Boston, New England, 1731. [SCS]
TAYLOR, ROBERT, a founder in St Ninian's Row, Edinburgh, a sasine, 1752. [NRS.RS27.139.391]
TAYLOR, ROBERT, a sailor in Leith, husband of Jean Rannie, 1773. [SL.109]
TAYLOR, THOMAS, son of Thomas Taylor a merchant, appr. to Robert Orrock a barber wigmaker burgess of Edinburgh, 1728. [ERA]
TAYLOR, THOMAS, from Edinburgh, transported to the colonies in August 1753. [NRS.JC3.29.268]
TAYLOR, THOMAS, a baker burgess of Edinburgh, 1770, former appr. of John Middlemist a baker burgess. [EBR]

The People of Edinburgh, 1725-1775

TAYLOR, WILLIAM, appr. to Patrick Gibb a cordiner in Edinburgh, 1726. [ERA]

TAYLOR, WILLIAM, son of Robert Taylor a baxter in Canongate, appr. to William Gilchrist a goldsmith in Edinburgh, 1754. [ERA]

TELFER, JOHN, son of Samuel Telfer a minister, appr. to William Carmichael a merchant burgess of Edinburgh, 1728. [ERA]

TELFER, JOHN, a cow-feeder in Portsburgh, Edinburgh, and his wife Janet Aikman, a sasine, 1757. [NRS.RS27.149.44]

TELFERT, JOSEPH, a sailor in Leith, husband of Margaret Anderson, 1775. [SL.112]

TENNANT, CHARLES, a hair merchant burgess of Edinburgh, 1776, son of George Tennant a merchant. [EBR]

TENNANT, JOHN, a burgess and guilds-brother of Edinburgh, 1763. [EBR]

TENNANT, ROBERT, a merchant in Leith, 1740. [NRS.AC10.277]

THAIN, ALEXANDER, a merchant in Leith, a decreet, 1767. [NRS.CS16.1.130]

THOM, JAMES, a vintner burgess of Edinburgh, 1763. [EBR]

THOM, WALTER, from the Orphan Hospital, appr. to Patrick Thomson a freeman weaver burgess of Edinburgh, 1739. [ERA]

THOMKINS, LAURENCE, son of Sergeant William Thomkins, appr. to Charles Watkins a barber burgess of Edinburgh, 1737. [ERA]

THOMSON, ALEXANDER, a cordiner burgess of Canongate, 1726. [CBR]

THOMSON, ALEXANDER, a skipper from Leith, master of the John of Portsmouth, New Hampshire, 1739. [NRS.AC7.44.185]

THOMSON, ALEXANDER, son of James Thomson a brewer, appr. to James Johnston a freeman weaver burgess of Edinburgh, 1740. [ERA]

THOMSON, ALEXANDER, son of John Thomson in Edinburgh, appr. to Thomas Simpson a pewterer burgess of Edinburgh, 1748. [ERA]

THOMSON, ALEXANDER, son of Patrick Thomson a merchant, appr. to William Taylor, a goldsmith in Edinburgh, 1759-1766. [ERA]

THOMSON, ALEXANDER, a merchant burgess and guilds-brother of Edinburgh, 1766, husband of Lillias dau. of Alexander Anderson a merchant burgess and guilds-brother. [EBR]

THOMSON, ANDREW, a merchant in Edinburgh, trading with Maryland, 1745; 1748. [NRS.CS16.1.75; AC11.183]

THOMSON, ANDREW, a merchant in Edinburgh, later in New York, 1769. [NRS.CS16.1.134]

THOMSON, CHARLES, in Edinburgh, a deed, 1775. [NRS.RD4.218/79]

THOMSON, DAVID, a merchant burgess and guilds-brother of Edinburgh, 1768, former appr. of David Loch a merchant burgess and guilds-brother. [EBR]

THOMSON, DAVID, son of John Thomson a flax-dresser, appr. to Robert Gordon, a goldsmith in Edinburgh, 1762-1769. [ERA]

The People of Edinburgh, 1725-1775

THOMSON, ELIZABETH, in Edinburgh, a will, 1775. [NRS.RD4.215/514]
THOMSON, FRANCIS, son of Thomas Thomson a minister, appr. to John Dunsmuir a merchant in Edinburgh, 1747. [ERA]
THOMSON, GEORGE, master of Trinity House, Leith, 1741. [South Leith Kirk Session Records, 5.8.1741]
THOMSON, GEORGE, son of William Thomson a maltster burgess, appr. to George Nicol a merchant burgess of Edinburgh, 1744. [ERA]
THOMSON, JAMES, son of Alexander Thomson in Portsburgh, Edinburgh, appr. to Alexander Somervaill a tanner and merchant burgess of Edinburgh, 1729. [ERA]
THOMSON, JAMES, son of John Thomson a Writer to the Signet, appr. to William Hog a merchant burgess of Edinburgh, 1730. [ERA]
THOMSON, JAMES, son of Andrew Thomson a merchant burgess, appr. to Nathan Porteous a skinner burgess of Edinburgh, 1739. [ERA]
THOMSON, JAMES, a merchant in Edinburgh, 1742/1743. [NRS.AC10.305; AC11.22]
THOMSON, JAMES, a barber and wigmaker burgess of Edinburgh, 1765, son of James Thomson a wigmaker burgess. [EBR]
THOMSON, JAMES, a weaver burgess of Edinburgh, 1772, son of William Thomson a weaver burgess. [EBR]
THOMSON, JAMES, a skipper in Broad Wynd, Leith, 1773. [WED.78]
THOMSON, JAMES, a founder burgess of Edinburgh, 1775, son of Joseph Thomson a merchant burgess. [EBR]
THOMSON, JOHN, a sailor in Leith, husband of Margaret Ross, 1731. [SL.30]
THOMSON, JOHN, a skipper in Leith, dead by 1742. [SL.49]
THOMSON, JOHN, a merchant, died 1746, his wife Elizabeth Ronaldson died 1750. [Greyfriars MI, Edinburgh]
THOMSON, JOHN, appr. to his brother-german James Thomson a skinner in Edinburgh, 1752. [ERA]
THOMSON, JOHN, a journeyman wright in Edinburgh, a sasine, 1756. [NRS.RS27.148.320]
THOMSON, JOHN, from Edinburgh, a merchant in Charleston, probate, 1763, South Carolina.
THOMSON, JOHN, a carver and guilder burgess of Edinburgh, 1767. [EBR]
THOMSON, JOHN, a merchant burgess and guilds-brother of Edinburgh, 1769, son of Andrew Thomson a baxter burgess and guilds-brother. [EBR]
THOMSON, JOHN, a merchant burgess and guilds-brother of Edinburgh, 1771, former appr. of Thomas Rainnie a merchant burgess and guilds-brother. [EBR]
THOMSON, JOHN, a flesher burgess of Edinburgh, 1773, former appr. of John Melliss a flesher burgess. [EBR]

The People of Edinburgh, 1725-1775

THOMSON, JOHN, a merchant burgess and guilds-brother of Edinburgh, 1776. [EBR]

THOMSON, JOHN, a skipper in North Leith, husband of Euphemia Scott, 1766. [NRS.S/H][SL.106]; a skipper in Broad Wynd, Leith, 1773. [WED.78]; a burgess and guilds-brother of Edinburgh, 1772. [EBR]

THOMSON, MATTHEW, a writer in Edinburgh, a sasine, 1752. [NRS.RS27.140.42]

THOMSON, PATRICK, a merchant from Edinburgh, later in New York, 1768, 1769. [NRS.CS16.1.134; CS17.1.133]

THOMSON, PETER, son of Adam Thomson in Causewayside, Edinburgh, appr. to Alexander Thomson, a merchant in Edinburgh, 1772-1777. [ERA]

THOMSON, ROBERT, from Edinburgh, transported to Jamaica in January 1740. [NRS.JC3.23.13]

THOMSON, THOMAS, son of Robert Thomson a mason, appr. to Robert Brown, a founder in Edinburgh, 1770-1777. [ERA]

THOMSON, WILLIAM, a barber and wigmaker in Canongate, a burgess there in 1712, a sasine, 1751. [NRS.RS27.138.228][CBR]

THOMSON, WILLIAM, appr. to David MacLellan a wright in Edinburgh, 1726. [ERA]

THOMSON, WILLIAM, a merchant burgess and guilds-brother of Edinburgh, 1761. [EBR]

THOMSON, WILLIAM, son of John Thomson in Edinburgh, appr. to James Lightbody, a barber in Edinburgh, 1759-1764. [ERA]

THOMSON, WILLIAM, a druggist burgess and guilds-brother of Edinburgh, 1772, son of Adam Thomson a merchant burgess and guilds-brother. [EBR]

THORBURN, JOHN, a journeyman mason, a burgess of Edinburgh, 1771. [EBR]

TIBBETS, THOMAS, son of Thomas Tibbets a smith in Portsburgh, Edinburgh, appr. to Joseph Smeaton, a hatter in Edinburgh, 1763-1770. [ERA]; a burgess of Edinburgh, 1768. [EBR]

TOD, ALEXANDER, a skipper in Leith, test., 1745, C.E. [NRS]

TOD, ANDREW, son of John Tod a cutler, appr. to Patrick Cargill a cutler burgess of Edinburgh, 1734. [ERA]

TOD, Major CHARLES, of the East India Company at Madras, a burgess and guilds-brother of Edinburgh, 1765, son of Archibald Tod of Hayfield a burgess and guilds-brother. [EBR]

TODD, GEORGE, a mariner in Leith, husband of Agnes Rew, 1761; a skipper in Tolbooth Wynd, Leith, 1773; a burgess of Edinburgh, 1778. [ECL.14][WED.78][EBR]

TOD, JOHN, son of William Tod in Pleasance, Edinburgh, appr. to John Spalding, a saddler in Edinburgh, 1762-1768. [ERA]

The People of Edinburgh, 1725-1775

TOD, JOHN, son of Alexander Tod in Edinburgh, appr. to Alexander Aitchison, a goldsmith in Edinburgh, 1768-1775. [ERA]

TOD, OLIVER, a skipper in Leith, 1738. [NRS.S/H]

TOD, OLIVER, a merchant in Edinburgh trading with Jamaica, dead by 1762. [NRS.AC7.50]

TOD, PATRICK, a merchant in Edinburgh, a sasine, 1751. [NRS.RS27.138.409]

TOD, RICHARD, a merchant in Leith, 1745; a sasine, 1756; a bond, 1773. [NRS.AC11.165; RS27.147.198; RD4.216/209]

TOD, THOMAS, a merchant in Edinburgh, a sasine, 1759. [NRS.RS27.154.316]

TOD, WILLIAM, a merchant in Edinburgh, 1735; 1737; master of the Leith Linen Company, 1743; a sasine, 1759. [NRS.AC10.206/247/300; RS27.154.316]

TOD, WILLIAM, son of Alexander Tod in Edinburgh, appr. to William Anderson, a saddler in Edinburgh, 1761-1767. [ERA]

TOD, WILLIAM, a coach-builder from Edinburgh, to Philadelphia, Pennsylvania, before 1775. [NRS.RD4.718.858]

TOWART, JAMES, a merchant burgess of Edinburgh, 1769. [EBR]

TOWRIE, EDWARD, son of William Towrie a land surveyor of the Customs at Leith, appr. to Hart and Polson, linen drapers in Edinburgh, 1767-1772. [ERA]

TRAILL, GEORGE, a surgeon from Edinburgh, died in North America, probate 1759 PCC

TRANER, ARCHIBALD, a merchant in Edinburgh, a sasine, 1757. [NRS.RS27.149.332]

TROTTER, JOHN, a merchant burgess and guilds-brother of Edinburgh, 1766, husband of Mary, dau. of Robert Bartleman a baxter burgess and guilds-brother. [EBR]

TROTTER, THOMAS, a brewer in Edinburgh, a decreet, 1762. [NRS.CS16.1.114]

TROTTER, WILLIAM, a merchant burgess and guilds-brother of Edinburgh, son of Thomas Trotter a merchant burgess and guilds-brother. [EBR]

TROTTER, WILLIAM, a merchant burgess and guilds-brother of Edinburgh, 1763. [EBR]

TULLIDEPH, WALTER, in Antigua, a burgess and guilds-brother of Edinburgh, 1757. [EBR]

TULLY, THOMAS, a merchant burgess of Edinburgh, 1762, son of Thomas Tully a merchant burgess. [EBR]

TURNBULL, GEORGE, a writer in Edinburgh, nephew of George Turnbull in Haddington, a sasine, 1751. [NRS.RS27.138.126]

TURNBULL, GEORGE, son of George Turnbull a baker in Portsburgh, Edinburgh, appr. to Adam Murray, a baker in Edinburgh, 1770-1775. [ERA]

TURNBULL, JAMES, a merchant burgess and guilds-brother of Edinburgh, 1764. [EBR]

The People of Edinburgh, 1725-1775

TURNBULL, JAMES, son of James Turnbull a candlemaker in Pleasance, Edinburgh, appr. to Young and Trotter, upholsterers in Edinburgh, 1771-1776. [ERA]

TURNBULL, PATRICK, a goldsmith burgess of Edinburgh, test., 1725, C.E. [NRS]

TURNBULL, PATRICK, a skinner burgess of Edinburgh, 1762, son of William Turnbull a litster burgess. [EBR]

TURNBULL, RICHARD, a sailor in Leith, husband of Frances Warden, 1764. [SL.97]

TURNBULL, ROBERT, son of John Turnbull a farmer, appr. to John Turnbull a wright burgess of Edinburgh, 1728. [ERA]

TURNBULL, THOMAS, son of George Turnbull a baker in Potterrrow, Edinburgh, appr. to Arthur Miller, a merchant in Edinburgh, 1764-1769. [ERA]; a burgess of Edinburgh, 1771. [EBR]

TURNBULL, WILLIAM, a clock and watchmaker burgess of Edinburgh, 1770, former appr. to John Dalgleish a clock and watch maker burgess. [EBR]

TURPY, ALEXANDER, a boy from the Charity Workhouse, appr. to Patrick Taylor, a locksmith in Edinburgh, 1770-1776. [ERA]

TURPIE, WILLIAM, son of David Turpie a staymaker, appr. to Thomas Robertson a barber burgess of Edinburgh, 1731. [ERA]

TYRIE, JOHN, a writer in Edinburgh, a sasine, 1759. [NRS.RS27.153.438]

TYRIE, WILLIAM, son of Alexander Tyrie a porter, appr. to Alexander Nicolson a plumber burgess of Edinburgh, 1755. [ERA]

URE, JAMES, a jeweller in Edinburgh, test., 1755, C.E. [NRS]

URQUHART, ALEXANDER, a skipper in Tolbooth Wynd, Leith, 1773. [WED.79]

URQUHART, ANDREW, a mariner from Leith, escaped from Peterhead Tolbooth, 1743. [NRS.AC10.302]

URQUHART, JOHN, a tailor burgess of Edinburgh, 1762, husband of Elizabeth dau. of Alexander Coutts a tailor burgess. [EBR]

URQUHART, JOHN, son of Leonard Urquhart, a Writer to the Signet, appr. to John Hope and Company, merchants in Edinburgh, 1768-1773. [ERA]

URQUHART, LENNARD, a carpenter from Edinburgh, probate, 1758, South Carolina.

VAIR, Mrs JANET, widow of George Vair in South Carolina, and their dau. Margaret, in Edinburgh, a decreet, 1776. [NRS.CS16.1.168]

VAIR, WILLIAM, a peruke-maker in Edinburgh, a decreet, 1776. [NRS.CS16.1.168]

VALLANCE, GEORGE, a sailor in Leith, 1751. [SL.67]

VAN WYNGARDEN, HENRY, a merchant in Edinburgh, 1748. [NRS.AC11.183]

The People of Edinburgh, 1725-1775

VEITCH, GEORGE, a merchant burgess and guilds-brother of Edinburgh, 1764, former appr. to Adam Cleghorn and John Livingstone merchant burgesses and guild-brothers, [EBR]; trading with Virginia, 1768. [NRS.CS16.1.134]

VEITCH, JOHN, a marble-cutter in Edinburgh, a bond, 1771; a decreet, 1779. [NRS.RD2.217/2/184; CS16.1.175]

VEITCH, ROBERT, son of John Veitch a tailor, appr. to Norman McPherson, a clock and watch maker in Edinburgh, 1774-1781. [ERA]

VOGIL, JOHN, son of John Vogil a journeyman goldsmith, appr. to Charles Dickson a goldsmith in Edinburgh, 1748. [ERA]

WACHOPE, HENRY, a burgess and guilds-brother of Edinburgh, 1763. [EBR]

WADDELL, JAMES, a skipper on The Shore, Leith, 1773. [WED.84]

WADDELL, ROBERT, a writer in Edinburgh, sasines, 1759-1760. [NRS.RS27.154/324/38; 155/381]

WADDEL, WILLIAM, a smith burgess of Edinburgh, 1767. [EBR]

WAITE, WILLIAM, St David's Street, Edinburgh, a sasine, 1778. [NRS.RS27.240.226]

WALKER, ALEN, in Canongate, a deed, 1775. [NRS.RD4.217/952]

WALKER, ALEXANDER, nephew of Patrick Walker, in Canongate, a sasine, 1771. [NRS.RS27.194.67]

WALKER, ALEXANDER, a brewer in Canongate, heir to his father Alexander Walker a brewer there, 1775. [NRS.S/H]

WALKER, ANDREW, a mariner in Leith, husband of Mary Walker, 1730. [SL.29]

WALKER, CHARLES, son of William Walker a schoolmaster, appr. to James McKay a coppersmith in Edinburgh, 1754. [ERA]

WALKER, CHARLES, a vintner burgess and guilds-brother of Edinburgh, 1774, husband of Jean, dau. of Christopher Alexander a vintner burgess and guilds-brother. [EBR]

WALKER, GEORGE, a mariner in Leith, husband of Sarah Geyler, 1763; 1764. [SL.96][NRS.S/H]

WALKER, GEORGE, son of George Walker a fruit seller, appr. to George Hutchison, a painter in Edinburgh, 1775-1781. [ERA]

WALKER, JAMES, a writer in Leith, 1738. [NRS.AC11.111]

WALKER, JAMES, son of William Walker a schoolmaster, appr. to Patrick Murray a goldsmith burgess of Edinburgh, 1743. [ERA]

WALKER, JAMES, MA, born 1680, minister of Canongate from 1713 until his death on 3 March 1752, a burgess of Canongate in 1719, husband of Isobel Oliphant, parents of Samuel. [F.I.25][CBR]

WALKER, JAMES, a merchant in Edinburgh, 1742/1743. [NRS.AC10.305; AC11.226]

WALKER, JAMES, in Leith, a deed, 1751. [NRS.RD4.715/98]

The People of Edinburgh, 1725-1775

WALKER, JAMES, a merchant burgess of Edinburgh, 1778. [EBR]

WALKER, JOHN, son of John Walker a merchant in Leith, appr. to John Yetts a merchant burgess of Edinburgh, 1727. [ERA]

WALKER, JOHN, son of John Walker a porter, appr. to William Dick, a merchant in Edinburgh, 1764-1769. [ERA]

WALKER, JOHN, a merchant in Edinburgh, a sasine, 1775. [NRS.RS27.223.211]

WALKER, PATRICK, in Canongate, a sasine, 1771. [NRS.RS27.194.67]

WALKER, PATRICK, in Edinburgh, a bond, 1775. [NRS.RD3.234/80]

WALKER, ROBERT, son of James Walker a writer in Leith, appr. to Joseph Gibson a surgeon apothecary burgess of Edinburgh, 1734. [ERA]

WALKER, ROBERT, a mason in Edinburgh, a sasine, 1771. [NRS.RS27.191.273]

WALKER, WILLIAM, eldest son of James Walker minister in Canongate, appr. to Thomas Gardner a merchant burgess of Edinburgh, 1733. [ERA]

WALKER, WILLIAM, a sailor in Leith, husband of Isabel Simpson, 1739. [SL.43]

WALKER, WILLIAM, a writer in Edinburgh, a decreet, 1775. [NRS.CS16.1.161]

WALLACE, ALEXANDER, a mason in Leith, a sasine, 1772. [NRS.RS27.197.186]

WALLACE, ANDREW, appr. to Archibald Wallace a merchant in Edinburgh, 1726. [ERA]

WALLACE, CHARLES, a merchant burgess and guilds-brother of Edinburgh, 1766, son of Archibald Wallace a merchant burgess and guilds-brother. [EBR]

WALLACE, DAVID, a horse hirer burgess of Canongate, 1729. [CBR]

WALLACE, JAMES, a barber burgess of Edinburgh, 1761, husband of Annabella dau. of Robert Drummond a barber burgess. [EBR]

WALLACE, JOHN, late of Jamaica, a merchant burgess and guilds-brother of Edinburgh, 1752. [EBR]

WALLACE, JOHN, a maltman in Leith, a sasine, 1775. [NRS.RS27.222.144]

WALLACE, ROBERT, son of Robert Wallace a writer, appr. to John Hamilton a cordiner burgess of Edinburgh, 1736. [ERA]

WALLACE, ROBERT, died 1757. [Greyfriars MI, Edinburgh]

WALLACE, THOMAS, a shoemaker burgess of Edinburgh, 1766, son of John Wallace a wright burgess. [EBR]

WALLACE, THOMAS, a mason in Leith, a sasine, 1775. [NRS.RS27.223.197]

WALLACE, WILLIAM, a merchant in Jamaica, a burgess and guilds-brother of Edinburgh, 1752. [EBR]

WALLACE, WILLIAM, professor of Scots Law at Edinburgh University, a burgess and guilds-brother of Edinburgh, 1765. [EBR]

WALLACE, WILLIAM, in Crosscauseway, Edinburgh, a sasine, 1774. [NRS.RS27.214.223]

WALLS, JOHN, a sailor in Leith, husband of Isabel Kilgour, 177. [SL.113]

The People of Edinburgh, 1725-1775

WALTERS, CATHERINE, born 1764 in Edinburgh, died in Georgia on 22 September 1808. [Savannah Death Register]

WANTWORTH, JOHN, from Portsmouth, New Hampshire, a burgess and guilds-brother of Edinburgh, 1764. [EBR]

WARDEN, ALEXANDER, son of Henry Warden in Leith Mills, appr. to Thomas Letham, a locksmith in Edinburgh, 1763-1769. [ERA]

WARDEN, EBENEZER, son of Henry Warden a miller at Leith Mills, appr. to James Ker, a wright in Edinburgh, 1763-1769, [ERA]; a journeyman wright from Leith, to Port Oxford, Maryland, in 1771. [NRS.JC27.10.3]

WARDEN, GEORGE, a stabler in Edinburgh, a sasine, 1772. [NRS.RS27.196.268]

WARDLAW, ANDREW, son of Henry Wardlaw, appr. to William Armstrong a coppersmith in Edinburgh, 1729. [ERA]

WARDROP, ALEXANDER, son of John Wardrop a writer, appr. to William Reoch a wright in Edinburgh, 1744, [ERA]; a wright in Edinburgh, a sasine, 1773. [NRS.RS27.207.231]

WARDROPE, ANDREW, a surgeon burgess of Edinburgh, 1777, son of Andrew Wardrope a merchant burgess and guilds-brother. [EBR]

WARDROP, DAVID, a merchant in Edinburgh, a sasine, 1760, a decreet, 1775. [NRS.RS27.155.151; CS16.1.165]

WARDROPE, DAVID, son of Alexander Wardrope minister at Whitburn, appr. to John Wallace a surgeon apothecary in Edinburgh, 1748, [ERA]; a surgeon in Edinburgh, a decreet. 1783. [NRS.CS17.1.2]

WARDROP, JAMES, a wright in Edinburgh, a sasine, 1759. [NRS.RS27.154.140]

WARDROPE, JOSEPH, son of David Wardrope of Easter Quill, appr. to John Wardrope a wright burgess of Edinburgh, 1710, [ERA]; a house-carpenter from Edinburgh, to Georgia in 1733. [TNA.CO5.670.128]

WARE, JOHN, a comedian in Edinburgh, 1735. [NRS.AC10.213]

WARES, FRANCIS, a vintner burgess of Edinburgh, 1773, husband of Margaret, dau. of John Miller a burgess. [EBR]

WARRANDER, HUGH, a writer in Edinburgh, a sasine, 1774. [NRS.RS27.209.270]

WARROCK, ANNE, spouse of John Pursel a baker in Crosscauseway, Edinburgh, a sasine, 1772. [NRS.RS27.234.230]

WARROCK, JAMES, son of John Warrock a brewer, appr. to James Seton jr a merchant burgess of Edinburgh, 1748. [ERA]

WAST, WILLIAM, a poultryman burgess of Edinburgh, 1770, son of John Wast a poultryman burgess, 1770. [EBR]

WASTON, THOMAS, a merchant burgess of Edinburgh, 1770. [EBR]

WATKINS, PHILIP, a writer in Edinburgh, and his dau. Janet, a sasine, 1775. [NRS.RS27.223.44]

The People of Edinburgh, 1725-1775

WATSON, ADAM, a tanner in Canongate, a sasine, 1772. [NRS.RS27.200.152]

WATSON, ALEXANDER, son of Alexander Watson a merchant, appr. to James Tait, a wright in Edinburgh, 1757-1763. [ERA]

WATSON, ALEXANDER, a merchant burgess and guilds-brother of Edinburgh, 1764. [EBR]

WATSON, ALEXANDER, an upholsterer in Edinburgh, 1773. [NRS.RS27.205.276]

WATSON, DAVID, from Leith, a wigmaker in Charleston, probate, 1732, South Carolina

WATSON, DAVID, son of James Watson late dean of the litsters in Edinburgh, appr. to Charles Butter a merchant burgess and guilds-brother of Edinburgh, 1749. [ERA]

WATSON, DAVID, in Canongate, a sasine, 1771. [NRS.RS27.191.366]

WATSON, DAVID, son of John Watson a shoemaker in Potterrow, appr. to Walter Brunton, a saddler in Edinburgh, 1774-1780. [ERA]

WATSON, JAMES, a merchant in Edinburgh, trading with Boston, New England, before 1739. [NRS.AC7.44.185]

WATSON, JAMES, son of George Watson a brewer, appr. to John Reoch a painter burgess of Edinburgh, 1747, [ERA]; a burgess of Edinburgh, 1768. [EBR]

WATSON, JAMES, son of James Watson a merchant, appr. to James Yorston a cutler burgess of Edinburgh, 1754, [ERA], a cutler burgess of Edinburgh, 1767. [EBR]

WATSON, JAMES, a smith in Edinburgh, a sasine, 1774. [NRS.RS27.214.17]

WATSON, JOHN, son of John Watson a merchant, appr. to Alexander Grant a barber wigmaker burgess of Edinburgh, 1725. [ERA]

WATSON, JOHN, a cooper in Leith, 1730. [NRS.CH2.621.90]

WATSON, JOHN, junior, a merchant from Edinburgh, son of Robert Watson a merchant in the Luckenbooths, settled in Charleston, South Carolina, by 1743, died there 1756, test., 1756, C.E. [NRS.CC8.8.116]

WATSON, JOHN, a feuar in Edinburgh, a sasine, 1771. [NRS.RS27.194.41]

WATSON, JOHN, a cooper in Leith, a burgess and guilds-brother of Edinburgh, 1773, husband of Euphemia dau. of James Fyfe a merchant burgess and guilds-brother, 1773. [EBR]

WATSON, JOSEPH, a writer in Edinburgh, 1742. [NRS.AC11.153]

WATSON, LAURENCE, son of Alexander Watson a chairmaster in Pleasance, Edinburgh, appr. to Alexander Runciman, a painter in Edinburgh, 1766-1773. [ERA]

WATSON, MUNGO, a porter burgess of Edinburgh, 1778. [EBR]

WATSON, NICOL, a shipmaster in Leith, trading with America, 1759-1765. [NRS.CS96.1085]; test., 1764, C.E. [NRS]

The People of Edinburgh, 1725-1775

WATSON, PETER, son of Peter Watson a waterman, appr. to John Finn a waulker burgess of Edinburgh, 1736. [ERA]

WATSON, ROBERT, in Canongate a feu contract, 1773. [NRS.RD2.216/482]

WATSON, ROBERT, a mason in Edinburgh, a sasine, 1771. [NRS.RS27.192.70]

WATSON, ROBERT, formerly a student in Edinburgh, a decreet, 1775. [NRS.CS16.1.165]

WATSON, SAMUEL, a merchant burgess and guilds-brother of Edinburgh, 1764, husband of Anne dau. of David Somerville a merchant burgess and guilds-brother. [EBR]

WATSON, SAMUEL, a writer in Edinburgh, a sasine, 1772. [NRS.RS27.197.120]

WATSON, THOMAS, son of George Watson a brewer, appr. to David Boswell a glazier burgess of Edinburgh, 1742. [ERA]

WATSON, THOMAS, a merchant burgess of Edinburgh, 1776. [EBR]

WATSON, WILLIAM, a sailor in Leith, husband of Elizabeth Watson, 1742. [SL.48]

WATSON, WILLIAM, a skipper in Leith, husband of Agnes Ferguson, 1755. [SL.79]; test., 1759, C.E. [NRS]

WATSON, WILLIAM, son of Alexander Watson a merchant, appr. to James Caddell, an upholsterer in Edinburgh, 1760-1766. [ERA]

WATSON, WILLIAM, a smith and farrier in Musselburgh, a burgess of Edinburgh, 1775, husband of Sophia dau. of John Wilson a cordiner burgess. [EBR]

WATT, GEORGE, a founder burgess and guilds-brother of Edinburgh. 1777. [EBR]

WATT, HELEN, a shopkeeper in Leith, a sasine, 1772. [NRS.RS27.202.103]

WATT, JAMES, son of George Watt a maltman in Leith, appr. to William Montgomery a wright burgess of Edinburgh, 1731. [ERA]

WATT, JOHN, a skipper in Leith, test., 1772, C.E. [NRS]

WATT, ROBERT, a merchant in New York, a burgess and guilds-brother of Edinburgh, 1717, former appr. of Sir Patrick Johnston late Lord Provost of Edinburgh. [EBR]

WATT, ROBERT, a mason in Leith, a sasine, 1772. [NRS.RS27.201.67]

WATTERS, ALEXANDER, a wright on Crosscauseway, Edinburgh, a sasine, 1771. [NRS.RS27.193.365]

WAUCHOP, JAMES, son of Andrew Wauchop a merchant, appr. to Robert Selkirk the younger a merchant burgess of Edinburgh, 1739. [ERA]

WAUGH, ANDREW, a flesher in Leith, a sasine, 1755. [NRS.RS27.146.217]

WAUGH, DAVID, a flesher in Leith, a sasine, 1771. [NRS.RS27.193.169]

The People of Edinburgh, 1725-1775

WAUGH, GILBERT, a baxter burgess of Edinburgh, 1766, son of Gavin Waugh a baxter burgess. [EBR]

WAUGH, JOHN, a merchant in Edinburgh, 1750. [NRS.AC10.355]

WAUGH, JOHN, son of James Waugh a baler at the Water of Leith, appr. to George Fairbairn, a baker in Edinburgh, 1774-1779. [ERA]

WEBSTER, ALEXANDER, a minister in Edinburgh, a sasine, 1753. [NRS.RS27.141.302]

WEBSTER, DAVID, a baxter in St Ninian's Row, Edinburgh, 1776, husband of Euphame dau. of William Smith a founder burgess. [EBR]

WEBSTER, Dr EBENEZER, a deed of attorney, 1774. [NRS.RD4.215/667]

WEBSTER, GEORGE, a merchant burgess and guilds-brother of Edinburgh, 1768, son of Rev. Dr Alexander Webster in Edinburgh. [EBR]

WEIR, ALEXANDER, son of Walter Weir a stabler, appr. to James Miller a painter burgess of Edinburgh, 1747. [ERA]

WEIR, ALEXANDER, in Edinburgh, a sasine, 1774. [NRS.RS27.215.189]

WEIR, ELIZABETH, in Edinburgh, a deed, 1767. [NRS.RD4.216/168]

WEIR, JAMES, son of Adam Weir a wright in Leith, appr. to Adam Keir, a baker in Edinburgh, 1774-1779. [ERA]

WEIR, JOHN, son of Thomas Weir one of the Royal Household trumpeters, appr. to David Clelland a painter in Edinburgh, 1741. [ERA]

WEIR, JOHN, a merchant burgess and guilds-brother of Edinburgh, 1761, husband of Jean dau. of Reverend John Hepburn in Edinburgh. [EBR]

WEIR, ROBERT, son of Walter Weir a stabler, appr. to Walter and Thomas Ruddiman printers in Edinburgh, 1744. [ERA]

WEIR, ROBERT, a mason in Edinburgh, a sasine, 1771. [NRS.RS27.228.105]

WEIR, WILLIAM, son of William Weir a cowfeeder, appr. to Thomas Gray a cordiner burgess of Edinburgh, 1739. [ERA]

WELSH, ALEXANDER, a tenant in Potterrow, Edinburgh, a sasine, 1775. [NRS.RS27.221.218]

WELSH, GEORGE, son of Alexander Welsh, appr. to James Miller, a furrier in Edinburgh, 1769-1775. [ERA]

WELSH, JOHN, a merchant from Leith, in Jamaica, 1769. [NRS.AC7.53]

WELSH, SAMUEL, a merchant in Edinburgh, trading with Jamaica before 1734, and with Boston, New England, 1736; 1738. [NRS.AC10.94/246; AC13.1; AC7.43.493]

WEMYSS, JAMES, appr. to David Penman a goldsmith in Edinburgh, 1727. [ERA]

WEMYSS, JOHN, Deputy Governor of Edinburgh Castle, a burgess and guilds-brother of Edinburgh, 1762. [EBR]

The People of Edinburgh, 1725-1775

WEMYSS, ROBERT, a dyer burgess of Edinburgh, 1778, son of John Wemyss a litster burgess. [EBR]

WESTWATER, JOHN, son of James Westwater a coach-wright, appr. to George Hutchison and Company, painters in Edinburgh, 1768-1774. [ERA]

WESTWATER, ROBERT, son of Robert Westwater a whipmaker, appr. to David Anderson, a hatter in Edinburgh, 1771-1778. [ERA]

WHARTON, THOMAS, deputy solicitor of Excise, a burgess and guilds-brother of Edinburgh, 1761. [EBR]

WHITE, DAVID, a merchant in Edinburgh, 1738. [NRS.AC11.112]

WHITE, GEORGE, son of James White a tailor in Crosscauseway, Edinburgh, appr. to John and George Dunsmure, merchants in Edinburgh, 1761-1766. [ERA]

WHITE, JAMES, a wigmaker burgess of Edinburgh, 1772. [EBR]

WHITE, JAMES, a candlemaker burgess of Edinburgh, 1775, former appr. to John Sprott a candlemaker burgess. [EBR]

WHITE, JOHN, son of James White in Edinburgh, appr. to John Blyth a weaver burgess of Edinburgh, 1748. [ERA]

WHITE, JOHN, son of Alexander White, an architect's clerk, appr. to Thomas Miln a mason in Edinburgh, 1755. [ERA]

WHITE, JOHN, a merchant burgess and guildsbrother of Edinburgh, 1768, former appr. to Robert Thomson. [EBR]

WHITE, ROBERT, a merchant burgess of Edinburgh, 1765, former appr. to Patrick Drummond a merchant burgess. [EBR]

WHITE, ROBERT, of Bennochie, a physician and professor of medicine at Edinburgh University, a burgess and guilds-brother of Edinburgh, 1761. [EBR]

WHITE, ROBERT, born 1710, a smith and feuar in Portsburgh, died 13 September 1780, and his wife Margaret Bernar, born 1717, died 29 August 1787. [St Cuthbert's MI]

WHITE, THOMAS, a skipper in Leith, 1732. [NRS.S/H]

WHITE, THOMAS, a baxter burgess of Edinburgh, 1768, former appr. to William Richardson a baxter burgess. [EBR]

WHITE, WILLIAM, a brewer in Pleasance, a burgess of Canongate, 1727. [CBR]

WHITE, WILLIAM, son of Robert White a smith in Portsburgh, Edinburgh, appr. to John Richardson, a smith in Edinburgh, 1759-1765. [ERA]; a burgess of Edinburgh, 1776. [EBR]

WHITEHEAD, JAMES, born 1756, a cordiner from Edinburgh, to Virginia in December 1773. [TNA.T47.9/11]

WHITEHEAD, ROBERT, son of James Whitehead a plasterer, appr. to John Murdoch, a watchmaker in Edinburgh, 1770-1776. [ERA]

WHITEHEAD, ROBERT, a wright in Canongate, a decreet, 1783. [NRS.CS17.1.2]

The People of Edinburgh, 1725-1775

WHITEHILL, WILLIAM, son of Richard Whitehill in Edinburgh, appr. to George Drummond a white iron smith in Edinburgh, 1753. [ERA]

WHITELAW, ADAM, a tailor burgess of Canongate, 1727. [CBR]

WHYTE, ROBERT, of Bannochy, born 1715, royal physician, professor of medicine at Edinburgh University, Fellow of the Royal Society, died 15 April 1766; his wife Louis Balfour born 1718, died 25 May 1764. [Greyfriars MI, Edinburgh]

WHYTE, WILLIAM, a sailor in Leith, 1736. [ECL.17]

WIGHT, JOHN, a baxter burgess and guilds-brother of Edinburgh, 1766, son of William Wight a baxter burgess. [EBR]

WIGHT, WILLIAM, a baxter burgess and guilds-brother of Edinburgh, 1768, son of Robert Wight a baxter burgess and guilds-brother. [EBR]

WIGHTMAN, ARCHIBALD, a merchant in Edinburgh, a sasine, 1752. [NRS.RS27.140.186]

WIGHTMAN, JAMES, son of William Wightman a stabler, appr. to Patrick Bowie, an orris and livery lacemaker in Edinburgh, 1770-1777. [ERA]

WIGHTMAN, Captain WILLIAM, shoremaster at Leith, 1741. [NRS.AC11.140]

WIGHTMAN, WILLIAM, a skipper in Leith, dead by 1746, husband of Grizel Calendar. [SL.55]

WILKIE, JOHN, a mason burgess of Edinburgh, 1762. [EBR]

WILKIE, ROBERT, a mariner in Leith, a sasine, 1756. [NRS.RS27.147.249]

WILKIE, ROBERT, a candlemaker burgess of Edinburgh, 1767, son of James Williamson a candlemaker burgess. [EBR]

WILKIE, THOMAS, a sailor in Leith, husband of Euphan Mitchell, 1759. [SL.85]

WILL, ROBERT, son of Robert Will a shoemaker, appr. to James Ranken a barber burgess of Edinburgh, 1730. [ERA]

WILLIAMS, WAKEFIELD, son of Rodger Williams, appr. to Thomas Marr a wigmaker burgess of Edinburgh, 1728. [ERA]

WILLIAMSON, ANDREW, a merchant burgess of Canongate, 1728. [CBR]

WILLIAMSON, ARCHIBALD, son of Thomas Williamson a weaver, appr. to Archibald Shiels a merchant burgess of Edinburgh, 1736. [ERA]

WILLIAMSON, CHARLES, born 1757 in Edinburgh, a former army officer who settled in America 1790, estate agent for Pultenet, western New York State from 1790-1800, died in New Orleans during September 1808. [TSA]

WILLIAMSON, DAVID, a burgess and guilds-brother of Edinburgh, 1763, son of Joseph Williamson an advocate and grandson of David Williamson minister of the West Kirk. [EBR]

WILLIAMSON, HUGH, late student of physic, a burgess and guilds-brother of Edinburgh, 1765. [EBR]

WILLIAMSON, JOHN, a skipper in Leith, test., 1759, C.E. [NRS]

The People of Edinburgh, 1725-1775

WILLIAMSON, JOHN, a burgess and guilds-brother of Edinburgh, 1763, grandson of David Williamson minister of the West Kirk. [EBR]
WILLIAMSON, JOHN, a skipper in Leith, husband of Janet Yetts, 1765. [NRS.S/H]
WILLIAMSON, JOSEPH, son of David Williamson a vintner, appr. to James McEwen a barber and wigmaker burgess of Edinburgh, 1734. [ERA]
WILLIAMSON, JOSEPH, an advocate burgess and guilds-brother of Edinburgh, 1763, grandson of David Williamson minister of the West Kirk, [EBR]; sasines, 1771-1774. [NRS.RS27.193.142, etc.]
WILLIAMSON, JOSIAH, a merchant in Edinburgh, 1740s. [NRS.CS229.K1/29]
WILLIAMSON, THOMAS, a clerk from Edinburgh transported to Jamaica in 1747. [TNA.CO137.58]
WILLIAMSON, THOMAS, a flesher burgess of Edinburgh 1767, son of James Williamson a flesher burgess, [EBR]; heir to his mother Helen Watson, wife of James Williamson a flesher there, 1776. [NRS.S/H]
WILLIAMSON, THOMAS BRUCE, a surgeon burgess and guilds-brother of Edinburgh, 1769, [EBR]; a sasine, 1776. [NRS.RS27.230.93]
WILLIAMSON, WILLIAM, a merchant in Edinburgh, a sasine, 1776. [NRS.RS27.229.6]
WILLISON, JOHN, in Leith, a deed, 1775. [NRS.RD2.218/491]
WILSON, ADAM, a mariner in Leith, husband of Jean McNabb, 1764. [SL.98]
WILSON, ALEXANDER, a sailor in Leith, husband of Catherine Christie, 1741. [SL.46]
WILSON, ANDREW, a flesher burgess of Edinburgh, 1767, husband of Janet, dau. of Alexander Clark a flesher burgess. [EBR]
WILSON, ARCHIBALD, a merchant burgess of Edinburgh, 1766, son of John Wilson a merchant burgess. [EBR]
WILSON, BASIL, son of Robert Wilson in Edinburgh, appr. to William Heriot, a gunsmith in Edinburgh, 1770-1776. [ERA]
WILSON, CLAUD, a tailor in North Leith, a burgess of Canongate, 1725. [CBR]
WILSON, DAVID, son of John Wilson a schoolmaster, appr. to James Farquhar a merchant burgess of Edinburgh, 1732. [ERA]
WILSON, DAVID, a brewer in Canongate, a sasine, 1755. [NRS.RS27.144/401]
WILSON, EBENEZER, a founder burgess of Edinburgh, 1775, son of James Smith a smith burgess. [EBR]
WILSON, FRANCIS, a skipper in Leith, 1760. [NRS.S/H]
WILSON, GEORGE, a surgeon apothecary, a burgess of Canongate, 1727. [CBR]
WILSON, HENRY, son of John Wilson a musician, appr. to Adam Cockburn a lorimer burgess of Edinburgh, 1725. [ERA]

The People of Edinburgh, 1725-1775

WILSON, HUGH, son of William Wilson a journeyman mason, appr. to Laurence Dalgleish, a watchmaker in Edinburgh, 1774-1782. [ERA]

WILSON, JEAN, widow of James Laurie a baker in Edinburgh, 1744. [NRS.AC11.161]

WILSON, JOHN, son of John Wilson a tailor in Canongate, appr. to Patrick Lawson a weaver burgess of Edinburgh, 1737. [ERA]

WILSON, JOHN, a sailor in Leith, 1744. [ECL.29]

WILSON, JOHN, second son of William Wilson a writer, appr. to William Richardson a smith burgess of Edinburgh, 1748. [ERA]

WILSON, JOHN, son of John Wilson a silk dyer, appr. to Robert Gordon, a goldsmith in Edinburgh, 1759-1766. [ERA]

WILSON, JOHN, a gardener from Edinburgh, transported to the colonies in July 1769. [NRS.HCR.I.104]

WILSON, JOHN, an architect burgess of Edinburgh, 1775. [EBR]

WILSON, JOHN, born 1767 in Leith, a cartman, naturalised in New York on 31 March 1821.

WILSON, MARION, in Edinburgh, a deed, 1771. [NRS.RD4.215/233]

WILSON, PETER, a silk-dyer burgess of Edinburgh, 1764, son of John Wilson deacon of the bonnetmakers and dyers. [EBR]

WILSON, PETER, a school-master from Edinburgh, transported to the colonies in 1768. [NRS.JC27.10.3]

WILSON, PETER, an innkeeper in Canongate, a sasine, 1771. [NRS.RS27.192.225]

WILSON, PHILIP, a planter in St Kitts, eldest son of William Wilson of Soonhope, a writer in Edinburgh, decreets/deeds, 1780, 1781, 1782, 1783. [NRS.CS16.1.173/179/183/184; CS17.1.1/2; RD4.775.589; RD2.234.787]

WILSON, RICHARD, a printer in Edinburgh, a sasine, 1775. [NRS.RS27.222.159]

WILSON, ROBERT, a baxter burgess of Edinburgh, 1762, son of John Wilson a baxter burgess. [EBR]

WILSON, ROBERT, a writer in Edinburgh, a sasine, 1772. [NRS.RS27.198.147]

WILSON, SAMUEL, son of John Wilson a minister, appr. to Thomas Lumsden a printer burgess of Edinburgh, 1738. [ERA]

WILSON, THOMAS, appr. to John More a merchant in Edinburgh, 1725. [ERA]

WILSON, THOMAS, born 1758 in Edinburgh, a gentleman, husband of Matilda ......, naturalised in New York on 1 November 1818.

WILSON, WILLIAM, son of James Wood, a smith burgess of the Canongate, 1726. [CBR]

WILSON, WILLIAM, a sailor in Leith, husband of Isabel Sommerville, 1749. [SL.64]

The People of Edinburgh, 1725-1775

WILSON, WILLIAM, son of William Wilson a mason in Canongate, appr. to James Mack, mason in Edinburgh, 1756-1762. [ERA]
WINCHESTER, JOHN, a clerk in the Leith Customs House, 1732. [NRAS.AC11.52]
WINTER, WILLIAM, in Edinburgh, appr. to George Winter, a barber and wigmaker in Edinburgh, 1762-1768. [ERA]
WISHART, DAVID, a mariner in Leith, a sasine, 1777. [NRS.RS27.231.34]
WISHART, PETER, a sailor in North Leith, test., 1764, C.E. [NRS]
WODDROP, WILLIAM, son of John Woddrop a writer in Edinburgh, a merchant from Edinburgh, settled in Tappahannock, Virginia, before 1772. [NRS.S/H.22.1.1772]
WOMBLES, GEORGE, a wright in Edinburgh, husband of Sibilla Robertson, sasines, 1758, 1760. [NRS.RS27.152/368, 156/189, 394]
WOOD, AMBROSE, son of Alexander Wood a port waiter in Edinburgh, appr. to Andrew Cockburn a white iron smith burgess of Edinburgh, 1753. [ERA]
WOOD, ANDREW, a surgeon burgess and guilds-brother of Edinburgh, 1770, son of William Wood a surgeon burgess and guilds-brother of Edinburgh. [EBR]
WOOD, DAVID, a skipper in Leith, 1767; commander of the William and Elizabeth, a witness in Antigua, 1773. [NRS.RD3.232.432]
WOOD, GEORGE, appr. to Duncan Campbell a merchant in Edinburgh, 1726. [ERA]
WOOD, JAMES, appr. to John Ferguson a merchant in Edinburgh, 1725. [ERA]
WOOD, JAMES, son of Charles Wood a cooper, appr. to Lawrence Kyll a weaver burgess of Edinburgh, 1736. [ERA]
WOOD, JAMES, son of James Wood in Edinburgh, appr. to William Hamilton a bookseller burgess of Edinburgh, 1745. [ERA]
WOOD, JAMES, son of James Wood a journeyman candlemaker, appr. to Robert Sprott, a candlemaker in Edinburgh, 1767-1773. [ERA]
WOOD, JAMES, a tailor in Canongate, father of Ann and Catherine, a sasine, 1774. [NRS.RS27.209.197]
WOOD, JOHN, a mariner in Leith, husband of Catherine Haig, 1760. [SL.90]
WOOD, JOHN, from Edinburgh, to St Kitts before 1775. [NRS.RD4.227.789]
WOOD, THOMAS, a surgeon in Leith, husband of Margaret Home, a sasine, 1771. [NRS.RS27.193.236]
WOOD, WILLIAM, a surgeon apothecary, a burgess of Canongate, 1725. [CBR]
WOODHEAD, HUGH, son of John Woodhead, an Excise supervisor, appr. to James Burton a tanner burgess of Edinburgh, 1742. [ERA]
WOODROP, WILLIAM, a merchant from Edinburgh, settled in Tappahannock, Virginia, before 1772; a merchant late from Virginia, a sasine in Edinburgh, 1779. [NRS.S/H.1772; RS27.243.29]

The People of Edinburgh, 1725-1775

WORDIE, JAMES, son of John Wordie a tailor, appr. to Archibald Punton a baxter in Edinburgh, 1733. [ERA]

WORDIE, JOHN, a merchant burgess of Edinburgh, 1768, former appr. to Coutts brothers. [EBR]

WOTHERSPOON, JOHN, son of John Wotherspoon a baxter in Canongate, appr. to Thomas Lumsden a printer burgess of Edinburgh, 1754, [ERA]; a printer burgess of Edinburgh, 1761, [EBR]; a printer in Edinburgh, a sasine, 1773. [NRS.RS27.204.169]; a guilds-brother of Edinburgh, 1774, husband of Janet dau. of William Mitchell an accountant burgess. [EBR]

WRIGHT, CHARLES, a book-seller in Edinburgh, a sasine, 1754. [NRS.RS27.144.247]

WRIGHT, DAVID, a merchant in Edinburgh, sasines, 1752, 1755. [NRS.RS27.140/286, 146/107]

WRIGHT, DAVID, a distiller in Edinburgh, a sasine, 1775. [NRS.RS27.222.159]

WRIGHT, DUNCAN, a potmaker to the Edinburgh Glasshouse Company, a sasine, 1759. [NRS.RS27.153.232]

WRIGHT, GEORGE, a sailor in Leith, 1759. [SL.85]

WRIGHT, JAMES, a wright burgess of Edinburgh, 1761, son of Charles Wright. [EBR]

WRIGHT, JOHN, a baxter burgess of Edinburgh, 1763, former appr. to John Bell a baxter burgess. [EBR]

WRIGHT, MALCOLM, a merchant burgess and guilds-brother of Edinburgh, 1776, husband of Ann dau. of Charles Little a vintner burgess. [EBR]

WRIGHT, REBEKAH, born 1708, spouse to James Finlay of Walyford, died 30 May 1780. [St Cuthbert's MI]

WRIGHT, ROBERT, born 1749, a tinker from Edinburgh, to Philadelphia, Pennsylvania, in October 1774. [TNA.T47.12]

WRIGHT, ROBERT, a merchant in North Leith, a burgess of Canongate, 1729. [CBR]

WRIGHT, ROBERT, a mason in Edinburgh, a sasine, 1776. [NRS.RS27.227.106]

WRIGHT, WILLIAM, a wright in Edinburgh, a sasine, 1772. [NRS.RS27.202.198]

WRIGHT, WILLIAM, born 1751, a tinker from Edinburgh, to Philadelphia, Pennsylvania, in October 1774. [TNA.T47.12]

WYLD, JAMES, a wright in Portsburgh, Edinburgh, 1773. [NRS.RS27.206.295]

WYLD, JOHN, a mason burgess and guilds-brother of Edinburgh, 1772. [EBR]

WYLIE, JAMES, a mason in Edinburgh, husband of Agnes Smellie, a sasine, 1771. [NRS.RS27.192.279]

WYLIE, WILLIAM, a sailor in Leith, husband of Agnes Bell, 1764. [SL.101]

WYLIE, WILLIAM, son of John Wylie a teacher of English, appr. to Robert Clydesdale, a watchmaker in Edinburgh, 1762-1770. [ERA]

The People of Edinburgh, 1725-1775

YETTS, CATHERINE, in Leith, a deed, 1768. [NRS.RD4.215/607]
YETTS, JANET, in Leith, a deed, 1768. [NRS.RD4.215/610]
YETTS, JOHN, a merchant in Edinburgh, later in Leith, a sasine, 1756. [NRS.RS27.148.167]; a deed, 1774. [NRS.RD2.216/376]
YETTS, WILLIAM, a merchant burgess and guilds-brother of Edinburgh, 1777. [EBR]
YORKSTON, JACOBINA, spouse of John Hunter a brewer at the back of the Canongate, a sasine, 1772. [NRS.RS27.199.186]
YOUNG, ADAM, appr. to John Webster a candlemaker in Edinburgh, 1726. [ERA]
YOUNG, ADAM, son of Adam Young a causeway-layer, appr. to Robert Gordon a goldsmith burgess of Edinburgh, 1754. [ERA]
YOUNG, AGNES, in Edinburgh, a deed, 1767. [NRS.RD3.234/534]
YOUNG, ALEXANDER, a brewer in Potter Row, Edinburgh, a decreet, 1752. [NRS.CS16.1.88]
YOUNG, ALEXANDER, a wright in the New Town of Edinburgh, a sasine, 1776. [NRS.RS27.229.277]
YOUNG, ARCHIBALD, son of Archibald Young a coach-driver, appr. to Andrew Boag, a cutler in Edinburgh, 1771-1778. [ERA]
YOUNG, ELIZABETH, born 1755, a servant from Edinburgh, to Philadelphia, Pennsylvania, in May 1775. [TNA.T47.12]
YOUNG, GEORGE, a physician in Edinburgh, 1741; sasines, 1751. [NRS.AC10.284; RS27.138/413, 139/90]
YOUNG, GEORGE, son of George Young a causeway layer, appr. to James Young, jr., a barber in Edinburgh, 1761-1768. [ERA]
YOUNG, GEORGE, a merchant burgess and guilds-brother of Edinburgh, 1769. [ERA]
YOUNG, GILBERT, son of Andrew Young a shoemaker, appr. to Colin Campbell a bookbinder burgess of Edinburgh, 1748. [ERA]
YOUNG, JAMES, son of James Young in Edinburgh, appr. to David Oliphant a bookbinder burgess of Edinburgh, 1731. [ERA]
YOUNG, JAMES, son of Garshom Young in Edinburgh, appr. to John Blyth a freeman burgess of Edinburgh, 1743. [ERA]
YOUNG, JAMES, son of William Young in the Abbey of Holyroodhouse, appr. to Archibald Stratoun a watchmaker in Edinburgh, 1753. [ERA]
YOUNG, JAMES, a brewer burgess of Edinburgh, 1763, husband of Elizabeth dau. of George Meikle a brewer burgess. [EBR]
YOUNG, JAMES, a skipper in Rotten Row, Leith, 1773. [WED.85]
YOUNG, JOHN, a skipper in Leith, 1736. [ECL.48]
YOUNG, JOHN, a sailor in Leith, 1736. [SL.78]

The People of Edinburgh, 1725-1775

YOUNG, JOHN, a smith burgess of Edinburgh, 1772, son of David Young a smith burgess. [EBR]

YOUNG, JOHN, a merchant in Edinburgh, a sasine, 1773. [NRS.RS27.203.141]

YOUNG, ROBERT, son of William Young, appr. to Adam Anderson a barber wigmaker burgess of Edinburgh, 1728. [ERA]

YOUNG, ROBERT, born 1741, a carpenter from Edinburgh, to Dominica in December 1773. [TNA.T47.9/11]

YOUNG, ROBERT, a sailor in Leith, test., 1775, C.E. [NRS]

YOUNG, THOMAS, son of Alexander Young a writer, appr. to James Grant a merchant and former bailie of Edinburgh, 1751. [ERA]

YOUNG, THOMAS, a surgeon in Edinburgh, a sasine, 1751. [NRS.RS27.138.413]

YOUNG, THOMAS, a brewer at the Water of Leith, a sasine, 1754. [NRS.RS27.143.329]

YOUNG, THOMAS, son of George Young a vintner in Canongate, appr. to James Wemyss a goldsmith in Edinburgh, 28 July 1767. [ERA]

YOUNG, THOMAS, a physician in Edinburgh, a sasine, 1774; a feu charter, 1774. [NRS.RS27.212.97; RD2.216/311]]

YOUNG, THOMAS, second son of James Young a brewer in Leith, died in Jamaica on 24 October 1798. [AJ#2661]

YOUNG, WILLIAM, appr. to George Auld a locksmith in Edinburgh, 1727. [ERA]

YOUNG, WILLIAM, son of Robert Young a minister, appr. to Samuel Graham a bookbinder burgess of Edinburgh, 1733. [ERA]

YOUNG, WILLIAM, a stabler burgess of Edinburgh, 1764, [EBR]; Edinburgh, a sasine, 1773. [NRS.RS27.203.192]

YOUNG, WILLIAM, a baker burgess of Edinburgh, former appr. to John Hardie a baker burgess, 1775. [EBR]

YOUNG, WILLIAM, from Edinburgh, a British Army surgeon, married Elizabeth Clauson in Annapolis Royal, Nova Scotia, on 5 January 1785, settled on Staten Island, New York. [ANY.II.43]

YOUNGER, ELIZABETH, spouse of John Fletcher a baker on Crosscaseway, Edinburgh, sasines, 1773. [NRS.RS27.209.103/109]

YULE, JAMES, a flesher burgess of Edinburgh, former appr. to John Greig a flesher burgess, 1777. [EBR]

YULE, MARY, spouse of David Hay a mason in Edinburgh, a sasine, 1778. [NRS.RS27.237.100]

ZIEGLER, ALEXANDER, son of George Ziegler a glover at the Windmill, Edinburgh, appr. to Alexander Campbell a goldsmith in Edinburgh, 1747. [ERA]

www.ingramcontent.com/pod-product-compliance
Lightning Source LLC
Chambersburg PA
CBHW051104160426
43193CB00010B/1315